Nuclear Reactors, Materials, and Waste Sector-Specific Plan

An Annex to the National Infrastructure Protection Plan

2010

Homeland Security

Preface

The National Infrastructure Protection Plan (NIPP) provides the unifying structure for the integration of critical infrastructure and key resources (CIKR) protection efforts into a single national program. The NIPP provides an overall framework for integrating programs and activities that are underway in the various sectors, as well as new and developing CIKR protection efforts. The NIPP includes 18 Sector-Specific Plans (SSPs) that detail the application of the overall risk management framework to each specific sector.

The Nuclear SSP describes the collaborative effort between the private sector; State, local, tribal, and territorial governments; nongovernmental organizations; and the Federal Government to ensure the protection and resilience of the Nuclear Reactors, Materials, and Waste Sector. This collaboration includes the prioritization of protection initiatives and investments to ensure resources are applied where they contribute the most to risk mitigation by reducing vulnerabilities, deterring threats, and minimizing the consequences of attacks and other incidents.

The 2010 Nuclear SSP builds on the original Nuclear SSP, published in 2007, but reflects the increased emphasis on resilience, all hazards, and cybersecurity included in the 2009 NIPP. In addition, the 2010 SSP includes a broader array of protective programs and resilience strategies than the 2007 Nuclear SSP, to encompass a more robust spectrum of programs underway to protect nuclear and radiological materials as well as nuclear facilities.

Examples of Nuclear Sector accomplishments since publication of the 2007 SSP include the following:

- Regulatory programs:
  - Finalized a new rule updating security requirements for the Nation's civilian nuclear power reactors.
  - Launched the National Source Tracking System to securely inventory high-risk radiation sources licensed in the United States.
  - Published a new rule requiring nuclear power plants to provide high assurance that digital computer and communication systems and networks are adequately protected against cyber attacks.
  - Made substantial progress through Nuclear Regulatory Commission collaboration with the nuclear industry, to develop a regulatory guide and cybersecurity plan template to facilitate compliance with the new digital computer and communications system rule.
- Voluntary programs:
  - Completed an Integrated Pilot Comprehensive Exercise at the Limerick Nuclear Generating Station in December 2008.
  - Established a voluntary program to improve the security of Research and Test Reactor facilities.
  - Facilitated, as appropriate, the implementation of voluntary security enhancements identified during Comprehensive Reviews conducted between 2005 and 2007.

- Implemented a voluntary national program to harden radiological facilities and install in-device delay kits to make unauthorized removal of radioactive materials from high-risk irradiators more difficult.
- Continued progress within the Joint Cyber Subcouncil to develop a strategic roadmap to secure control systems within the Nuclear Sector.

Nuclear Sector partners will continue to implement voluntary and regulatory CIKR protection and resilience programs, such as those referenced above, and will work with DHS and each other to ensure continued progress toward the sector vision and goals through a broad set of risk mitigation activities, including some which are not addressed in detail in this plan due to their sensitive nature.

Each year, the Nuclear Sector CIKR Protection Annual Report will provide updates on the sector's efforts to identify, prioritize, and coordinate the protection of its critical infrastructure. The Sector Annual Report provides the current priorities of the sector as well as the progress made during the past year in following the plans and strategies set out in the Nuclear SSP.

Preparation of the 2010 Nuclear SSP involved input from a wide range of public and private Nuclear Sector partners, including the membership of the Nuclear Sector Coordinating Council (NSCC) and Nuclear Government Coordinating Council (NGCC).

By signing this letter, the NGCC and NSCC commit to:

- Support SSP development, concepts and processes, and carry out their assigned functional responsibilities regarding the protection of CIKR as described herein;

- Work with the Department of Homeland Security (DHS) as the Nuclear Reactors, Materials, and Waste Sector-Specific Agency (SSA), as appropriate and consistent with Homeland Security Presidential Directive 7 (HSPD-7) (and their own agency-specific authorities, resources, and programs, where appropriate) to coordinate and implement programs that enhance and facilitate CIKR protection;

- Develop and maintain partnerships for CIKR protection with appropriate State, regional, local, tribal, and international entities; the private sector; and nongovernmental organizations; and

- Protect critical infrastructure information according to the Protected Critical Infrastructure Information Program or other appropriate guidelines, and share CIKR protection-related information, as appropriate and consistent with their own agency-specific authorities and the process described herein.

Todd M. Keil	W. Craig Conklin	Michael J. Wallace
Assistant Secretary for Infrastructure Protection U.S. Department of Homeland Security	Director SSA Executive Management Office U.S. Department of Homeland Security Chair, Nuclear GCC	Chair Nuclear Sector Coordinating Council

Table of Contents

List of Figures

List of Tables

Executive Summary

Introduction

Protection of critical infrastructure and key resources (CIKR) is a necessary component of overall protection of the United States. Terrorist attacks, as well as unintentional manmade accidents and natural disasters, threaten CIKR and, therefore, threaten public health and safety, economic vitality, and the American way of life. As a critical step toward the overarching goal of nationwide CIKR protection, President George W. Bush issued Homeland Security Presidential Directive 7 (HSPD-7) in 2003, which called for establishment of a National Infrastructure Protection Plan (NIPP) to address critical infrastructure identification, prioritization, and protection for all 17 CIKR sectors.[1]

HSPD-7 assigned responsibility for coordinating protection of CIKR in each sector to Sector-Specific Agencies (SSAs). The SSA for the Nuclear Reactors, Materials, and Waste Sector[2] is the U.S. Department of Homeland Security (DHS). In DHS, the Office of Infrastructure Protection (IP), Sector-Specific Agency Executive Management Office (SSA EMO) has been assigned SSA responsibilities.

Because each sector is unique in various ways, the SSAs were instructed to create Sector-Specific Plans (SSPs) to supplement the NIPP and explain how partners, including the private sector; Federal, State, local, tribal, and territorial governments; and international entities, can work together to improve protection and resilience in the current 18 CIKR sectors. SSPs explain how to identify and prioritize assets, assess risks, implement protective programs and resiliency strategies, and measure progress in CIKR security and resilience.

The 2010 Nuclear SSP builds on the original Nuclear SSP, published in 2007, but reflects the increased emphasis on resilience, all-hazards, and cybersecurity included in the 2009 NIPP. In addition, the 2010 SSP includes a broader array of protective programs and resiliency strategies compared to the 2007 Nuclear SSP, to include the full spectrum of programs to protect nuclear and radiological materials, as well as nuclear facilities.

Preparation of the 2010 Nuclear SSP involved input from a wide range of Nuclear Sector partners, including the membership of the Nuclear Sector Coordinating Council (NSCC) and the Nuclear Government Coordinating Council (NGCC). In accordance with DHS guidance, the Nuclear SSP will be updated annually and reissued every 3 years. The 2010 Nuclear SSP is the first reissue of the Nuclear SSP.

---

[1] An 18th CIKR sector, Critical Manufacturing, was designated in 2008.

[2] The Nuclear Reactors, Materials, and Waste Sector is also referred to as the Nuclear Sector. This document, the Nuclear Reactors, Materials, and Waste SSP, is also referred to as the Nuclear SSP.

1. Sector Profile and Goals

The Nuclear Sector sets a high standard for CIKR preparedness with its approach to the security of nuclear reactors, materials, and waste, and the extensive emergency planning and exercise programs around nuclear power plants, as well as other nuclear and radiological facilities. The strong regulatory role of the Nuclear Regulatory Commission (NRC) sets the baseline for security in the Nuclear Sector. The security and resilience of sector assets, systems, networks, and functions are further improved by the involvement of a wide range of public and private sector partners, at the Federal, State, and local levels.

The Nuclear Sector is comprised of the elements listed in Table ES-1 below.

Table ES-1: Nuclear Reactors, Materials, and Waste Sector Components

Nuclear Power Plants:
- Boiling water reactors; and
- Pressurized water reactors.

Research, Training, and Test Reactors:
- Government research and test reactors;
- University research and training reactors; and
- Private research and test reactors.

Deactivated Nuclear Facilities:
- Deactivated reactors; and
- Other deactivated nuclear facilities.

Fuel Cycle Facilities:
- Uranium mining or in situ uranium leaching;
- Uranium ore milling or leachate processing;
- Uranium conversion facilities;
- Uranium enrichment facilities;
- Fuel fabrication facilities:
  - Category I (special nuclear materials) facilities;
  - Category II (special nuclear materials - moderate strategic significance) facilities; and
  - Category III (special nuclear materials - low strategic significance) facilities.

Nuclear Materials Transport:
- Low hazard radioactive materials transport; and
- High hazard radioactive materials transport, including spent nuclear fuel.

Radioactive Materials:
- Medical facilities with radioactive materials;
- Research facilities using radioactive materials;
- Irradiation facilities; and
- Industrial facilities with radioactive materials.

Radioactive Source Production and Distribution Facilities:

- Radioactive device manufacturers;
- Radioactive source producers;
- Radioactive source importers;
- Radioactive source manufacturers; and
- Radioactive source distributors.

Nuclear Waste:

- Low-level radioactive waste processing and storage facilities;
- Sites managing accumulations of naturally occurring radioactive materials (NORM);
- Spent nuclear fuel processing and storage facilities:
  - Spent nuclear fuel wet storage facilities;
  - Spent nuclear fuel dry storage facilities;
- Transuranic waste processing and storage facilities;
- High-level radioactive waste storage and disposal facilities; and
- Mixed waste processing.

The Nuclear Sector does not include Department of Defense (DoD) and Department of Energy (DOE) nuclear facilities, or radioactive material associated with defense-related activity.

The Nuclear Sector is interdependent with a number of other sectors. For example, the Nuclear Sector relies on the Transportation Systems Sector for shipping nuclear and radioactive material, and as both a producer and consumer of electricity, the Nuclear Sector is interdependent with the Energy Sector. In addition, nuclear and radiological facilities and materials play a key role in the Healthcare and Public Health Sector. Protective programs in the Nuclear Sector and other sectors must take into account and mitigate impacts that may arise from these dependencies and interdependencies.

Nuclear Sector partners have agreed on a vision statement and seven overarching goals for Nuclear CIKR protection and resilience, included in Table ES-2.

Table ES-2: Nuclear Sector Vision and Goals[3]

Nuclear Sector Vision
The Nuclear Sector will support national security, public health and safety, public confidence, and economic stability by enhancing, where necessary and reasonably achievable, its existing high level of readiness to promote the protection and resiliency [a] of the Nuclear Sector in an all-hazards [b] environment; and to lead by example to improve the Nation's overall critical infrastructure readiness.

Nuclear Sector Goals	
Awareness	
Goal 1	Establish permanent and robust collaboration and communication among sector partners having security and emergency responsibilities for the Nuclear Sector.
Goal 2	Obtain information related to dependencies and interdependencies of other CIKR to the Nuclear Sector and share it with sector partners.

---

[3] The numbering of the goals is not to set priorities, but for identification purposes only.

Goal 3	Increase public awareness of sector protective measures, consequences, and proper actions following a release of radioactive material.
Prevention	
Goal 4	Improve security, tracking, and detection of nuclear and radioactive material in order to prevent it from being used for malevolent purposes.
Goal 5	Coordinate with sector partners to develop protective measures and procedures to prevent, protect, respond and recover from all hazard disasters impacting Nuclear Sector assets.
Protection, Response, and Recovery	
Goal 6	Protect against the exploitation of the Nuclear Sector's cyber assets, systems, networks, and the functions they support.
Goal 7	Use a risk-informed approach that includes protection and resilience considerations to make budgeting, funding, and grant decisions on potential protection and emergency response enhancements.

[a] "Resilience" is the ability to resist, absorb, recover from, or successfully adapt to adversity or a change in conditions. (2009 National Infrastructure Protection Plan)

[b] "All Hazards" is a grouping classification encompassing all conditions, environmental or manmade, that have the potential to cause injury, illness, or death; damage to or loss of equipment, infrastructure services, or property; or, alternatively, causing functional degradation to social, economic, or environmental aspects. (2009 National Infrastructure Protection Plan)

2. Identify Assets, Systems, Networks

To implement protective measures in a sector, DHS needs to first identify what assets, systems,[4] networks,[5] and functions[6] the sector contains. The Infrastructure Data Warehouse (IDW) is an extensive DHS inventory of information pertaining to all 18 CIKR sectors. To date, information has been gathered through DHS-initiated data calls to Federal partners, State and local governments, and private sector owners and operators; the NRC specifically shares its own nuclear asset data with DHS. To keep sensitive security data from being improperly disclosed, this information is marked as Safeguards Information (SGI)[7] or Protected Critical Infrastructure Information (PCII),[8] as appropriate.

3. Assess Risks

The NIPP framework assesses risk as a function of consequence, vulnerability, and threat. DHS must understand the risk to a subset of CIKR in comparison with the risk to other CIKR assets, systems, networks, and functions, so that it can prioritize limited protection resources across the 18 CIKR sectors. Consequence assessments will determine the likely damage resulting

---

[4] A system is a collection of assets, resources, or elements that perform a process providing infrastructure services to the Nation.

[5] A network is a group of assets or systems that share information or interact with each other to provide infrastructure services within or across sectors.

[6] A function is the service, process, capability, or operation performed by specific infrastructure assets, systems, or networks.

[7] SGI is a special category of sensitive unclassified information authorized by Section 147 of the Atomic Energy Act to be protected. SGI concerns the physical protection of operating power reactors, spent fuel shipments, strategic special nuclear material (SSNM), or other radioactive material. While SGI is considered to be sensitive unclassified information, its handling and protection more closely resemble the handling of classified confidential information. The categories of individuals who are permitted access to SGI are listed in 10 CFR 73.22(b) and 10 CFR 73.59.

[8] The PCII program, established pursuant to the Critical Infrastructure Information Act of 2002, creates a new framework that enables members of the private sector to voluntarily submit sensitive information regarding the Nation's critical infrastructure to DHS with the assurance that the information, if it satisfies requirements of the act, will be protected from public disclosure. See 6 CFR Part 29 for the final rule for handling PCII.

from a given scenario and include public health and safety considerations, national security and governance impacts, and economic disruptions. Vulnerability assessments will determine aspects of an asset that might be exploited by a specific threat. In characterizing threat, DHS will consider potential modes of attack against a nuclear facility, theft of radioactive material from a facility, and possible breaches of a facility's digital computer and communication systems and networks. The NIPP risk management framework allows DHS to evaluate risk and partner with industry, the NRC, DOE, the Environmental Protection Agency (EPA), and other sector partners to help protect the assets at highest risk.

4. Prioritize Infrastructure

The Nuclear Sector uses the Strategic Homeland Infrastructure Risk Analysis (SHIRA) process to assess and manage its risks, which is the same process that is used to manage the risks faced by the other 17 CIKR sectors. When fully implemented, the SHIRA risk management approach will provide standardized consequence and vulnerability estimates to determine a quantitative assessment of risk for individual CIKR. Because of the significant interdependencies between CIKR sectors, the consequences of a successful attack in one sector may have impacts well beyond that sector. By using SHIRA, DHS will be able to normalize and prioritize risks across assets, systems, and networks in all sectors; this will allows cross-sector risk comparisons that can inform policy decisions and resource allocation. Ultimately, by carefully managing risk, DHS, industry, and other partners can most efficiently use limited resources—including DHS grants—to focus on those assets most in need of protection.

5. Develop and Implement Protective Programs and Resilience Strategies

A protective program is a coordinated plan of action to prevent, deter, and mitigate terrorist attacks on CIKR; to make potential targets more resilient; or respond to and recover from such acts as quickly and effectively as possible. DHS works with government and industry partners to develop and coordinate programs to protect our Nation's nuclear CIKR. This includes programs required by regulation and voluntary programs through which the Federal government and Nuclear Sector owners and operators enhance security beyond the level required by regulation.

6. Measure Progress

DHS is collaborating with its sector partners in government to identify and track a robust set of metrics and metrics data to measure the progress of the Nuclear Sector in its CIKR protection efforts. By setting goals and creating metrics to gauge performance, the SSA can identify and develop strategies to maintain the high level of security resilience already achieved and identify areas for further enhancement.

7. CIKR Protection Research and Development

Much of this Nuclear SSP addresses work that is being done currently or in the near future to prevent or mitigate effects of terrorist attacks, natural disasters, and manmade accidents on the Nuclear Sector. While nuclear facilities and systems are already hardened and robust, sector partners can work together to further strengthen sector security through various long-term activities. Some key elements of long-term protection are awareness, training, and education; research and development initiatives; and ongoing planning, management, and risk-based resource allocation. With persistent focus, the Nuclear Sector will continue to improve its security posture[9] and maintain its reputation as a leading sector in CIKR security, emergency preparedness, and resilience.

---

[9] The term "risk posture" will be used interchangeably with the NIPP's use of "protective posture."

8. Managing and Coordinating SSA Responsibilities

The Nuclear SSA in DHS IP is responsible for many coordination and partnership efforts in the Nuclear Sector. This includes monitoring protective program requirements, working with partners to fill gaps in programs or resources, and ensuring that the sector meets its goals. In addition, the Nuclear SSA plays a key role in facilitating communication among sector partners across government and industry to ensure that best practices are shared and that dependencies and interdependencies are identified and addressed in preparedness plans. The Nuclear SSA is also responsible for submitting an annual report on CIKR protection to the Secretary of Homeland Security by June 1st of each year. This report is used to compile the National CIKR Protection Annual Report (NAR), which is presented to the Executive Office of the President.

Introduction

Protecting and ensuring continuity of the critical infrastructure and key resources (CIKR) of the United States is essential to the Nation's security, public health and safety, economic vitality, and way of life. CIKR includes the assets, systems, networks, and functions that provide vital services to the Nation. Terrorist attacks and other manmade or natural disasters could significantly disrupt the functioning of government and business alike and produce cascading effects far beyond the affected CIKR and physical location of the incident. Direct and indirect impacts could include large-scale human casualties, property destruction, economic disruption, and significant degradation of national morale and public confidence. Terrorist attacks using components of the Nation's CIKR as weapons of mass destruction (WMD) could have even more devastating physical, psychological, and economic consequences.

Protection of the Nation's CIKR is essential for making America safer, more secure, and more resilient to terrorist attacks and other natural and manmade hazards. Protection includes actions to mitigate the overall risk to physical, cyber, and human CIKR assets, systems, and networks, or their interconnecting links, resulting from exposure, injury, destruction, incapacitation, or exploitation. In the context of the NIPP, this protection includes actions to deter threats, mitigate vulnerabilities, or minimize consequences associated with a terrorist attack or other incident. Protection can include a wide range of activities, such as improving business protocols, hardening facilities, building resilience and redundancy, incorporating hazard resistance in initial facility design, initiating active or passive countermeasures, installing security systems, leveraging self-healing technologies, promoting workforce surety programs, and implementing cybersecurity measures. The NIPP and its complementary Sector-Specific Plans (SSPs) provide a consistent, unifying structure for integrating both existing and future CIKR protection efforts. The NIPP also provides the core processes and mechanisms that enable all levels of government and private sector partners to work together to implement CIKR protection in an effective and efficient manner.

The NIPP was developed through extensive coordination with CIKR partners at all levels of government and the private sector. NIPP processes are designed to be adapted and tailored to individual sector and partner requirements. Implementation of the NIPP enables the government and private sector to use collective expertise and experience to more clearly define CIKR protection issues and practical solutions, as well as to ensure that existing CIKR protection approaches and efforts, including business continuity and resilience planning, are recognized.

Purpose

The NIPP requires each CIKR sector to develop an SSP to provide a framework for reducing risk and fostering cooperation and information sharing among sector partners, including all levels of government, the private sector, and international partners.

The SSAs are responsible for development of the SSPs, in coordination with sector partners. The Nuclear SSP[10] follows and supports the risk management approach and key steps outlined in the NIPP:

- Setting goals and objectives;

- Identifying sector CIKR assets, systems, and networks;

- Identifying and assessing the vulnerabilities and interdependencies among CIKR and analyzing potential risks based on threats, vulnerabilities, and consequences;

- Prioritizing assets based on analysis and normalization of risk, and prioritizing protection initiatives on a cost-benefit basis so that they offer the most efficient reduction of risk;

- Developing and implementing sustainable programs to protect assets and implementing information-sharing and protection measures in the sector; and

- Using metrics to measure and communicate the effectiveness of SSP implementation.

Through a process similar to that established for review and maintenance of the NIPP, the SSP will be reviewed to ensure that protection efforts remain effective, efficient, and correspond to sector risk. This review process will include input from various sector officials, including representatives from the private sector and multiple government agencies. The SSP will be reviewed annually and reissued every three years. Changes may also be made to the document as a result of changes in the risk environment or lessons learned from actual events or exercises.

Figure I-1 shows the interaction of core elements of the NIPP based on a dynamic risk environment, with threat information provided by DHS. The resulting outputs are sector-specific strategies to protect assets based on sector priorities. The ultimate objective of this SSP is to have Federal, State, local, tribal, and territorial governments and the private sector work with the SSA to implement the plan in a way that is consistent, sustainable, effective, and measurable.

Figure I-1: NIPP Risk Management Framework

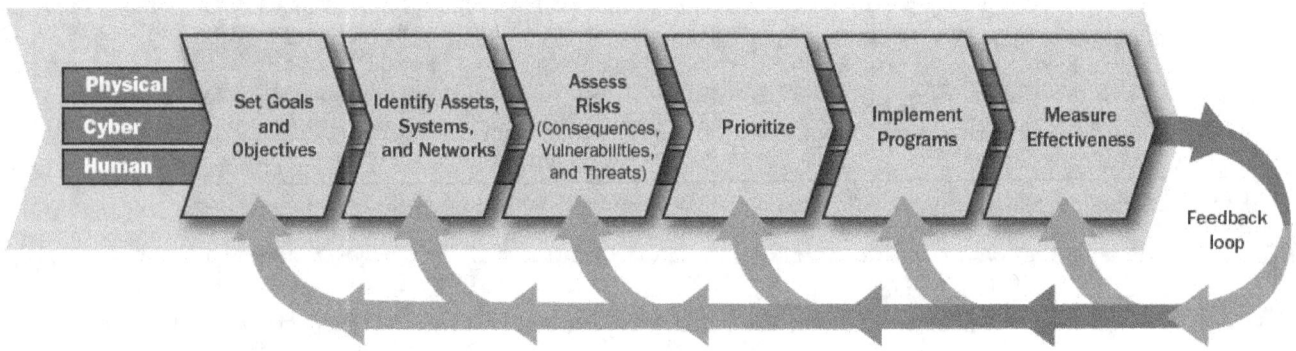

Continuous Improvement to enhance protection of CIKR

The Nuclear SSP provides a detailed description of: specific processes used to identify, assess, prioritize, and protect Nuclear Sector CIKR; processes used to measure effectiveness; the approach required to implement protective activities, including

---

[10] The Nuclear Reactors, Materials, and Waste Sector is also referred to as the Nuclear Sector. This document, the Nuclear Reactors, Materials, and Waste Sector-Specific Plan, is also referred to as the Nuclear SSP.

descriptions of projects, initiatives, activities, periods, milestones, and resources. The purpose of this document is to describe at the unclassified, unrestricted level the efforts through which Nuclear Sector assets, systems, and networks are protected.

Continued implementation of the programs and processes described in this SSP enable Federal, State, local, tribal, and territorial governments, and the private sector to work together in protecting the Nuclear Sector. Nothing in this SSP is intended to alter or impede the ability of any of these partners to perform their respective responsibilities under the law.

Scope and Applicability

Homeland Security Presidential Directive 7 (HSPD-7) directs protection of commercial nuclear reactors used for generating electrical power and non-power reactors used for research, testing, and training; nuclear material[11] in medical, industrial, and academic settings and facilities that fabricate nuclear fuel; and transportation, storage, and disposal of nuclear materials and waste. In accordance with the NIPP and the guidance published by the DHS NIPP Program Management Office, this SSP is focused on protecting the Nuclear Sector from a terrorist attack, while supporting an all-hazards approach in the context of other events. The intent of this SSP is to increase overall preparedness and resilience to manage natural and unintentional manmade disasters, while also providing protection against acts of terrorism, using the same protective strategies and initiatives when possible. Sector protective measures are also addressed in the context of international relationships and cross-sector partnerships.

The Nuclear Sector is generally comprised of the following assets, systems, and networks necessary for their secure and resilient operation:

- Nuclear power plants;
- Research and test reactors (RTRs);
- Nuclear fuel cycle facilities;
- Radioactive waste management;
- Nuclear material transport;
- Deactivated nuclear facilities;
- Radioactive materials;
- Radioactive source production and distribution facilities; and
- Other nuclear facilities.

All Hazards and CIKR Protection and Resilience

The 2010 Nuclear SSP builds on the original Nuclear SSP, published in 2007, but it now reflects the increased emphasis on resilience, all hazards, and cybersecurity included in the 2009 NIPP. In addition, the 2010 SSP includes a broader array of protective programs and resilience strategies compared to the 2007 Nuclear SSP, to include the full spectrum of programs to protect nuclear and radiological materials, as well as nuclear facilities.

---

[11] Nuclear materials for medical purposes include source, byproduct (nuclear material other than special nuclear material (SNM) that is produced or made radioactive in a nuclear reactor), and SNM (uranium-233 or uranium-235, enriched uranium, or plutonium).

By focusing on security and preparedness from the all-hazards approach, the United States can use prevention, protection, and response capabilities not only to reduce the threat of a terrorist attack on its nuclear facilities,[12] but also to prevent or mitigate damage in the event of a natural or unintentional manmade disaster. This comprehensive approach strengthens the sector so that it is fully prepared to face the challenges ahead. The SSA, working with DHS, other Federal agencies, and additional Nuclear Sector partners, ensures seamless linkage between the NIPP and Nuclear Sector steady-state protection and incident management activities.

Planning Assumptions

- The Nuclear Sector depends on other sectors for its full operation; in many cases, a failure in another sector may affect the ability of the Nuclear Sector to perform its necessary functions;

- CIKR protection requires participation and communication among all CIKR partners;

- CIKR protection activities take place in a highly dynamic threat environment that changes as the capabilities and intentions of terrorists evolve;

- Given the uncertain nature of the terrorist threat, the full range of threats—not just the most likely or those involving the most frequent reporting—must be considered for actions to enhance CIKR protection and resilience;

- Protecting all assets, systems, and networks against every possible terrorist attack is not practical. A risk-based approach driven by intelligence analysis and reporting is crucial to an effective risk management strategy and efficient resource allocation;

- Successful CIKR protection requires robust baseline information on assets, systems, and networks that function within and across CIKR sectors, regions, and specific localities;

- Owners and operators conduct risk management planning and invest in security from a business perspective;

- Efforts to enhance CIKR protection against terrorist attacks also support all-hazards preparedness and response, including threats such as natural and unintentional manmade disasters; and

- The Nuclear Sector does not include the Department of Defense (DoD) and Department of Energy (DOE) nuclear facilities or radioactive material associated with defense-related activity.

---

[12] A term that includes all facilities that are part of the Nuclear Sector, such as commercial nuclear power plants, research and test reactors, nuclear fuel cycle facilities, radioactive waste management facilities, deactivated nuclear facilities, facilities housing radioactive material, and radioactive source production and distribution facilities.

1. Sector Profile and Goals

Figure 1-1: NIPP Risk Management Framework: Set Goals and Objectives

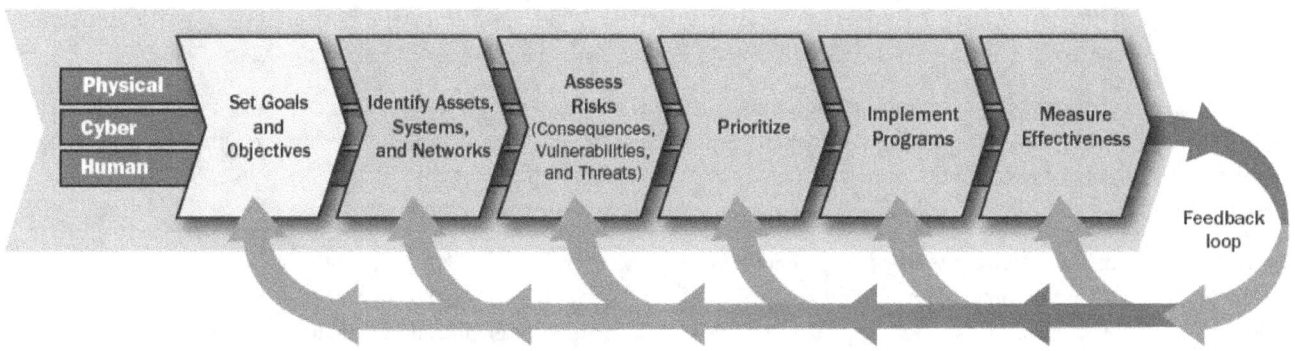

Continuous Improvement to enhance protection of CIKR

The NIPP describes the organizational framework for coordination of CIKR protection efforts at all levels of government, as well as within and across sectors (see Figure 1-1). Sector-specific planning and coordination are addressed through coordinating councils that are established for each sector. Sector Coordinating Councils (SCCs) include representatives from owners and operators, generally from the private sector, while Government Coordinating Councils (GCCs) include the Sector-Specific Agency (SSA), other relevant Federal departments and agencies, and representatives from State, local, tribal, and territorial governments.

Collaboration between the Nuclear SCC (NSCC) and Nuclear GCC (NGCC) is protected by the Critical Infrastructure Partnership Advisory Council (CIPAC), which provides a legal framework that enables members of the SCCs and GCCs to engage in protected CIKR protection-related discussions. DHS published a Federal Register notice on March 24, 2006, announcing the establishment of CIPAC as a Federal Advisory Committee Act (FACA)-exempt body, according to section 871 of the Homeland Security Act. This exemption supports government CIKR protection collaboration with the private sector in a number of areas, such as planning, risk assessments, coordination, NIPP implementation, and operational activities, including incident response and recovery.

The Nuclear SSP is the result of the combined efforts of many public and private sector partners. In the public sector, the Nuclear Regulatory Commission (NRC), DOE, Department of Transportation (DOT), Federal Bureau of Investigation (FBI), State regulators, and numerous other offices in DHS all make valuable contributions. The contribution from the private sector is just as important and includes inputs from the nuclear industry's owners and operators and the Nuclear Energy Institute (NEI).

The Nuclear Sector consists of a wide variety of assets, systems, and networks. While the Nation's 104 nuclear power plants are the most recognizable assets in the sector, they are only part of a much larger nuclear CIKR landscape. In addition to the infrastructure dedicated to creating and processing the fuel used in the Nation's nuclear power plants (also known as "fuel cycle facilities"), radioactive materials[13] are used tens of thousands of times every day for a wide variety of medical, research, and industrial purposes. These materials are created (or imported), distributed, and transported throughout the Nation, and they are important components of the Nation's Chemical, Critical Manufacturing, Energy, Food and Agriculture, and Healthcare and Public Health Sectors. In addition, there are 32 nuclear RTRs in the sector, most at major universities. These reactors are used for various research purposes, as well as for training the next generation of nuclear engineers. Because radioactive waste and disused radioactive sources may pose a safety or security threat, the proper disposal of radioactive materials is also a key sector concern. Decommissioned reactors are also part of the sector; the protection of nuclear materials still in storage at these sites is important because these materials may be targets.

The Nuclear Sector is designated a key resource in paragraph 29 of HSPD-7, defined as including the following: "(1) commercial nuclear reactors for generating electric power and non-power nuclear reactors used for research, testing, and training; (2) nuclear materials in medical, industrial, and academic settings and facilities that fabricate nuclear fuel; and (3) the transportation, storage, and disposal of nuclear materials and radioactive waste." The "nuclear materials" referenced in the definition include source, byproducts,[14] and special nuclear material (SNM),[15] as defined by the Atomic Energy Act of 1954 (AEA).

HSPD-7 assigned responsibility for coordinating protection of CIKR within each sector to SSAs. The Nuclear SSA resides within DHS. More specifically, the Sector-Specific Agency Executive Management Office (SSA EMO) within the Office of Infrastructure Protection (IP) has been assigned the oversight responsibility for six SSAs including the Nuclear SSA (SSA EMO is also responsible for the Chemical, Commercial Facilities, Critical Manufacturing, Dams, and Emergency Services Sectors).

Pursuant to the AEA, as amended by the Energy Reorganization Act of 1974, as well as other authorities, the NRC is responsible for ensuring the secure commercial use and management of radioactive material in the United States. The NRC requires its licensees, including nuclear power reactors, RTRs, and radioactive material users to follow a wide variety of security orders and regulations.[16] However, HSPD-7 states that the Secretary of Homeland Security "will continue to work with the NRC and, as appropriate, DOE in order to ensure the necessary protection" of the Nuclear Sector. The NRC works with DHS, DOE, other Federal agencies, State and local partners, and the private sector to improve security beyond the level required by law. The breadth, scope, and importance of the Nation's nuclear critical infrastructure require that all Nuclear Sector partners cooperate to ensure the secure use of nuclear materials in the United States.

1.1 Sector Profile

The Infrastructure Data Warehouse (IDW), which will be discussed in greater detail in chapter 2, employs a taxonomy that divides the Nuclear Sector into several subsectors. This taxonomy,[17] which is detailed in Table 1-1, provides a high-level overview of the Nuclear Sector.

---

[13] Material that undergoes spontaneous emission of radiation (alpha particles, beta particles, and gamma rays) directly from unstable atomic nuclei.

[14] The term "byproduct material" generally includes nuclear material (other than SNM) that is produced or made radioactive in a nuclear reactor. Also, it includes the tailings and waste produced by extraction or concentration of uranium or thorium from an ore processed primarily for its source material content. Under the EPAct of 2005, byproduct material now includes discrete sources of radium and other naturally occurring radioactive material, as well as accelerator-produced radioactive material.

[15] Uranium-233 or uranium-235, enriched uranium, or plutonium.

[16] Section 274b of the Atomic Energy Act allows the NRC to relinquish its regulatory authority over certain materials and certain activities in a State if three conditions are met. First, the State must have laws, regulations, and safety standards compatible with those of the NRC. Second, it must have a regulatory program that provides a degree of protection for the public health and safety comparable to that of the NRC program. Third, the governor, on behalf of the State, must enter into a formal agreement with the NRC to assume regulatory responsibility over the materials.

[17] The order in which the various subsectors are listed does not reflect the amount of risk, threat, vulnerability, or consequence associated with these types of assets relative to a terrorist attack.

Table 1-1: The Nuclear Sector Taxonomy

Nuclear Power Plants:
- Boiling water reactors (BWR); and
- Pressurized water reactors (PWR).

Research, Training, and Test Reactors:
- Government research and test reactors;
- University research and training reactors; and
- Private research and test reactors.

Decommissioned Nuclear Facilities:
- Deactivated reactors; and
- Other deactivated nuclear facilities.

Fuel Cycle Facilities:
- Uranium mining or in situ uranium leaching;
- Uranium ore milling or leachate processing;
- Uranium conversion facilities;
- Uranium enrichment facilities;
- Fuel fabrication facilities:
  - Category I (special nuclear materials) facilities;
  - Category II (special nuclear materials—moderate strategic significance) facilities; and
  - Category III (special nuclear materials—low strategic significance) facilities.

Nuclear Materials Transport:
- Low-hazard radioactive materials transport; and
- High-hazard radioactive materials transport.

Radioactive Materials:
- Medical facilities with radioactive materials;
- Research facilities using radioactive materials;
- Irradiation facilities; and
- Industrial facilities with nuclear materials.

Radioactive Source Production and Distribution Facilities:
- Radioactive device manufacturers;
- Radioactive source producers;
- Radioactive source importers; and
- Radioactive source manufacturers.

Nuclear Waste:
- Low-level radioactive waste processing and storage facilities;
- Sites managing accumulations of naturally occurring radioactive materials (NORM);
- Spent nuclear fuel processing and storage facilities:
  - Spent nuclear fuel wet storage facilities; and
  - Spent nuclear fuel dry storage facilities;
- Transuranic waste processing and storage facilities;
- High-level radioactive waste storage and disposal facilities; and
- Mixed waste processing.

1.1.1 Reactors

Commercial Nuclear Power Reactors

The NRC licenses 104 commercial nuclear power reactors to operate at 65 sites in 31 States. These commercial nuclear power reactors account for approximately 20 percent of the electricity-generating capacity in the United States. Nuclear power plants are among the best defended and most physically hardened of the Nation's privately owned CIKR, designed to withstand such extreme events as hurricanes, tornadoes and tornado-generated missiles, and earthquakes. While loss of the electricity generated by a single nuclear power plant may have only a minor impact on the Nation's overall electrical capacity, a terrorist attack would be a significant security event, especially if it resulted in release of radioactive material to the environment.

Commercial nuclear power plants in the United States can be owned by a number of separate entities, each with varying ownership proportions. Each of these owners may in turn have a parent or subsidiary relationship with other companies. The operator of the plant may be a different entity as well. The NRC Information Digest (NUREG-1350) published annually in August, provides a compilation of the owners and operators for all commercial nuclear power reactors in the United States.

A nuclear facility with a single power reactor may have a staff of approximately 500 to 700 employees; however, some sites have two or even three reactors, with staffing levels up to 1,500 people. Staffing consists of operations, training, quality assurance, maintenance, engineering, technical support, management, and security personnel.

Research and Test Reactors

The NRC licenses 32 RTRs to operate in 23 States. RTRs, also called non-power reactors, are nuclear reactors used primarily to conduct research, develop theoretical practices, produce radioactive sources, and for educational or medical purposes. Most RTRs are at universities or colleges, while several others are operated by private companies or the Federal Government.

RTRs are typically licensed according to the total thermal (heat) energy produced by the reactor. These facilities range in size from 0.1 watt to 20 megawatts (MW) (thermal). In contrast, a typical commercial nuclear power reactor is rated at 3,000 MW (thermal). Because of this large difference in power generated, the consequence of an accident at an RTR is limited when compared to that of a commercial power reactor. However, several RTRs operate on highly enriched uranium (HEU) fuels which may present a threat if diverted or stolen. In addition, many RTRs are collocated with significant quantities of radiological materials which could be used in a radiological dispersal device (RDD). Adequate emergency planning zones (EPZs)[18] to protect the public from potential radiological accidents at RTRs are, in some cases, within owner-controlled areas. RTRs take many varieties and forms. Reactors may be classified by the type of material, called the moderator,[19] used to slow the neutrons that cause fission.

The NRC requires RTRs to maintain security and emergency plans in accordance with regulations established in 10 CFR 73. Because of the relatively low power output of research reactors, the more extensive security requirements for power reactors are not mandated for RTR facilities. The NRC also imposes varying RTR security requirements based on its evaluation of a particular RTRs' site-specific criteria, such as source-term (quantity and enrichment of special nuclear material), thermal power output, physical design, etc.

In addition, all RTRs have automatic shutdown systems. Before an unsafe condition occurs, control rods rapidly shut down the reactor. Redundant systems that initiate a reactor shutdown also help to protect the public. Most of the reactors do not generate enough heat to be of concern in a loss-of-coolant accident. Others have auxiliary features and systems capable of adding water from a tank or city water supply to provide core cooling. Because of the low power levels at which RTRs operate, they require

---

[18] To facilitate a preplanned strategy for protective actions during an emergency, there are two EPZs around each nuclear power plant (the Plume Exposure Pathway EPZ and Ingestion Exposure Pathway EPZ). The exact size and shape of each EPZ is a result of detailed planning, which includes consideration of the specific conditions at each site, unique geographical features of the area, and demographic information.

[19] A material such as ordinary water, heavy water, or graphite that is used in a reactor to slow down high-velocity neutrons, thus increasing the likelihood of fission.

Nuclear Power Plants

A nuclear power plant is an arrangement of structures, systems, and components used to generate electrical power. Because the Nation's nuclear power plants were built at different times by numerous vendors using different plant designs, each reactor facility is unique. However, the following are some major components common to all current U.S. nuclear power plants and their functions:

- Nuclear reactor cores produce energy to heat water. Heat transfer/working fluid loops transfer thermal energy from the reactor to electricity-generating components. Steam-driven turbines operate generators to produce electrical power. Generating transformers convert electricity into suitable voltage for transmission and consumption.

- Reactor vessels house and provide for proper control of the reactor core. Containment structures and systems prevent release of radioactivity to the environment if the reactor coolant system and reactor core are damaged. Pools and casks store spent nuclear fuel (SNF).

- Heat sinks (e.g., cooling tower, river, lake, ocean) and associated normal cooling water systems condense steam and cool plant equipment during normal operation.

- Plant control room and reactor control systems allow for proper control of the reactor under normal and emergency conditions.

Nuclear power plants also have the following for accident mitigation:

- Nuclear power plant design and safety procedures support prevention or mitigation of damage associated with a robust series of design-basis accidents, including earthquakes, fires, floods, loss of off-site power, and extreme winds such as hurricanes and tornadoes.

- Three distinct barriers are designed to prevent radioactive material from being released into the environment: the cladding that contains actual fuel pellets; the reactor vessel itself where the fuel resides, which is made of thick, high-strength steel; and the containment building that encloses the reactor components, made of heavily reinforced concrete many feet thick.

- Redundant emergency systems with redundant electrical power supplies are designed to preclude overheating, melting of the core, and release of radioactive material during an accident. Redundant instrumentation and control features automatically initiate reactor shutdown and emergency systems activation during an accident.

- Emergency plans and procedures and severe accident management strategies are designed to reduce accident consequences and minimize the public's radiation exposure. Strong training programs and frequent emergency plan testing integrated with Federal, State, and local agency involvement are designed to ensure that emergency response organizations are well prepared.

Nuclear power plants also have the following security features:

- Nuclear power plant security is premised on the principle of defense-in-depth, in which independent, redundant layers of defense are employed to enhance security and guard against single-point failures.

- Specific elements of a defense-in-depth strategy may include hardware, such as barrier and surveillance systems; procedures, including access controls, security operations, and emergency-response planning; and facility design.

- Nuclear power plants and Category I fuel cycle facilities must possess security adequate to protect against the relevant Design Basis Threat (DBT). Adherence to this requirement is regularly inspected and is tested through Force-on-Force Exercises employing a mock adversary force.

this cooling only for short periods after shutdown. Many of these RTRs are located in pools, under enough water to provide necessary radiation shielding.

Decommissioned Nuclear Facilities

Decommissioning is the regulated process by which a licensed nuclear facility is safely removed from operational service. The NRC requires that decommissioned facilities adhere to the regulations requiring protection of the radioactive material onsite.

1.1.2 Materials and Waste

Fuel Cycle Facilities

The NRC licenses eight major fuel fabrication and production facilities to operate in six States. In addition, the NRC regulates two gaseous diffusion fuel enrichment facilities, one operational and one in cold shutdown. Both are operated by the United States Enrichment Corporation (USEC) and leased from DOE. The NRC regulates nine additional facilities (other than reactors) that possess small quantities of SNM or process source material[20] (other than uranium recovery facilities, where uranium is extracted from the ground or from mined ore). Table 1-2 lists the categories of fuel cycle facilities.

Table 1-2:   Categories of Fuel Cycle Facilities

Category I Fuel Cycle Facilities: Two operating facilities in the United States:
- Licensed to receive, possess, use, and store a Category I quantity of strategic special nuclear material (SSNM). SSNM consists of uranium-235 (contained in uranium enriched to 20 percent or more in the U-235 isotope), uranium-233, or plutonium
- Category I quantity of SSNM is 5,000 grams or more in any combination computed by the formula: (grams contained U-235) + 2.5(grams U-233 + grams plutonium)

Category II Fuel Cycle Facilities: Two NRC-licensed facilities in the United States authorized to possess Category II-level SNM (however, these facilities do not fabricate fuel):
- Licensed to receive, possess, use, and store SNM of moderate strategic significance;
- Category II quantity of material is either:
  - Less than Category I quantity of SSNM, but more than 1,000 grams of uranium-235 (contained in uranium enriched to 20 percent or more in the U-235 isotope), or more than 500 grams of uranium-233 or plutonium, or the combination of more than 1,000 grams computed by the formula: (grams contained U-235) + 2 (grams U-233 + grams plutonium)
  - 10,000 grams or more of uranium-235 (contained in uranium enriched to 10 percent or more, but less than 20 percent in the U-235 isotope)

Category III Fuel Cycle Facilities: Four operating fuel fabrication facilities in the United States that manufacture fuel assemblies for commercial nuclear reactors:
- Licensed to receive, possess, use, and store SNM of low strategic significance;
- Category III quantity of material is any one of the following:
  - Less than an amount of SNM of moderate strategic significance, but more than 15 grams of uranium-235 (contained in uranium enriched to 20 percent or more in the U-235 isotope), or 15 grams of uranium-233 or plutonium, or the combination of 15 grams when computed by the formula: (grams contained U-235) + (grams plutonium) + (grams U-233)
  - Less than 10,000 grams but more than 1,000 grams of uranium-235 (contained in uranium enriched to 10 percent or more but less than 20 percent in the U-235 isotope)
  - 10,000 grams or more of uranium-235 (contained in uranium enriched above natural, but less than 10 percent in the U-235 isotope)

[20] Natural uranium or thorium or depleted uranium that is not suitable for use as reactor fuel. The Department of Energy (DOE) regulates activities undertaken by it or on its behalf. In addition, DOE is responsible for promoting common defense and security, conducting research and development, and other activities to support the use of byproduct, source, and special nuclear materials for medical, biological, health, and other uses in assuring public health and safety in accordance with Section 102(13) of the DOE Organization Act, as amended.

Category III Fuel Enrichment Facilities:

- Gaseous Diffusion Plants (GDPs)
  - One operating GDP and one in cold shutdown in the United States, both operated by USEC, which was created as a government corporation under the Energy Act of 1992 and privatized by legislation in 1996
  - Certified to receive, possess, use, and store source material (or natural uranium, less than 5.5 percent enriched) and SNM
  - Manufacture feed materials—enriched uranium hexafluoride (UF6)—for commercial fuel fabricator facilities
- Gas Centrifuge Uranium Enrichment Facilities
  - One facility in the United States (not operational)
  - Certified to receive, possess, use, and store source material (or natural uranium, up to 5 percent enriched) and SNM
  - Manufactures feed materials—enriched UF6—for commercial fuel fabricator facilities

Uranium Conversion Facilities (UF6 Production Facilities):

- Licensed to receive, possess, use, and store source material (natural uranium)
- Manufacture feed materials in the form of UF6 for commercial fuel enrichment facilities. Currently, there is one UF6 production facility licensed by the NRC in the United States

The principal potential hazard at fuel cycle facilities is from chemical releases. An offsite release of these chemicals may have substantially greater consequences than those associated with the release of radioactive material from a nuclear reactor.

Fuel cycle facilities are categorized based on the type of nuclear material that they store or produce. [21] SNM is given different designations depending on its level of enrichment and the amount of material a facility possesses.

Uranium mining and milling facilities are also part of the fuel cycle facility category. A uranium mill is a chemical plant designed to extract uranium from mined ore. The mined ore is brought to the milling facility by truck and the ore is crushed and leached. In most cases, sulfuric acid is used as the leaching agent, but alkaline leaching can also be used. The leaching agent extracts not only uranium from the ore, but also several other constituents such as molybdenum, vanadium, selenium, iron, lead, and arsenic. The uranium product from the mill is referred to as "yellow cake" because of its yellowish color.

Uranium is extracted from ore at uranium mills and at in situ leach (ISL) facilities. The yellow cake generated by both processes is sent to a conversion facility for the next step in manufacturing nuclear fuel. The uranium milling and disposal of byproduct material by the NRC licensees is regulated under Title 10 of the Code of Federal Regulations (CFR)[22] Part 40, Appendix 3.

Conventional mills crush the pieces of ore and extract 90 to 95 percent of the uranium. Mills are typically located in areas of low population density, and they process ore from mines within about 30 miles. Most mills in the United States are being decommissioned. One is in cold shutdown mode, and one is in operation.

ISL facilities are another means of extracting uranium from underground mines. ISL facilities recover uranium from ores that may not be economically recoverable by other methods. In this process, a leaching agent such as oxygen with sodium carbonate is injected through wells into the ore body to dissolve the uranium. The leach solution is pumped from the formation, and ion exchange separates the uranium from the solution. Twelve such facilities exist in the United States.

Low-Level Radioactive Waste Disposal

Low-level waste includes items that have become contaminated with radioactive material or have become radioactive through exposure to neutron radiation. This waste typically consists of contaminated protective shoe covers and clothing, wiping rags,

---

[21] Uranium, plutonium, or another substance that is or may be used to extract nuclear energy (nuclear fuel), or a compound containing such a substance; thorium or another substance suited for conversion into nuclear fuel, or a compound containing such a substance; and SNF that has not been placed in final storage.

[22] Codification of the general and permanent rules published in the Federal Register by the executive departments and agencies of the Federal Government. It is divided into 50 titles that represent broad areas subject to Federal regulation. Each volume of the CFR is updated once each calendar year and is issued quarterly.

mops, filters and resins, reactor water treatment residues, equipment and tools, luminous dials, catheters, swabs, injection needles, syringes, and disused radioactive sealed sources. Also included is radioactive waste identified as greater than Class C (GTCC)[23] low-level waste. The radioactivity can range from just above background levels found in nature to very high levels in certain cases, such as parts from inside a nuclear power plant reactor vessel. Low-level waste can be stored onsite by licensees until the radioactivity has decayed and the items can be disposed of as ordinary trash, or the waste can be accumulated and shipped to a low-level waste disposal site in containers specified or approved by DOT or the NRC.

Commercial low-level waste disposal facilities must be licensed by either the NRC or an Agreement State (the Agreement State program is described later in this chapter), in accordance with health and safety requirements. The facilities must be designed, constructed, and operated to meet safety and environmental protection standards. The operator of a facility must also extensively characterize the site where the facility is located and analyze how the facility will perform for at least 500 years.

Low-level waste disposal facilities occasionally provide storage for chemical waste as well. In those cases, facilities are considered to be in both the Nuclear and Chemical Sectors.

There are currently three low-level commercial waste disposal facilities in the United States that accept various types of low-level waste from certain States. These facilities, situated in and regulated by Agreement States, are in Barnwell, SC; Richland, WA; and Clive, UT.

High-Level Radioactive Waste Disposal

High-level radioactive wastes are the highly radioactive material produced as a byproduct of the reactions that occur inside nuclear reactors. High-level wastes take one of three forms:

- Irradiated nuclear fuel;
- Highly radioactive material remaining after spent fuel is reprocessed;[24] or
- Other highly radioactive material that the NRC, consistent with existing law, determines by rule requires permanent isolation.

High-level waste and spent fuel must be handled and stored with care because of their highly radioactive fission products. Radioactive waste becomes radioactively harmless through decay. The waste must be stored and finally disposed of in a manner that provides adequate public protection.

Spent Fuel Storage

All operating nuclear power reactors store spent fuel under the NRC licenses in spent fuel pools located within the protected area.

In addition, the United States has 42 licensed independent spent fuel storage installations (ISFSIs) in the United States. Twenty-eight operating power plants have ISFSIs, as do eight decommissioned power plant sites; four power plant sites that are in the decommissioning process; an interim storage facility operated by DOE at the Idaho National Laboratory near Idaho Falls; and the General Electric Morris operation in Illinois (which is licensed for wet storage of spent fuel).

---

[23] Defined in the Low Level Waste (LLW) Policy Amendments Act of 1985 as LLW that exceeds the Class C limits in 10 CFR Part 61.55, Licensing Requirements for Land Disposal of Radioactive Waste. This section classifies LLW as Class A, B, or C, according to concentration of specific short and long lived radionuclides; it also sets varying requirements on waste forms for disposal. Most forms of GTCC waste are generated by routine operations at nuclear power plants, fuel research facilities, and manufacturers of radiopharmaceuticals, as well as sealed sources used in medical and industrial applications and moisture and density gauges and contaminated trash. GTCC waste is generally unacceptable for near surface disposal.

[24] Reprocessing of spent fuel from commercial nuclear reactors is not currently performed in the United States.

In 1990, the NRC amended its regulations to authorize storage of spent fuel at reactor sites in dry cask storage systems that it approves. Dry cask storage allows spent fuel that has already been cooled in the spent fuel pool to be transferred to an NRC-certified storage cask. Dry storage, which is almost completely passive, is simpler and uses fewer support systems than spent fuel pools. Dry storage is not suitable for spent fuel until it has been out of the reactor for several years and the amount of heat generated by radioactive decay has been reduced. The casks are typically steel cylinders that are either welded or bolted closed. The cylinders provide robust containment and confinement of the spent fuel. Each cylinder is surrounded by additional steel, concrete, or other material to provide radiation shielding to workers and the public. Some cask designs, referred to as dual-purpose canisters, can be used for both storage and transportation.

Radioactive Sealed Sources

Radioactive materials have numerous applications in the United States. They provide critical capabilities in the public health, oil and gas, electrical power, construction, and food industries. They are used to treat millions of patients each year in diagnostic and therapeutic medical procedures and in various law enforcement and military applications. In addition, they are used in many areas for technology research and development (R&D) at academic, government, and private institutions.

The radioactive material for medical diagnostic procedures and for R&D may be used in many chemical and physical forms. Industrial uses principally involve encapsulated radioactive material or sealed sources. There are millions of radioactive sources in the United States and tens of thousands of authorized users (licensees). The amount of radioactive material authorized for use by these licensees varies from 1 one-millionth of a curie to millions of curies (used, for instance, in large irradiators). A graded regulatory approach to safety and security is generally consistent with the potential radiation risk from these materials.

Oversight of regulated radioactive material is commensurate with the level of risk to workers and the public that the materials pose under ordinary or accident-related conditions, when used for their intended purposes. These risk-significant radioactive materials[25] require implementation of additional security measures and increased controls to enhance their protection from theft or sabotage.

Byproduct material is radioactive material (except for SNM) yielded or made radioactive by exposure to radiation incident to the process of producing or utilizing SNM, and the tailings or wastes produced by the extraction or concentration of uranium or thorium from any ore primarily for its use as source material content. Under the Energy Policy Act of 2005 (EPAct), byproduct material now also includes discrete sources of radium and other naturally occurring radioactive material, as well as accelerator-produced radioactive material. Examples of byproduct material include cobalt-60, cesium-137, and iridium-192. Source material is uranium or thorium, or any combination of them, in any physical or chemical form, or ores that contain, by weight, one-twentieth of 1 percent of these elements.

The AEA, as amended, gives the NRC the responsibility and authority for control of commercial SNM, source material, and byproduct material. Under the AEA, the NRC is authorized to transfer some of its authority to the States on a State-specific basis. To date, 37 States, known as Agreement States, have entered into agreements with the NRC to regulate byproduct and source material and very small quantities of SNM. More information and a complete list of Agreement States as of November 2009 are provided in section 1.2.5.

---

[25] Radioactive material that is considered to be Category 1 and 2 sources, based on the definitions of Category 1 and 2 sources in the International Atomic Energy Agency (IAEA) Code of Conduct on Safety and Security of Radioactive Sources. That document states that Category 1 sources, if not safely managed or securely protected, would be likely to cause permanent injury to a person who handled them or was otherwise in contact with them for more than a few minutes. It would probably be fatal to be close to this amount of unshielded material for longer than a few minutes. Category 2 sources, if not safely managed or securely protected, could cause permanent injury to a person who handled them or was otherwise in contact with them for a short time (minutes to hours). It could possibly be fatal to be close to this amount of unshielded radioactive material for a period of hours to days.

Radioactive Material Transportation

Licensed radioactive material is shipped in accordance with the hazardous material transportation safety and security regulations of DOT and the NRC. The responsibilities of the two agencies are generally divided as follows:

- DOT regulates shippers and carriers of hazardous material, including radioactive material. DOT is responsible for such safety requirements as vehicle safety, routing, shipping papers, hazard communications, certain packaging requirements, emergency response information, and shipper/carrier training requirements, as well as security requirements for highway route controlled quantities (HRCQ) of radioactive material and other quantities of radioactive material that require placards for transport.

- The NRC regulates users of radioactive material and approves design, fabrication, use, and maintenance of transportation packages for domestic radioactive material shipments. It also regulates the physical protection of commercial spent fuel and large quantities of radioactive material in transit against sabotage or other malicious acts.[26]

Packages of low-hazard radioactive material are shipped throughout the United States by rail, air, sea, and road. They contain small quantities of radioactive material typically used in industry and medicine. They are designed to provide a safe and economical means of transporting relatively small quantities of radioactive material. The regulations prescribe limits on the amount of radioactivity that can be transported in these packages, such that doses from an accident will have no substantial health risks. Examples include transport of smoke detectors, exit signs, watch dials, some radiopharmaceuticals,[27] and such slightly contaminated equipment as syringes used to administer radiopharmaceuticals.

Safety standards for the more hazardous radioactive material packaged in casks are set forth in NRC regulations. Casks must be designed to withstand a series of impacts, punctures, fires, and a deep-water immersion test to provide reasonable assurance that they will withstand serious transportation accidents. An approval certificate for the design must be issued by the NRC before a cask can be used to domestically transport more hazardous radioactive material, such as spent fuel or the high-activity sources used in panoramic irradiators. DOT, in consultation with the NRC, revalidates foreign certificates for casks used in international shipments.

The standards established in NRC regulations require that transportation packages, or casks, prevent the loss or dispersion of their radioactive contents, provide adequate shielding and heat dissipation, and prevent nuclear criticality (a self-sustaining nuclear chain reaction) under both normal and accident conditions of transport.

Nuclear Sector partners also coordinate, as appropriate, with the Transportation Security Administration (TSA) and the U.S. Coast Guard (USCG), which are assigned SSA responsibilities, respectively, for the Transportation Systems Sector and its maritime mode, and with other relevant partners to enhance the security of Nuclear Sector assets in transit.[28]

1.1.3 Cross-cutting Sector Human and Cyber Elements

There is a human element to be considered relative to each Nuclear Sector asset, system, and network. This human element consideration requires:

- Identifying and preventing the potential insider threat resulting from infiltration or individual employees determined to do harm;

---

[26] While the NRC regulates the security measures applied to commercial shipments of SNF, it does not regulate DOE's shipment of SNF to the Yucca Mountain repository. The DOE regulates those shipments, as well as shipments of its own SNF and radioactive material. The Nuclear Waste Policy Act, as amended, requires that the NRC certify the packages used by DOE for transport, and that DOE comply with the NRC's shipment pre-notification regulations. DOE regulates all other aspects of transportation, including physical security.

[27] Same as medical isotopes, which are defined as radioactive elements (atoms) used for medical purposes. Different radiopharmaceutical drugs are used for diagnostic imaging of the heart and other organs, and for therapy in treatment of cancers and other diseases.

[28] Discussion of plans, processes, and activities used by TSA, DOT, and other Transportation Systems Sector and modal subsector CIKR partners to promote the security and resiliency of the Nation's transportation CIKR may be found in the Transportation Systems Sector SSP.

- Identifying, protecting, and supporting (e.g., through cross training) employees and other people with critical knowledge or functions; and

- Identifying and mitigating tactics used by terrorist agents and insider attackers.

Some of the ways that the Nuclear Sector addresses these parameters include running background checks on employees, providing extra protective measures to safeguard the most critical employees, and conducting exercises and drills to physically and mentally prepare employees for potential terrorist activity.

A cyber element also requires consideration for each Nuclear Sector asset, system, and network. Functions at nuclear facilities that are provided by digital and analog devices, equipment, and systems include:

- Acquiring and displaying real-time information about plant and equipment parameters that aid in plant operation, maintenance, management, security, or safety;

- Providing real-time calculation of plant parameters or limits based on instrumented or manually entered information;

- Maintaining safe and secure operations of nuclear power plants;

- Providing an alarm or warning when a parameter exceeds a limit;

- Controlling equipment position or function based on an internal algorithm; and

- Acquiring and storing information about the plant or plant operations to support data analysis and decision making on plant operations and maintenance.

For example, for each of these functions, a compromise in cybersecurity could affect a facility in one of three ways:

- Confidentiality: Confidentiality of information could be violated by having an individual or organization acquire information without authorization;

- Integrity: Digital devices or systems could be manipulated to provide erroneous data or to alter a critical function or process; or

- Availability: Authorized users could be denied access to a digital device or system.

1.1.4 Interdependencies and Overlapping Relationships With Other Sectors

This sector has multiple dependencies and interdependencies with other sectors, including Energy as a supplier of critical electrical power; Transportation Systems for the movement of radioactive material; Chemical for hazardous chemicals used at fuel cycle facilities; Healthcare and Public Health as related to nuclear medicine, radiopharmaceuticals, and sterilization of surgical supplies; and Government Facilities for Federal and State facilities that use radioactive material for myriad purposes. While nuclear power plants provide electrical power to the grid, the infrastructure protection requirement associated with the grid itself would be discussed in the Energy SSP. The Nuclear SSP addresses the grid only as it relates to nuclear power plant operations and vulnerabilities. In addition, the Nuclear Sector does not include DoD and DOE nuclear facilities or radioactive material associated with defense-related activities.

Many assets are dependent upon multiple elements and systems to maintain functionality. In some cases, a failure in one sector will have a significant impact on the ability of another sector to perform necessary functions. When one sector relies specifically on another sector, the relationship is called a dependency. [29] If two assets are dependent upon one another, then they are

---

[29] The NIPP defines a dependency as the one-directional reliance of an asset, system, network, or collection thereof, within or across sectors, on input, interaction, or other requirement from other sources to function properly.

interdependent.[30] It is extremely important to identify dependencies and interdependencies, both at the sector and asset levels, to fully understand the consequences of a manmade or natural disaster.

Overlaps exist where assets fit into more than one of the 18 CIKR sectors described in the NIPP based on their operating characteristics or functions. For example, the Hoover Dam is a key resource placed in the Dams Sector, but it also could be classified as an Energy Sector asset due to its hydroelectric power generation capabilities, a Transportation Systems Sector asset due to the highway that runs over the dam, and a National Monuments and Icons Sector asset. Identifying cross-sector overlaps is important to minimize duplication of effort and ensure that critical considerations are not being ignored because of shared security responsibilities and authorities.

Table 1-3 identifies the CIKR sectors that are interdependent or overlap with the Nuclear Sector. DHS is working with the SSAs responsible for each of the sectors identified to enhance the security of assets that are interdependent or overlap with the Nuclear Sector.

Table 1-3: Nuclear Sector Interdependencies and Overlaps With Other CIKR Sectors

Sector (SSA)	Interdependency/Overlap With the Nuclear Sector
Transportation Systems (DHS/TSA)	The Nuclear Sector overlaps with and is dependent upon the Transportation Systems Sector for transportation of materials by land, water, and air. Modes of transportation used to ship nuclear and radioactive material in various stages of the value chain include ships, barges, trains, trucks, and airplanes. Disruption of the Transportation Systems Sector has the potential to seriously hinder the movement of materials and cause cascading effects throughout the Nuclear Sector. Nuclear, like all other sectors, is dependent upon enhanced airport screening and other security measures as the most effective strategy for protection of CIKR against air attacks.
Energy (DOE)	The Nuclear Sector overlaps with the Energy Sector because of its production of electricity. The Energy Sector has primary responsibility for electric power. In addition, like most other sectors, the Nuclear Sector depends on Energy for power. An interruption to the power supply would directly affect nuclear facilities in the region serviced by a downed electrical grid.
Emergency Services (DHS IP)	Because of its uniquely hazardous characteristics, the Nuclear Sector relies on many distinct entities at the Federal, State, local, and tribal level to provide emergency response services in an incident.
Healthcare & Public Health (Department of Health and Human Services (HHS))	The Healthcare and Public Health (HPH) Sector depends on the Nuclear Sector for many items, including pharmaceuticals and diagnostic and therapeutic substances. A successful attack on the Nuclear Sector could have a cascading impact on the HPH Sector. Conversely, the Nuclear Sector depends on HPH to ensure the well being of its workers during a major disease outbreak, such as pandemic flu.
Information Technology (DHS, National Cyber Security Division (NCSD))	As in all other sectors, the Nuclear Sector depends on the Information Technology (IT) Sector. Many sector facilities rely heavily on IT to control critical processes, manage day-to-day operations, and store sensitive information. In addition, DHS, the Nuclear SCC, NRC, industry associations, and other sector partners use IT to facilitate information sharing, including dissemination of security and threat data.

---

[30] Mutually reliant relationship between entities (objects, individuals, or groups). The degree of inter-dependency does not need to be equal in both directions.

Sector (SSA)	Interdependency/Overlap With the Nuclear Sector
Communications (DHS, National Communications System (NCS))	Like all other sectors, the Nuclear Sector depends on the Telecommunications Sector for much of its communications capability.
Chemical (DHS IP)	The Nuclear and Chemical sectors are interdependent because the principal hazard to public health and safety during an accident at a fuel cycle facility would be from the release of onsite chemicals.
CIKR in close physical proximity to Nuclear Sector assets	If an attack occurs on CIKR in close proximity to Nuclear Sector assets, that attack can also affect the nuclear assets in the area. Likewise, attacks on Nuclear Sector assets can potentially impact other nearby CIKR.

In addition to the dependencies and interdependencies identified above, the NIPP requires the Federal Government to create a comprehensive inventory of infrastructure outside the United States that, if disrupted or destroyed, would lead to loss of life in the United States, or would critically affect the Nation's economic, industrial, or defensive capabilities. In response, DHS, working with the Department of State (DOS), developed the Critical Foreign Dependencies Initiative (CFDI), an effort designed to ensure that a classified National Critical Foreign Dependencies List will be inclusive, representative, and leveraged in a coordinated and responsible manner.

To accomplish this mission, CFDI involves the following three initial phases that were started in 2008:

- Phase I – Identification: DHS is coordinating with infrastructure protection community partners to develop the first-ever National Critical Foreign Dependencies List, reflecting the critical foreign dependencies of all 18 CIKR sectors, as well as critical foreign dependencies of interest to the Nation as a whole.

- Phase II – Prioritization: After the list is developed, DHS, again working with its CIKR partners, and in particular DOS, will prioritize the National Critical Foreign Dependencies List based on factors such as overall criticality of the element to the United States and foreign partner willingness and capability to engage in risk management activities.

- Phase III – Engagement: Phase III involves leveraging the prioritized National Critical Foreign Dependencies List to guide U.S. bilateral and multilateral incident and risk management activities with foreign partners.

1.2 CIKR Partners

1.2.1 Department of Homeland Security

The national approach for CIKR protection is provided through the unifying framework established in HSPD-7. This directive establishes the U.S. policy for "enhancing protection of the Nation's CIKR" and mandates a national plan to actuate that policy. In HSPD-7, the President designates the Secretary of Homeland Security as the "principal Federal official to lead CIKR protection efforts among Federal departments and agencies, State and local governments, and the private sector" and assigns responsibility for coordination of CIKR sectors to the SSAs. The SSAs are responsible for working with DHS and their respective GCCs and are responsible for: implementing the NIPP sector partnership model and risk management framework; developing protective programs, resiliency strategies, and related requirements; and providing sector-level CIKR protection guidance in line with the overarching guidance established by DHS pursuant to HSPD-7. In accordance with HSPD-7, SSAs are also responsible for collaborating with private sector partners and encouraging the development of appropriate voluntary information-sharing and analysis mechanisms within the sector. This includes encouraging voluntary security-related information sharing, where possible, among private entities within the sector, as well as among public and private entities.

DHS Office of Infrastructure Protection

The Nuclear SSA works closely with other divisions within IP to execute its responsibilities:

- The Contingency Planning and Incident Management Division (CPIMD) coordinates and implements IP's CIKR preparedness activities in the areas of exercises, contingency planning, concept of operations development, and incident management in a manner that is consistent with and supportive of the NIPP and the National Response Framework (NRF), as well as established DHS and Federal inter-agency incident management coordination structures.

- The Infrastructure Analysis and Strategy Division (IASD) leads the Nation's premier analytical team in the conduct of CIKR-related modeling, simulation, and analysis, in close collaboration with DHS and NIPP partners.

- The Infrastructure Information Collection Division (IICD) leads DHS' efforts to acquire and provide standardized, relevant, and customer-focused infrastructure data to various public and private sector homeland security partners.

- The Infrastructure Security Compliance Division (ISCD) leads the implementation of the Chemical Facility Anti-Terrorism Standards (CFATS), balancing regulatory authority with the need to secure the nation's highest risk chemical facilities while sustaining the economic vitality of the chemical industry. The ISCD program assesses high-risk chemical facilities, promotes collaborative security planning, and ensures that covered facilities meet risk-based performance standards.

- The Partnership and Outreach Division (POD) develops and sustains viable strategic relationships and information-sharing systems and processes with the SSAs and owners and operators of the Nation's CIKR that support program execution across the spectrum of preparedness, prevention, protection, response, and recovery activities. Additionally, POD provides coordination and management of the NIPP process and its supporting SSPs, as well as the National CIKR Protection Annual Report, which tracks progress of NIPP and SSP implementation, including performance metrics.

- The Protective Security Coordination Division (PSCD) reduces the risk of a terrorist attack on the Nation's CIKR by: assessing vulnerabilities and consequences; developing, implementing, and providing national coordination for protective programs and resiliency strategies; and facilitating CIKR response and recovery operations in an all-hazards environment.

In addition, DHS has numerous responsibilities in its role as the focal point for cybersecurity and for leading, integrating, and coordinating the overall national effort to enhance CIKR protection. Some of the responsibilities that directly pertain to the Nuclear Sector are:

- Coordinating, facilitating, and supporting the overall process for building partnerships and leveraging sector-specific security expertise, relationships, and resources across CIKR sectors, including oversight and support of the sector partnership model;

- Working with DOS, the SSAs, and other partners to ensure that U.S. CIKR protection efforts are fully coordinated with international partners;

- Facilitating the sharing of CIKR protection best practices and processes and risk assessment methodologies and tools across sectors and jurisdictions;

- Coordinating multiagency efforts to optimize use of resources and avoid duplicative activities;

- Sponsoring CIKR protection-related R&D, demonstration projects, and pilot programs; and

- Promoting national CIKR protection education, training, and awareness through State, local, tribal, and territorial government partners, as well as private sector partners.

Other organizations within DHS that are engaged in Nuclear Sector activities include the Federal Emergency Management Agency (FEMA), DHS Science and Technology Directorate (S&T), TSA, USCG, the DHS Domestic Nuclear Detection Office (DNDO), and DHS' Office of Cyber Security and Communications (CS&C).

National Infrastructure Protection Plan Coordinating Councils

The NIPP describes the organizational framework for coordination of CIKR protection efforts at all levels of government, as well as within and across sectors. Sector-specific planning and coordination are addressed through the GCCs and SCCs.

The NGCC and the NSCC were established on October 13, 2004. The NGCC and NSCC meet quarterly to continue developing this important partnership. The councils are part of the overall sector partnership model that is described in the NIPP and they provide a structure through which representative groups from all levels of government and the private sector can collaborate and share approaches to Nuclear CIKR protection.

Figure 1-2: The Sector Partnership Structure in the Nuclear Sector

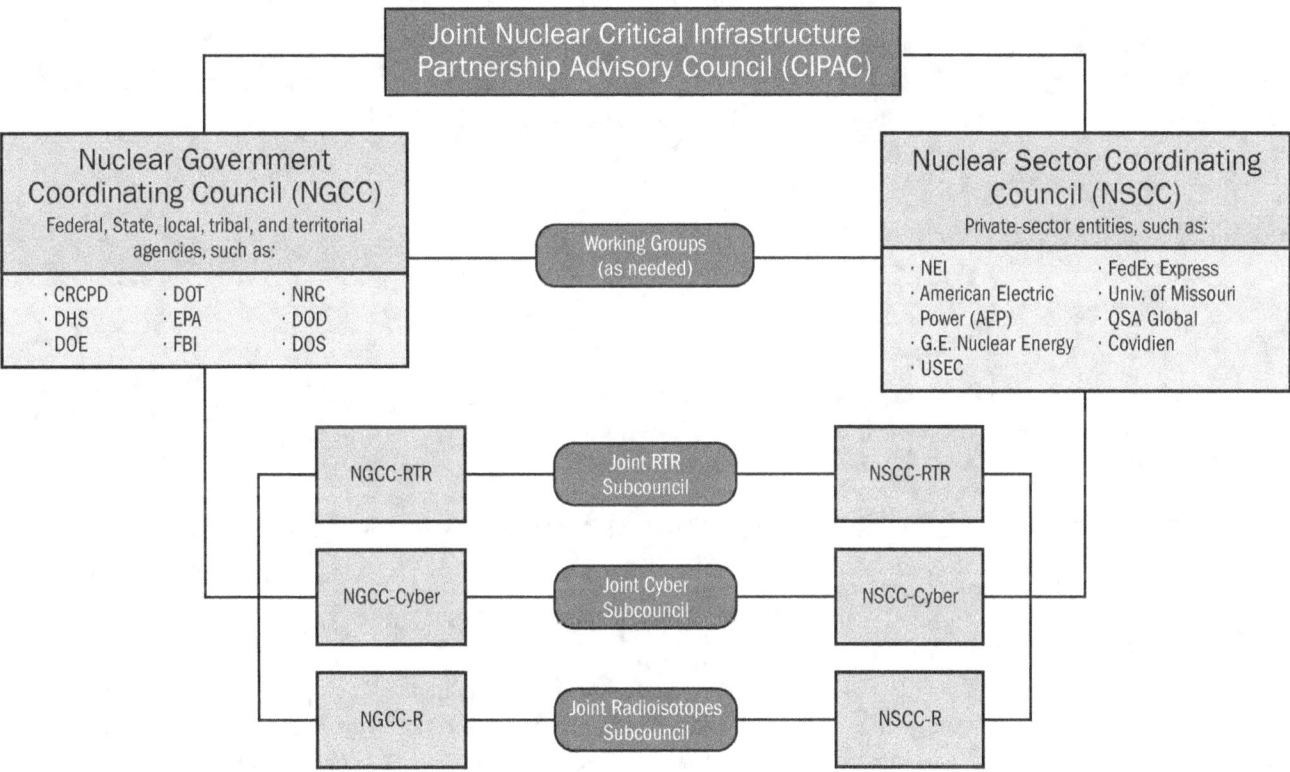

Nuclear Government Coordinating Council

The NGCC is the principal Federal interagency body responsible for coordinating domestic civilian nuclear and radiological security strategies, activities, policies, and communications, including those activities conducted in partnership with State and local partners, and those between government and industry to support the Nation's homeland security mission. In addition, the NGCC coordinates with existing emergency management and public health and safety communities regarding response and recovery issues associated with a terrorist act or other disasters involving radioactive materials. The NGCC accomplishes these objectives through the following types of activities:

- Identification and facilitation of activities that benefit from public-private coordination;

- Identification and facilitation of improvements to plans, programs, policies, procedures, technologies, and strategies that affect Nuclear Sector partners;

- Initiatives to encourage, acknowledge, and recognize successful non-regulatory programs and practices within the Nuclear Sector and interdependent sectors; and

- Initiatives to leverage complementary resources within the Federal Government and between Federal Government and industry to support the Nation's homeland security mission.

The NGCC is co-chaired by the DHS Assistant Secretary for Infrastructure Protection and the Director, SSA Executive Management Office. Membership comprises the organizations listed in Table 1-4.

Table 1-4: Nuclear Government Coordinating Council Membership

Voting Members[a]	Ad Hoc Members	Ex Officio Members
· DHS IP · Commonwealth of Massachusetts · Commonwealth of Pennsylvania · DOE · DOS · DOT · Environmental Protection Agency (EPA) · FBI · NRC · State of Delaware · State of Florida · State of Texas	· Customs and Border Protection (CBP) · DNDO · FEMA · TSA · USCG	· DoD, Homeland Defense

[a] Note: State partners also represent the Organization of Agreement States and/or the Conference of Radiation Control Program Directors, Inc. (CRCPD).

Nuclear Sector Coordinating Council

The mission of the NSCC is to advance the physical, cybersecurity, and emergency preparedness posture of the Nation's commercial nuclear infrastructure in the context of overall national infrastructure protection. This mission will be accomplished through the voluntary interaction of infrastructure owners and operators with the NGCC, as outlined in HSPD-7 and the NIPP.

The NSCC consists of representatives from the nuclear industry and covers the broad interests of Nuclear Sector security. The scope of the NSCC includes companies licensed to operate nuclear power plants in the United States, nuclear plant designers, major nuclear architect and engineering firms, fuel supply and fabrication facilities, research reactors, radioisotope manufacturers and suppliers, commercial nuclear waste management and transportation firms, and other organizations and individuals involved in the nuclear industry. The NSCC is a consensus-driven body with secretariat staff provided by NEI. The NSCC members include those listed in Table 1-5.

Table 1-5: Nuclear Sector Coordinating Council Membership

Members of the Nuclear Sector Coordinating Council	
• American Association of Physicists in Medicine • American Electric Power • Arizona Public Service Company • Constellation Energy Generation Group • Covidien • Dominion Energy • Dominion Generation • Edlow International Company • Entergy Operations • Exelon Generation Company, LLC • FirstEnergy Corp.	• Florida Power & Light Company • General Electric • National Institute of Standards and Technology • Nuclear Energy Institute • Oregon State University • QSA Global • Southern Nuclear Company • University of Missouri • USEC Inc.

While the precise makeup of the NSCC may change, it will generally conform to the following guidelines:

• Six members from companies owning or operating at least one commercial nuclear power reactor;

• One member from owners of fuel manufacturing or fuel fabrication facilities;

• One member from manufacturers of nuclear reactors or components;

• One observer from the National Organization of Test, Research, and Training Reactors (TRTR);

• One member from a nuclear waste management or transportation company;

• One member from NEI; and

• Representative(s) from the Nuclear Sector Coordinating Council-Radioisotopes Subcouncil (NSCC-R).

NEI is a member of the NSCC because it represents a large portion of the overall sector, including constituents of the Radioisotopes Subcouncil. All domestic operators of commercial nuclear power plants and fuel processing facilities are members of NEI. Through NEI, the industry can undertake initiatives that commit the entire industry to specific action.

Joint Critical Infrastructure Partnership Advisory Council Meetings

The NGCC and NSCC meet quarterly within the coordination framework provided by the CIPAC to address issues of mutual concern to partners in the public and private sectors. The NGCC and NSCC each oversee three subcouncils: Radioisotopes, RTRs, and Joint Cybersecurity, which meet both separately and jointly and report their progress to the sector councils.

Radioisotopes Subcouncils

The NSCC Radioisotopes Subcouncil (NSCC-R) consists of members representing the radioisotope industry and covers the broad interests of radioisotope sector security. The NSCC-R has representatives from companies in the United States that are licensed to operate radioisotope manufacturing, handling, or processing facilities; companies in the United States that are licensed to distribute radioisotope products; and other organizations, individuals, and users involved in the nuclear industry, including nuclear materials licensees. The mission of the NSCC-R is to develop and recommend strategies that will enhance the physical security and emergency preparedness of the radioisotope industry under the auspices of the NIPP. The NSCC-R works closely with the NGCC Radioisotopes Subcouncil (NGCC-R) in fulfillment of this objective.

The NGCC-R includes a broad range of Federal and State partners engaged in security and risk management in the Nuclear Sector. The NGCC-R develops and recommends policies, strategies, plans, and measures to enhance the physical security and emergency preparedness of the Nation's radioisotope industry. This includes coordinating appropriate public-private collaboration with the NSCC-R. In recognition of the unique characteristics associated with the manufacture, transportation, use, and disposal of radioisotopes, the NGCC-R includes representation from Federal, State, and local agencies that may not be formal members of the full NGCC, such as the CBP, TSA, DOT, and the Council of Radiation Control Program Directors.

Research and Test Reactor Subcouncils

The NGCC Research and Test Reactor Subcouncil (NGCC-RTR) coordinates security strategies, policies, activities, and communications across the U.S. Government and between the U.S. Government and the RTR community. The Subcouncil also coordinates with emergency management and public health and safety communities with regard to security and emergency preparedness in the RTR subsector. Members include:

- DHS, Nuclear SSA;

- DOE, National Nuclear Security Administration (NNSA)

- FBI; and

- NRC.

Like the NGCC-RTR, the NSCC Research and Test Reactor Subcouncil (NSCC-RTR) addresses the security issues associated with research, test, and training reactors, with a primary focus on university facilities. The NSCC-RTR's primary member is the TRTR, which represents U.S. RTR facilities operated by the government, major universities, national laboratories, and private industry.

The NSCC-RTR and NGCC-RTR coordinate implementation of programs seeking to harden RTR facilities beyond the regulatory baseline.

Joint Nuclear Cyber Subcouncil

The Joint NGCC/NSCC Cyber Subcouncil was established in March 2007 and held its first meeting on August 14, 2007. The subcouncil comprises stakeholders with primary responsibility for cybersecurity in the Nuclear Sector. Members, including DHS, FBI, NRC, and private-sector representatives, identify cybersecurity risks potentially affecting the Nuclear Sector, serve as a forum for the sharing of relevant information within the CIPAC framework, and help coordinate Nuclear Sector participation in cross-sector bodies such as the NCSD Cross-Sector Cyber Security Working Group (CSCSWG) and Industrial Control Systems Joint Working Group (ICSJWG).

Domestic Nuclear Detection Office

DNDO plays an essential role in developing and implementing a defensive strategy with domestic and international programs to protect the Nation from a nuclear or radiological terrorist attack. DNDO is the primary agency within the U.S. Government responsible for developing the global nuclear detection architecture and acquiring and supporting the deployment of the domestic detection system to detect and report attempts to import or transport a nuclear device, fissile, or radiological material, intended for illicit use. DNDO's strategic objectives are to:

- Develop the global nuclear detection and reporting architecture;

- Develop, acquire, and support the domestic nuclear detection and reporting system;

- Fully characterize detector system performance before deployment;

- Establish situational awareness through information sharing and analysis;

- Establish operation protocols to ensure detection leads to effective response;

- Conduct a transformational research and development program; and

- Establish the National Technical Nuclear Forensics Center to provide planning, integration, and improvements to USG nuclear forensics capabilities.

1.2.2 Nuclear Regulatory Commission

For more than three decades, the NRC has regulated the civilian nuclear industry to ensure the necessary protection of: (1) commercial nuclear reactors for generating electrical power and non-power reactors used for research and testing; (2) nuclear materials in medical, industrial, and academic settings and fuel cycle facilities; and (3) transportation, storage, and disposal of nuclear materials and waste. The NRC is an independent agency headed by a five-member commission that formulates policies, develops regulations governing nuclear reactor and nuclear material safety and security, issues orders to licensees, and adjudicates legal matters.

Since September 11, 2001, the NRC and licensees have increased their attention on the possibility of malevolent acts at nuclear facilities or malicious use of radioactive material. The NRC has moved to provide for the common defense and security of the United States by requiring licensees to implement additional security measures appropriate for the current threat environment. This is a responsibility that the NRC is not permitted to transfer to the States; however, the AEA in section 274i permits the NRC to enter into agreements under which the States may inspect State licensees on behalf of the NRC. The NRC continues to develop 274i Agreements that allow interested Agreement States to inspect the Agreement State licensee implementation of additional security measures and orders issued under the NRC's common defense and security authority. In addition, some licensees have responded to the attacks of September 11 by collaborating with DOE/NNSA Global Threat Reduction Initiative (GTRI) to implement voluntary security enhancements at their facilities such as improved access control, assessment capabilities, response force training, and physical hardening and delay mechanisms.

The NRC exchanges technical information and operational data with various industry groups and standards organizations. These exchanges include participating in standards committees or sharing other publicly available documents with organizations such as NEI and the Institute of Nuclear Power Operations (INPO). NEI is the policy organization of the nuclear energy and technology industry that promotes the beneficial uses of nuclear energy and technology in the United States and around the world. With member participation, NEI develops policy on key legislative and regulatory issues affecting the industry.

In response to the terrorist attacks of September 11, 2001, and subsequent information provided by intelligence and law enforcement agencies, the NRC issued two security orders to nuclear power plant licensees to enhance cybersecurity at their facilities to address the threat environment at the time. In September 2002, in recognition of the potential cybersecurity-related issues resulting from increased use of digital technology at nuclear power plants and in conjunction with the DOE outreach program in support of Presidential Decision Directive 63, "Protecting America's Critical Infrastructures," the NRC initiated a project to develop a cybersecurity self-assessment method with cooperation from four volunteer "pilot" plants and NEI's Cyber Security Task Force.[31] The NRC published the developed method in a technical report in the U.S. Nuclear Regulatory Commission Regulation (NUREG) series.[32] This report provided a method that licensees used to systematically manage cyber risk at their facilities. Although the report does not provide a comprehensive approach to cybersecurity as described in National Institute of Standards and Technology (NIST) Special Publications, it did provide licensees information useful in developing an interim cybersecurity program for their facilities.

---

[31] According to NEI, the Cyber Security Task Force is a group of industry subject matter experts from NEI member companies. The subject matter experts normally come from the professional staffs of nuclear utilities.

[32] NUREG/CR-68476, Cyber Security Self-Assessment Method for U.S. Nuclear Power Plants, and NEI 04-04, Cyber Security Program for Power Reactors.

Using the report and the insights gained during the development of this method, NEI developed NEI 04-04, "Cyber Security Program for Power Reactors," to provide nuclear power reactor licensees a means for developing and maintaining a cybersecurity program at their sites. In December 2005, the NRC informed NEI that NEI 04-04, Rev. 1, provided an acceptable approach to formulate an interim cybersecurity program in lieu of comprehensive regulatory requirements from the NRC.

In March 2009, the NRC published a comprehensive cybersecurity rule that requires nuclear power plant licensees to provide high assurance that digital computer and communication systems and networks associated with safety, security, and emergency preparedness functions, as well as support systems and equipment, which, if compromised, would adversely impact safety, security, or emergency preparedness functions, are adequately protected against cyber attacks. The new cybersecurity rule also required each nuclear power plant licensee to submit its cybersecurity plans for NRC review and approval by November 23, 2009. Each submittal includes a proposed schedule for implementing a cybersecurity plan. The plans describe how criteria set forth in the new cybersecurity rule will be implemented. Applications for new reactors received on or after November 23, 2009 will also include a cybersecurity plan.

To facilitate rule compliance, the NRC developed a regulatory guide based on published NIST Special Publications to provide a method to comply with the cybersecurity rule. This regulatory guide, Regulatory Guide 5.71, Cyber Security Programs for Nuclear Facilities, also includes a cybersecurity plan template that licensees can use to develop their cybersecurity plan. The NRC published this regulatory guide in January 2010, but it had previously provided a draft copy to all power reactor licensees (as well as combined operating license applicants) in July 2009 and an updated version on September 21, 2009, which they could use to meet the above requirements. In addition, the stakeholders have been participating in the guidance development process since its inception. The industry also developed NEI 08-09, "Cyber Security Plan for Nuclear Power Reactors," which includes a template licensees and applicants can use when developing their plan submission.

In addition to these programmatic cybersecurity tasks, NRC reviews digital instrumentation and controls (I&C) system security as part of the regulatory review process for new reactors and digital upgrades included in license amendment requests. The intent is to ensure that cybersecurity engineering life-cycle activities are an integral part of the digital I&C system design and development processes, consistent with the "build security in" principle. Also, the NRC works with NEI's Cyber Security Task Force to address cybersecurity issues at nuclear power plants, and to develop guidance for future cybersecurity initiatives for the nuclear industry.

The NRC is also revising its oversight program for nuclear power reactors and nuclear material facilities to enhance the use of risk information to guide assessments of licensee performance. Among other components of this program, the NRC modified its physical protection oversight process to accommodate new security requirements imposed on reactor licensees since September 11. In February 2004, the NRC issued new inspection procedures for physical protection and security and, in January 2005, issued a new physical protection significance determination process. This process categorizes inspection findings into four bands: green (very low significance), white (low to moderate significance), yellow (substantial significance), and red (high significance). An action matrix for security and associated assessment processes has been developed and approved by the NRC for use. Although information specific to individual plants will be available to the associated licensee and Federal and State agencies, it will not be available to the general public, except to a limited extent.

To measure CIKR protection success against performance measures and strategic outcomes, the NRC collects and assesses security data involving licensed facilities and radioactive material and tracks it in databases maintained by the NRC. The NRC reports annually to Congress and the Executive Office of the President on its performance relative to the strategic and performance measures. In addition, the NRC reports annually to Congress on abnormal occurrences, including security incidents that satisfy the criteria. The criteria were stated in an NRC policy statement published in the Federal Register (FR) on December 19, 1996 (61 FR 67072). The NRC also reports to Congress annually on its security inspection programs, using both unclassified and SGI reports.

Nuclear Regulatory Commission Licensees

The NRC issues licenses to private sector entities and government agencies in the nuclear subsectors identified in section 1.1. The NRC oversees its licensees from its headquarters offices and four regional offices, and through on-site inspections at power reactors and certain fuel cycle facilities. It carries out its regulatory mission through five main components: (1) developing regulations, orders, and guidance; (2) licensing or certifying applicants to use nuclear materials or operate specific types of nuclear facilities; (3) overseeing licensee operations and facilities to ensure that licensees comply with safety and security requirements; (4) evaluating operational experience at licensed facilities or involving licensed activities; and (5) conducting research, holding hearings to address the concerns of parties affected by NRC decisions, and obtaining independent reviews to support NRC regulatory decisions.

Radiation Source Protection and Security Task Force

The EPAct required establishment of an interagency task force on radiation source protection and security under the lead of the NRC. The Task Force is to evaluate and provide recommendations to the President and Congress relating to the security of radiation sources in the United States from potential terrorist threats, including acts of sabotage, theft, or use of a radiation source in an RDD. The EPAct named 12 Federal agencies to the Task Force and named the NRC Chairman (or his designee) as its chair.

The Task Force is to evaluate and make recommendations for possible regulatory and legislative changes on several specific topics related to the protection and security of radiation sources. For the purposes of the Task Force, the EPAct defines a radiation source as a "Category 1 Source or a Category 2 Source as defined in the Code of Conduct and any other material that poses a threat such that the material is subject to this section, as determined by the Commission, by regulation, other than spent nuclear fuel and special nuclear material."

The Task Force is required to submit its reports to Congress and the President. The first report was submitted in August 2006, with subsequent reports to be submitted not less than once every four years. The reports will update current Federal actions and recommendations for future actions to better protect and control radiation.

1.2.3 Department of Energy

DOE regulates activities undertaken by it or on its behalf. In addition, DOE is responsible for promoting common defense and security, conducting research and development, and other activities to support the use of byproduct, source, and special nuclear materials for medical, biological, health, and other uses in assuring public health and safety in accordance with Section 102(13) of the DOE Organization Act, as amended.

NNSA within the DOE plays a key role in securing Nuclear Sector assets. Among NNSA's national security missions are to promote international nuclear safety and nonproliferation and to reduce global danger from WMDs. NNSA's GTRI provides voluntary security enhancements to civilian nuclear facilities at home and abroad. The mission of GTRI is to reduce and protect vulnerable nuclear and radiological material located at civilian sites worldwide, including within the United States. GTRI supports the DOE's nuclear security goal by reducing the risk of terrorists acquiring nuclear and radiological materials that could be used in WMDs or other acts of terrorism.

Three key subprograms of GTRI—Convert, Remove, and Protect—provide a comprehensive approach to denying terrorists access to nuclear and radiological materials.

Convert: The HEU Reactor Conversion subprogram supports the conversion of domestic and international civilian research reactors and isotope production facilities from the use of WMD-usable HEU fuel to low-enriched uranium (LEU) fuel. These efforts result in permanent threat reduction because the use of WMD-usable HEU in the civilian fuel cycle is minimized or eliminated. This subprogram includes assisting reactor operators in performing feasibility studies and safety analyses required for regulatory approval to convert; procuring LEU replacement fuels; developing and qualifying new high-density uranium-molybdenum (U-Mo) LEU fuel to convert high performance reactors; and supporting the development of a U-Mo LEU fuel fabrication capability to produce the new high-density fuel.

Remove: The Nuclear and Radiological Material Removal subprogram supports the removal or disposal of excess WMD-usable nuclear and radiological materials from civilian sites worldwide. The scope of work encompasses removal of Russian-origin nuclear material, U.S.-origin nuclear material, other nuclear materials not covered by the Russian and U.S. origin efforts, and removal of excess and vulnerable radiological material worldwide that could be used to make a dirty bomb. This includes removing domestic radiological materials by working in cooperation with Federal, State, and local agencies, and private industry to recover and permanently dispose of excess radiological sources in the United States. These efforts result in permanent threat reduction because WMD-usable material theft targets are eliminated.

Protect: The Nuclear and Radiological Material Protection subprogram supports the protection of at-risk WMD-usable nuclear and radiological materials worldwide against theft and sabotage until a more permanent threat reduction solution can be implemented. This includes protecting domestic materials by working in cooperation with Federal, State, and local agencies, and private industry to install security upgrades on high-priority nuclear and radiological materials located at civilian sites in the United States. These efforts result in threat containment because WMD-usable materials have increased protection against theft.

1.2.4 Other Federal Agencies and Departments

In addition to the central role played by DHS, NRC, and DOE, there is a wide range of cooperative interagency activities in the Nuclear Sector, including partners such as DOS, DOT, Environmental Protection Agency (EPA), FBI, and the Intelligence Community (IC). DOS roles and responsibilities are highlighted in section 1.2.7, which addresses the international community. DOT is responsible for regulating safety in transportation of all hazardous materials, including radioactive materials, while EPA has significant responsibilities with regard to radiation safety, including radioactive waste management, radiological site remediation, and radiological emergency preparedness and response. These programs focus on prevention, tracking, response, and recovery.

The FBI manages, leads, and coordinates all law enforcement and investigative activities in response to domestic terrorist acts or threats, including tactical operations, crime scene investigation, crisis negotiation, and intelligence gathering and dissemination. This includes coordination of law enforcement community activities to detect, prevent, preempt, and disrupt terrorist attacks against the United States. Under its memorandum of understanding (MOU) with the NRC,[33] FBI responsibilities include coordinating the Federal response to a nuclear threat incident involving NRC-licensed facilities, materials, or activities; managing the law enforcement and intelligence aspects of the response to a nuclear threat incident involving NRC-licensed facilities, materials, or activities; and establishing and maintaining contacts and coordinating the incident response with other Federal and local law enforcement agencies and military authorities, as appropriate. FBI has been an active participant in several Nuclear Sector initiatives, including Comprehensive Review Outcomes Working Network, Integrated Pilot Comprehensive Exercise, and information sharing through the Joint Nuclear Cybersecurity Subcouncil.

---

[33] The FBI-NRC MOU is dated May 16, 2000, and can be found in the Federal Register, Vol. 65, No. 95, pages 31197-98.

Led by the Office of the Director of National Intelligence (ODNI), the IC is a federation of executive branch agencies and organizations that work both jointly and independently to conduct intelligence activities necessary for the conduct of foreign relations and the protection of the national security of the United States. These activities include:

- Collection of information needed by the President, the National Security Council, the Secretaries of State and Defense, and other Executive Branch officials for the performance of their duties and responsibilities;

- Production and dissemination of intelligence;

- Collection of information concerning, and the conduct of activities to protect against, intelligence activities directed against the United States, international terrorist and international narcotics activities, and other hostile activities directed against the United States by foreign powers, organizations, people, and their agents;

- Special activities;

- Administrative and support activities within the United States and abroad necessary for the performance of authorized activities; and

- Such other intelligence activities as the President may direct from time to time.

By providing timely threat information, the IC plays a crucial role in implementation of the NIPP risk management framework. IC reporting, for example, informs the Design Basis Threat (DBT) against which nuclear power plants and Category I fuel cycle facilities must defend. In addition, DHS and the NRC work closely with intelligence-gathering agencies to identify potential physical and cyber threats to nuclear facilities. DOT and DOE also have a special relationship with the NRC because of their shared oversight responsibility for transportation of radioactive material.

1.2.5 Agreement States

Section 274b of the AEA authorizes the NRC to relinquish its regulatory authority over certain materials and certain activities in a State if three conditions are met. First, the State must have laws, regulations, and safety standards compatible with those of the NRC. Second, it must have a regulatory program that provides a degree of protection for the public health and safety comparable to that of the NRC program. Third, the governor, on behalf of the State, must enter into a formal agreement with the NRC to assume regulatory responsibility over the materials. Under the agreement, the State does not enforce Federal requirements on behalf of the NRC; rather, the State regulates the materials under its own authority.

Agreement States issue licenses[34] and regulate approximately 17,000 materials licensees, only a small fraction of which possess risk-significant radioactive material. Under the EPAct, the NRC received statutory authority to regulate certain radium-226 sources, accelerator produced radioactive material, and naturally occurring radioactive material as byproduct material; these materials are now subject to Section 274b agreements. States may continue to regulate radioactive material not regulated by the NRC under the AEA. The NRC issues licenses and regulates approximately 4,400 byproduct material licensees. As shown in Table 1-6, 37 States have section 274b agreements as of November 2009. In addition, Michigan has signed a letter of intent to become an Agreement State.

[34] A license is issued under the regulations of parts 30 through 36, 39, 40, or 70 of Title 10 of the CFR or by an Agreement State under its equivalent regulations. Specific licenses are issued for medical, academic, and industrial uses of nuclear materials. Reactor-produced radionuclides are used extensively throughout the United States for civilian and military industrial applications; basic and applied research; manufacture of consumer products; civil defense activities; academic studies; and for medical diagnostics, treatment, and research. The regulatory programs of the NRC and Agreement States are designed to ensure that licensees safely use these materials and do not endanger public health and safety or the environment.

Table 1-6: NRC Agreement States

Alabama	Kentucky	New Jersey	South Carolina
Arizona	Louisiana	New Mexico	Tennessee
Arkansas	Maine	New York	Texas
California	Maryland	North Carolina	Utah
Colorado	Massachusetts	North Dakota	Virginia
Florida	Minnesota	Ohio	Washington
Georgia	Mississippi	Oklahoma	Wisconsin
Illinois	Nebraska	Oregon	
Iowa	Nevada	Pennsylvania	
Kansas	New Hampshire	Rhode Island	

Under 274b agreements, the NRC interacts frequently with the States on matters of licensing, inspection, enforcement, incident response, training, and coordination of rulemaking. The NRC provides technical assistance, primarily to Agreement States, and sponsors conferences and special workshops on topics of interest when needed. Agreement States report significant incidents involving materials to the NRC Headquarters Operations Center. More detailed event descriptions are later entered into an events database. The NRC maintains Office of Management and Budget (OMB) clearances for the needed information collections.

The AEA requires the NRC to retain regulatory authority over nuclear reactors and SNM in quantities sufficient to form a critical mass, however possessed or used. The NRC also retains authority over shipment of materials into and out of the United States and matters related to common defense and security. The AEA also requires the NRC to periodically review the adequacy and compatibility of an Agreement State regulatory program under its Section 274b agreement. The NRC may terminate or suspend all or part of a 274b agreement if certain criteria are met.

1.2.6 Other States, Indian Tribes, and Related Organizations

DHS and NRC, as well as other sector partners, work with States, tribes, and other non-Federal organizations to enhance the protection and resilience of Nuclear CIKR. In addition to participation of State and local stakeholders in the NGCC and NSCC, subcouncils and focus groups, DHS works with State and local stakeholders to implement several key protective programs and resiliency strategies outlined in chapter 5.

The NRC shares safety, security, and emergency information with State and tribal governments, licensees, and stakeholder organizations, and disseminates nuclear safety information of interest to stakeholder organizations, including the Agreement States, CRCPD, Organization of Agreement States (OAS), National Governors Association, National Association of Regulatory Utility Commissioners, and National Congress of American Indians. The NRC also disseminates information on matters addressing nuclear regulation, nuclear security, and radiological public health and safety to State liaison officers. All States appoint, by governor designation, State liaison officers to interact with the NRC to improve Federal and State cooperation. The NRC looks to the State liaison officers to: (1) provide the primary communications channels between the States and the NRC; (2) serve as the key members in the States to keep the governors informed on issues under NRC's jurisdiction; and (3) provide the NRC with State information on particular nuclear safety, security, emergency, or environmental issues.

Licensees communicate information on the transport of spent reactor fuel and radioactive waste to the NRC and designated representatives of the States (either Agreement or non-Agreement). Both NRC and the States seek public comment for major actions. Stakeholder organizations meet publicly with the NRC to present information and concerns. State and local governments and stakeholder organizations also communicate through established channels with other Federal agencies active within the Nuclear Sector.

For events at nuclear reactors and fuel cycle facilities, the licensee, the NRC, and affected State and local government entities interact according to established and practiced emergency response plans. Event status information, recommended actions for public protection, and the status of implemented recommendations are shared through dedicated communications links and protocols.

1.2.7 International Community

As part of the global nuclear nonproliferation regime, Nuclear Sector partners participate in a wide variety of international activities to account for and control nuclear materials worldwide and encourage and assist other countries in the worldwide effort to ensure the protection and safe use of radiological materials. Following are descriptions of the agencies with international CIKR protection responsibilities that participate in the Nuclear Sector CIKR partnership.

DOE National Nuclear Security Administration Global Threat Reduction Initiative

GTRI supports the DOE Nuclear Security Goal of reducing the risk of terrorists acquiring nuclear and radiological materials that could be used in WMDs or other acts of terrorism. GTRI's international activities include:

- The conversion of nuclear reactors from the use of WMD-usable HEU to LEU;

- Removal and disposition of excess WMD-usable nuclear and radiological materials; and

- Protection of at-risk WMD-usable nuclear and radiological materials from theft and sabotage.

Since May 2004, 18 research reactors have been converted to operate with LEU instead of HEU, which can be used to make a nuclear weapon, and six have been shut down. In 2008–2009, the conversions included the following:

- The SAFARI-1 reactor in Pelindaba, South Africa, was converted in September 2008;

- Argentina's RA-6 reactor in Bariloche was converted in September 2008;

- The WWR-M reactor at the Kiev Institute of Nuclear Research in Ukraine was converted in September 2008;

- Washington State University's research reactor at its Nuclear Radiation Center was converted in September 2008;

- The research reactor at Oregon State University was converted in September 2008; and

- The ZPPR reactor at Idaho National Laboratories began decommissioning in September 2008.

In addition, since May 2004, GTRI has significantly increased the number of shipments to return Russian-origin research reactor fuel. These shipments include the return of the following nuclear material to Russia in 2008–2009:

- About 6.3 kilograms from Bulgaria in August 2008;

- Almost 173 kilograms from Hungary in October 2008 and July 2009;

- About 14.4 kilograms from Latvia in April 2008;

- About 53.8 kilograms from Romania in June 2009; and

- Almost 74 kilograms from Kazakhstan in four shipments between December 2008 and May 2009.

GTRI also safely recovers thousands of disused or "orphaned" sources and facilitates the security improvements at risk-significant radiological sites worldwide each year.

Nuclear Regulatory Commission

The NRC works with international organizations such as the International Atomic Energy Agency (IAEA), Organization for Economic Co-operation and Development (OECD), Nuclear Energy Agency (NEA), and International Nuclear Regulators Association (INRA) to help improve nuclear safety and security worldwide. The NRC provides for bilateral information exchange and cooperation on nuclear safety through letters of agreement with its foreign national regulatory counterparts. These exchanges and agreements ensure prompt notification of safety problems that warrant action or investigation. In addition, more than 60 joint international safety research agreements with other countries enable sharing of technical information, funding, technical support, and results of joint research projects and programs. For example, to improve nuclear safety regulation of Soviet-designed reactors, the NRC exchanges safety information with their foreign regulatory counterparts through workshops, peer reviews of regulatory documents, working group meetings, and technical information and specialist exchanges.

The NRC also issues import and export licenses for nuclear facilities, major components, materials, and related commodities and assists in development of legal instruments to address issues related to nuclear safety and security. It conducts interagency bilateral physical protection visits to ensure the adequacy of protection of U.S.-origin materials. The U.S. Government has nuclear trade agreements with some two dozen countries, the 27-nation European Union, the IAEA and, through appropriate channels, Taiwan. Pursuant to these nuclear trade agreements, the United States and these entities engage in nuclear trade for nonmilitary purposes. The U.S. Government actively supported the IAEA effort to develop the Code of Conduct on the Safety and Security of Radioactive Sources and the related Guidance on the Import and Export of Radioactive Sources. The goal of this activity, and the associated IAEA Safety Guide RS-G-1.9, Categorization of Radioactive Sources, is to create a harmonized global system of controls that focuses on sources of highest risk.

The NRC regularly exchanges classified or SGI information with a select group of countries regarding vulnerabilities, mitigation strategies, and security improvements. These exchanges ensure that U.S. security enhancements are better understood and, where needed, in harmony with foreign government activities.

The NRC Office of International Programs (OIP) implements policy guidance concerning NRC's international activities related to international conventions and treaties, export and import licensing, bilateral activities, multilateral organization programs, and cooperative research. In consultation with other program offices, OIP administers the NRC's international programs and provides policy advice and assistance to the Chairman, the Commission, and NRC management and staff. Accomplishments for FY 2009 include the following:

- Participation in the April 2009 review at the Joint Convention on the Safety of Spent Fuel Management and on the Safety of Radioactive Waste Management, and coordination of two dozen bilateral meetings at the annual IAEA General Conference;

- Promotion of activities related to implementing IAEA safeguards in the United States, including support for the U.S. ratification of the Additional Protocol (AP) and collecting information from NRC licensees as part of the first U.S. declaration under the AP (July 2009);

- Participation in international coordination activities relating to the implementation of the Code of Conduct on the Safety and Security of Radioactive Sources (Code of Conduct), including revising 10 CFR, part 110, which will be out as a final rule in 2010;

- Exchange of security-related information with designated countries, and work on IAEA security guidance documents; and

- Support for U.S. Government international activities leading up to the May 2010 Nuclear Non-Proliferation Treaty Review Conference and for the April 2010 Nuclear Security Summit.

U.S. Department of State

Several elements of the DOS support international engagement for CIKR protection. Two offices in the Department's Bureau of International Security and Nonproliferation (ISN) that are particularly important in the Nuclear Sector are described below, followed by a discussion of the Office of Coordinator for Counterterrorism.

Office of Nuclear Energy, Safety and Security

The role of the DOS Office of Nuclear Energy, Safety and Security (NESS) is to take the lead in developing U.S. policy on peaceful nuclear cooperation, nuclear energy, nuclear export controls, and the physical protection of nuclear materials and facilities in furtherance of U.S. nuclear nonproliferation, climate change, and energy security goals. In doing so, it consults multilaterally and bilaterally with other nations to advance U.S. interests, including through the IAEA, Nuclear Suppliers Group (NSG), and the Zangger Committee, NEA, Joint Standing Committees on Nuclear Energy Cooperation, and various mechanisms to implement U.S. bilateral nuclear cooperation agreements. NESS is the principal department liaison for most of these consultations. The office also advises and coordinates regularly with other relevant offices in the Bureaus of International Security and Nonproliferation, International Organizations, and Economic and Energy Affairs and the Department's various regional bureaus to advance U.S. nuclear energy and nonproliferation goals. NESS works closely with other agencies, including DOE, DoD, Department of Commerce, DHS, and NRC to help ensure consistent U.S. policy on nuclear energy, safety, and security issues, including physical protection and the minimization of the use of HEU in civil applications. NESS also has a leadership role in the development and direction of U.S. international policy on improving the security of nuclear material and facilities and of radioactive material usable in a RDD and on radioactive waste management through the Joint Convention on the Safety of Spent Fuel Management and on the Safety of Radioactive Waste Management peer reviews. NESS is leading efforts to strengthen IAEA guidance on security of nuclear and radioactive material and facilities and led earlier efforts to revise and build support for the IAEA Code of Conduct on the Safety and Security of Radioactive Sources and to develop the IAEA Guidance on the Import and Export of Radioactive Sources, released in 2005 with strong G-8 backing.

Office of Weapons of Mass Destruction Terrorism

The Office of Weapons of Mass Destruction Terrorism (WMDT) enhances international security against the threat of WMD terrorism by strengthening political and operational capability of international partners to deter, detect, defeat, and respond to terrorists and their facilitators. Adopting a joint counter proliferation and counterterrorism paradigm, ISN/WMDT establishes, maintains, and continues to improve upon U.S. Government efforts to combat WMD terrorism, to include diplomatic support and coordination activities funded and agreed to by other Federal agencies. Of particular relevance to the Nuclear Sector, ISN/WMDT serves as U.S. coordinator for the Global Initiative to Combat Nuclear Terrorism (GICNT). WMDT also leads several U.S. Government efforts to counter nuclear smuggling and promote nuclear forensics cooperation, which leverage U.S. expertise to advance broader counterterrorism and nonproliferation goals.

Office of Coordinator for Counterterrorism

The Office of the Coordinator for Counterterrorism (S/CT) works closely with DHS to implement international components of the NIPP, which includes both domestic and international critical infrastructure protection (CIP). S/CT collaborates on border and maritime security and other issues with foreign governments that critically impact U.S. national security, economic security, and/or public health or safety. In addition, S/CT has co-led the implementation of the international component of the NIPP, CFDI, and is leading in the development of an international CIP strategy. CIKR outside the United States are identified and prioritized based on input from diplomatic posts, 18 sectors of the economy, and other departments and agencies. S/CT takes the lead on coordinating engagement with priority countries to help secure those critical foreign dependencies or assets.

1.2.8 Owners and Operators, Industry Groups, Standards Organizations, and Professional Societies

All U.S. commercial nuclear power plants maintain membership in INPO, which provides oversight of the industry to enhance nuclear plant safety and reliability primarily through the cornerstone programs of on-site evaluations of each nuclear plant, training and accreditation, events analysis and information exchange, and assistance. The Atlanta Center of the World Association of Nuclear Operators (WANO) is co-located with INPO. WANO, formed by the international nuclear community, promotes worldwide improvements in the quality of nuclear plant operations. The Atlanta Center is one of its five worldwide regional centers. INPO provides operational support and facilities for the Atlanta Center and represents U.S. nuclear utility membership in WANO.

The industry's recognition that all nuclear utilities are affected by the action of any one utility motivated its support of INPO. Each member is responsible for the safe operation of its nuclear electricity-generating plants. The NRC has statutory responsibility for overseeing its licensees and verifying that each one operates its facility (or facilities) according to Federal regulations. Compliance with regulations alone, however, does not necessarily result in the best possible performance. INPO's role is to promote excellence in the operation of its members' nuclear power plants.

The World Institute for Nuclear Security (WINS), headquartered in Vienna, Austria, was formed in 2008. Modeled after WANO, WINS was established as an international forum for nuclear security professionals for discussion and exchange of best security practices.

All U.S. commercial nuclear power plants maintain membership in NEI, as do many material licensees. NEI provides the political and policy interface for the industry, and represents the various segments of the nuclear industry in a regulatory sense for generic issues with the NRC. Working groups and task forces organized through NEI provide information exchange and establish guidelines for performance on topics ranging from security to fire protection. NEI and the industry established the Security Working Group (SWG) to provide guidance and oversight of industry activities concerning physical and cyber security. The SWG comprises industry security managers and executives and meets frequently to coordinate and optimize security efforts. The SWG provides the means for industry to strategically approach improvements to its risk posture.[35]

Each nuclear utility has established a safety review committee that provides additional independent oversight of nuclear power plants. Reporting to the senior management of the utility, these committees perform the following activities:

- Independently review activities to provide additional assurance that the units are operated and maintained according to the operating license and applicable regulations that address nuclear safety; and

- Provide independent advice and counsel on the broad aspects of nuclear safety and operational performance.

Technical information is exchanged among other industry partners through participation in organizations and standards committees such as the American Concrete Institute (ACI), American Nuclear Society (ANS), American National Standards Institute (ANSI), American Society of Civil Engineers (ASCE), American Society of Mechanical Engineers (ASME), American Society for Nondestructive Testing (ASNT), Electrical Power Research Institute (EPRI), Health Physics Society (HPS), Institute of Electrical and Electronics Engineers (IEEE), Institute of Nuclear Materials Management (INMM), and Society for Nuclear Medicine.

Other industry groups represent manufacturers and distributors of radioactive material, including that used in diagnostic nuclear medicine, medical therapy, life science and biomedical research, nondestructive testing, and irradiation of food and medical products. Groups that have been active with the NRC and other agencies in the exchange of information in the process of rulemaking and policy development include the Council on Radionuclides and Radiopharmaceuticals and Society of Nuclear Medicine.

---

[35] Security posture will be used interchangeably with the NIPP's use of protective posture.

1.2.9 Federal Organizations With Specialized Capabilities to Respond to a Nuclear or Radiological Emergency

On March 23, 2008, the NRF replaced the National Response Plan (NRP). The NRF is the source of guiding principles that enables all response partners to prepare for and provide a unified national, all-hazards response to disasters and emergencies. The NRF was developed in response to repeated Federal, State, and local and private sector requests for a streamlined document that is less bureaucratic and more userfriendly. The framework also focuses on preparedness and encourages a higher level of readiness across all jurisdictions.

In addition to releasing the NRF base document, DHS released the Emergency Support Function Annexes and Support Annexes posted at the NRF Resource Center. The CIKR Support Annex provides the operational protocols for transitioning between steady-state and incident response. Similarly, the Nuclear/Radiological Incident Annex continues to provide the capability for a united Federal response, coordinated by DHS, to a nuclear or radiological incident.

The CIKR Support Annex for the NRF provides the operational protocols for transitioning between steady-state CIKR protection activities under the NIPP and incident-related operations under the NRF. The annex also provides concept of operations for information sharing, handling incident-related requests for assistance and information from the private sector, and risk management during periods of heightened threat, pre-incident coordination, and incident response.

The Nuclear SSA, working with FEMA, other Federal agencies, and other Nuclear Sector partners, will seek to ensure a seamless linkage between the NIPP and Nuclear SSP steady-state protection and incident management activities (e.g., NRF, National Incident Management System). This linkage includes the following:

- Increasing protective levels to correlate with the threat level communicated through the Homeland Security Advisory System (HSAS) or in accordance with sector-specific warnings using the NIPP and Nuclear SSP information-sharing networks;

- Using the NIPP, NRF, and Nuclear SSP information-sharing networks and risk management framework to review and establish national priorities for Nuclear Sector protection; facilitating communication between partners; and informing the NRF processes regarding priorities for response, recovery, and restoration of Nuclear Sector assets, systems, networks, and functions on a national scale and within the incident area; and

- Fulfilling roles and responsibilities as defined in the NRF for incident management activities.

Department of Energy National Emergency Response Assets

To address a nuclear weapons incident or radiological disaster, DOE maintains a response capability through the Nuclear Weapons Incident Response Program. This program supports first-responder teams of highly specialized scientists and technical personnel from DOE's NNSA sites who are deployed across the Nation to address immediate threats from nuclear material. These teams work with DHS and the FBI, making available DOE's nuclear expertise in response to suspected nuclear emergencies in the United States and around the world.

When the need arises, NNSA is prepared to respond immediately to any type of radiological accident or incident, regardless of location, with seven unique radiological emergency response assets. These assets include the Aerial Measuring System (AMS), National Atmospheric Release Advisory Capability (NARAC), Accident Response Group (ARG), Federal Radiological Monitoring and Assessment Center (FRMAC), Nuclear Emergency Support Team (NEST), Radiological Assistance Program (RAP), and Radiation Emergency Assistance Center/Training Site (REAC/TS). Each asset handles certain aspects of the radiological emergency and performs a comprehensive and rapid integrated response. Capabilities are outlined as follows:

- AMS detects, measures, and tracks radioactive releases after an emergency to determine contamination levels using both fixed and rotary wing aviation assets.

- NARAC develops predictive plumes generated by sophisticated computer models.

- ARG is deployed to manage or support successful resolution of a U.S. nuclear weapons accident anywhere in the world.

- FRMAC is an interagency asset that coordinates Federal emergency radiological monitoring and assessment activities with those of State and local agencies. The Consequence Management Response Team is DOE's asset that integrates into FRMAC.

- NEST provides the Nation's specialized technical expertise to DoD or the FBI in resolving nuclear and radiological terrorist incidents.

- RAP is usually the DOE/NNSA first responder for assessing emergencies and deciding what further steps should be taken to minimize the hazards of a radiological emergency.

- REAC/TS provides treatment and medical consultation for injuries resulting from radiation exposure and contamination, as well as a training venue.

FBI Emergency Response Assets

The FBI has various resources that, depending on the type of incident within the Nuclear Sector, may be important during the response phase. For example, each FBI field division has a crisis management coordinator, a WMD coordinator, special weapons and tactics (SWAT) teams, crisis negotiators, behavioral specialists, technical personnel, support personnel, and command and control personnel. The FBI Critical Incident Response Group at Quantico, VA, has resources, including a hazardous devices response unit, bomb data center, hostage rescue team, command post specialists, crisis negotiators, behavioral specialists, aviation support (fixed wing and helicopter), and SWAT team advisors. The FBI Laboratory Division supports response to incidents through its hazardous materials response unit, evidence response team unit, and scientific analysis section. The Information Resources Division has a crisis response team (communications and technical) and data-processing support.

DoD Emergency Response Assets

National Guard capabilities include the Civil Support Teams (CSTs) and Chemical, Biological, Radiological, Nuclear and Explosive Enhanced Response Force Packages (CERFPs). The mission of CSTs is to support State and local authorities at domestic WMD and Chemical, Biological, Radiological or Nuclear (CBRN) events by identifying agents and substances, assessing current and projected consequences, advising on response measures, and assisting with requests for additional military support. The CSTs were established to deploy rapidly to help local incident commanders determine the nature and extent of attacks or incidents; provide expert technical advice on WMD response operations; and help identify and support arrival of follow-on Federal, State, and military response assets. They are joint units and, as such, can consist of both Army National Guard and Air National Guard personnel, with some of these units commanded by Air National Guard lieutenant colonels.

CERFPs are regional task forces comprised of Army and Air National Guard units, which help locate and extract victims from contaminated environments, perform mass casualty and patient decontamination, and provide medical triage and treatment in response to CBRN events. Additional DoD Nuclear and Radiological Response teams include the Defense Threat Reduction Agency, Consequence Management Advisory Team, capable of hazard prediction, modeling, physical security assessment, public affairs assistance, and legal resources; Medical Radiobiology Advisory Team and Armed Forces Radiobiology Research Institute, capable of providing medical advice on radiation risk exposure, analysis of site restoration costs, and biodosimetry; Air Force Radiation Assessment Team, capable of providing comprehensive, onsite hazard assessment; Radiation Assistance Medical Team, capable of providing medical advice to military and civilian authorities and onsite hazard assessment and casualty management advice; and Hammer Ace, capable of providing secure voice and video communication in remote areas and trained and equipped for operations in down-range contaminated environments. These capabilities, and other forces, are tapped through State requests for the National Guard units and Federal Requests for Assistance for the DoD Title 10 forces needed to respond to incidents involving the Nuclear Sector.

EPA Emergency Response Assets

EPA's Emergency Response Special Teams work together, and with the Agency's On-Scene Coordinators, to prepare for and respond to emergency releases of hazardous substances. These teams play a critical role in helping the Agency accomplish its mission to protect human health and the environment during chemical, biological, and radiological emergency incidents. In addition to each team's specialized skills, they also maintain an extensive network of emergency response capabilities with other agencies and branches of the military. The Radiological Emergency Response Team (RERT) supports Federal, State, tribal, and local agencies responding to radiological incidents and emergencies. The RERT provides technical advice, monitoring, sampling, data assessment, and cleanup assistance. These services focus on minimizing threats to public health and the environment.

Along with a multidisciplinary cadre of highly trained staff, the RERT has specialized equipment, including two mobile laboratories capable of providing a wide range of radiation analyses at typical fixed-lab sensitivities, and a scanner van used for on-site field sample analysis and assessment. State-of-the-art communications equipment enables the RERT to keep in contact with responders both on- and off-site.

Domestic Emergency Support Team

The Domestic Emergency Support team is a specialized, rapidly deployable, inter-agency team comprising subject matter experts (SMEs) from the FBI, FEMA, DoD, DOE, EPA, and HHS. It provides guidance to the FBI special agent in charge concerning WMD threats and actual incidents, and has limited operational capacity.

1.3 Sector Vision and Goals

The Nuclear Sector vision statement concisely describes the ideal protective posture for the sector and informs the Nuclear Sector's seven CIKR goals (see Table 1-7).

Table 1-7: Nuclear Sector Vision and Goals

Nuclear Sector Vision
The Nuclear Sector will support national security, public health and safety, public confidence, and economic stability by enhancing, where necessary and reasonably achievable, its existing high level of readiness to promote the protection and resiliency [a] of the Nuclear Sector in an all-hazards [b] environment; and to lead by example to improve the Nation's overall critical infrastructure readiness.

Nuclear Sector Goals	
Awareness	
Goal 1	Establish permanent and robust collaboration and communication among sector partners having security and emergency responsibilities for the Nuclear Sector.
Goal 2	Obtain information related to dependencies and interdependencies of other CIKR to the Nuclear Sector and share it with sector partners.
Goal 3	Increase public awareness of sector protective measures, consequences, and proper actions following a release of radioactive material.

Prevention	
Goal 4	Improve security, tracking, and detection of nuclear and radioactive material in order to prevent it from being used for malevolent purposes.
Goal 5	Coordinate with sector partners to develop protective measures and procedures to prevent, protect, respond and recover from all-hazard disasters impacting Nuclear Sector assets.
Protection, Response, and Recovery	
Goal 6	Protect against the exploitation of the Nuclear Sector's cyber assets, systems, networks, and the functions they support.
Goal 7	Use a risk-informed approach that includes protection and resilience considerations to make budgeting, funding, and grant decisions on potential protection and emergency response enhancements.

[a] "Resilience" is the ability to resist, absorb, recover from, or successfully adapt to adversity or a change in conditions. (2009 National Infrastructure Protection Plan)

[b] "All Hazards" is a grouping classification encompassing all conditions, environmental or manmade, that have the potential to cause injury, illness, or death; damage to or loss of equipment, infrastructure services, or property; or, alternatively, causing functional degradation to social, economic, or environmental aspects. (2009 National Infrastructure Protection Plan)

Sector goals and objectives frame the comprehensive protective posture that the government and infrastructure owners and operators are working together to achieve for the sector. These goals reflect the overall risk management outcomes that owners and operators and government leaders seek. They also inform the various activities and initiatives undertaken to support the NIPP risk management framework. These goals were developed across a full spectrum of preparedness elements (i.e., awareness, prevention, protection, response, and recovery).

While the goals listed above pertain specifically to the Nuclear Sector, many also benefit other sectors and will require extensive coordination with them. Through the NIPP framework, organizations and processes are in place to facilitate industry and government coordination between sectors.

1.4 Value Proposition

The private sector has a strong incentive to participate in the SSP framework. The following are some reasons the private sector should consider such participation as an advantage:

- Proprietary or business-sensitive infrastructure information can be shared with government entities that share the private sector's commitment to a more secure homeland;

- Information sharing will result in better identification of risks and vulnerabilities, which will help industry partners with others to protect key assets;

- Industry is helping to prevent disruption to the U.S. economy and way of life;

- Private industry is demonstrating good corporate citizenship that may save lives and protect communities; and

- The nuclear industry recognizes that a successful attack on a nuclear facility would be devastating to the industry; therefore, it is in their best interest to detect and deter an attack before it occurs, or should one occur, to successfully defend against it.

2. Identify Assets, Systems, and Networks

Figure 2-1: NIPP Risk Management Framework: Identify Assets, Systems, and Networks

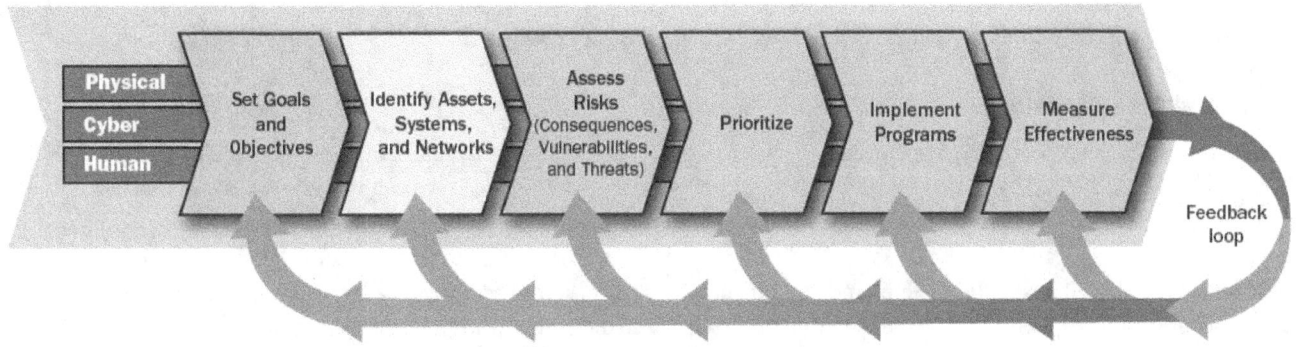

Continuous improvement to enhance protection of CIKR

In accordance with the 9/11 Commission Act of 2007, DHS is the lead coordinator in the national effort to identify and prioritize the country's CIKR. DHS executes this responsibility in collaboration with the SSAs through the National Critical Infrastructure Prioritization Program (NCIPP) that includes the Level 1 and Level 2 Program. Through this program, CIKR sector partners identify domestic infrastructure that, if disrupted, could critically impact the Nation's public health and safety, economic, and/or national security. These CIKR lists inform grant programs and are used during incidents as a tool for prioritizing Federal, State, and local response and recovery efforts. DHS also collaborates with international partners and DOS through CFDI, which identifies similarly critical infrastructure located outside of the United States. DHS/IP is now creating an IDW that will become part of the Infrastructure Information Collection System (IICS). This new approach will allow relevant critical infrastructure partners from Federal, State, local, and private entities to access various tools that house infrastructure data. The information in the IDW will help DHS conduct further risk analysis and meet the national data management requirements in Section 1001 of the 9/11 Commission Act. The Nuclear SSA will work with Nuclear Sector partners to ensure that appropriate sector information—including cyber assets, functions, and elements—is identified and included, as appropriate, in the IDW.

2.1 Defining Information Parameters

Nuclear Sector partners regularly collect Nuclear CIKR information to support their organizational missions, which is, in many cases, driven by regulatory and/or statutory requirements. These organizations independently determine the parameters required for this information and the specific methods used to collect and validate it. To support DHS in its responsibility to build, manage, refine, and improve a comprehensive inventory of the assets, systems, and networks that make up the Nation's CIKR, the NIPP obligates the SSA to work with its sector partners to collect sector-specific infrastructure information that includes:

- Voluntary submittals from CIKR partners, including owners and operators; State, local, tribal, and territorial governments; and Federal departments and agencies;

- Government or commercial databases developed as a result of studies undertaken by trade associations, advocacy groups, and regulatory agencies;

- Information submitted to annual DHS data calls, such as those conducted pursuant to the Homeland Infrastructure Threat and Risk Analysis Center's (HITRAC) NCIPP; and

- Assessments conducted in relation to specific assets, systems, and/or networks that DHS determines to be high-risk.

Identifying Cyber Infrastructure

By November 23, 2009, each licensee currently permitted to operate a commercial nuclear power plant under Title 10 CFR, section 73.54 (10 CFR 73.54) was required to submit a cybersecurity plan for NRC review and approval. When they are implemented, those plans must provide high assurance that digital computer and communication systems and networks are adequately protected against cyber attacks. Critical cyber systems associated with the safety, security, and emergency preparedness functions, as well as support systems and equipment which, if compromised, would adversely impact safety, important-to safety, security, and emergency preparedness functions are protected during the implementation of the plan. The DHS NCSD and the Nuclear SSA are collaborating on a cybersecurity roadmap, which will identify additional cyber infrastructure used in the Nuclear Sector, such as the cyber systems associated with non-power reactors and radiological facilities.

2.2 Collecting Infrastructure Information

DHS Data Collection Efforts in the Nuclear Sector

The Nuclear SSA collaborates with various Nuclear Sector partners in the exchange of information pertaining to Nuclear Sector assets, systems, and networks and to detect cross-sector interdependencies, in accordance with the NIPP and with HITRAC guidance on the NCIPP. These partners include:

- Federal departments and agencies: NRC, DOE, and other Federal partners collaborate with the Nuclear SSA to collect sector-specific information, as appropriate and consistent with their own responsibilities for protecting CIKR.

- State and local governments: The Nuclear SSA coordinates through the NGCC to identify, request, and appropriately utilize Nuclear CIKR information held by State and local partners.

- CIKR owners and operators: Successful implementation of the NIPP is predicated on the active participation of CIKR owners and operators in implementing each stage of the NIPP risk management framework. Acting on behalf of owners and operators of Nuclear Sector CIKR and as full NIPP partners, the NSCC supports NIPP information-collection requirements.

NRC Data Collection Efforts in the Nuclear Sector

A license or certificate from the NRC is required before any entity is permitted to operate a commercial nuclear facility or receive risk-significant nuclear or radioactive material. The NRC licenses the design, construction, operation, and decommissioning of nuclear power plants, nuclear fuel-cycle facilities, and non-power reactors. The NRC also licenses siting, design, construction, operation, and closure of radioactive waste disposal sites under its jurisdiction. In addition, the NRC licenses possession, use, processing, handling, and exporting of nuclear material and the operators of civilian nuclear power reactors. The NRC has a comprehensive program of inspections for commercial nuclear power plants, fuel cycle facilities, non-power reactors, and other facilities, and the reporting requirements of Title 10 of the CFR require that all licensees and Agreement States report certain events and conditions to the NRC. The NRC works closely with the Nuclear SSA and other elements within DHS to ensure that relevant information is shared with and through the Nuclear Sector partnership in pursuit of the Nation's homeland security mission.

NRC has also launched the National Source Tracking System (NSTS), which is a secure, Web-based database designed to enhance the accountability of IAEA Category 1 and 2 radioactive sources. As such, the NSTS meets the U.S. Government's commitment to implement a national source registry, as described in the Code of Conduct on the Safety and Security of Radioactive Sources, which the IAEA issued in January 2004. Toward that end, the NSTS helps the NRC and its Agreement States track and regulate the medical, industrial, and academic uses of certain nuclear materials from the time that they are manufactured or imported through the time of their disposal or exportation. As a result, the NSTS enhances the ability of the NRC and Agreement States to conduct inspections and investigations, communicate information to other government agencies, and verify legitimate ownership and use of nationally tracked sources.

Future Data Collection Efforts in the Nuclear Sector

Within DHS, the Nuclear SSA has primary responsibility for including relevant Nuclear Sector information in the IDW, the DHS data repository for analysis and integration. This tool provides DHS with the capability to identify, collect, catalog, and maintain a national inventory of information on assets, systems, and networks that may be critical to the Nation's well-being, economy, and security. The inventory is also essential to help inform decision making and specific response and recovery activities pertaining to natural disasters and other emergencies. In executing this responsibility, the Nuclear SSA coordinates with other Nuclear Sector partners to overcome any obstacles to the appropriate sharing of Nuclear CIKR inventory information. Specific conditions on how information may be handled, shared, or utilized will be addressed on a case-by-case basis in collaboration with the information holder and in accordance with all authorities pertaining to the exchange and use of such information.

The NRC and other Nuclear Sector Federal partners have information on numerous assets, systems, networks, and functions within the Nuclear Sector. After DHS defines the criteria for information inclusion within the IDW, these partners will work to provide information to DHS for inclusion in the IDW, as appropriate. The Nuclear SSA, with guidance from IICD within DHS/IP, will create a schedule for importing necessary data and will review the information in the IDW biannually to verify its accuracy. In future efforts, the Nuclear SSA will also collaborate with other Federal partners to gather and protect information on the foreign infrastructure on which the U.S. Nuclear Sector depends.

2.3 Verifying Infrastructure Information

Nuclear Sector infrastructure information submitted in accordance with regulatory or legal requirements is verified by the authorized department, agency, or other organization. For example, after an entity has submitted a license application for nuclear facility operation or possession and use of SNM, the NRC staff reviews the application to determine whether it meets all relevant regulations. For power reactors and Category I fuel cycle facilities, an application must include the licensee's safeguards contingency plan, which contains plans for dealing with threats, thefts, and radiological sabotage related to the SNM and nuclear facilities being licensed. The application must also include a physical security plan and security officer training and qualification plan. When the NRC completes its review, it prepares a safety evaluation report that documents the technical and legal basis for the NRC decision on whether the security plan meets NRC regulations and, if adequately implemented, provides adequate protection of health and safety, security, and environment. The NRC has reviewed and approved the physical security plans, security officer training and qualification plans, and contingency plans submitted in compliance with its April 29, 2003, orders for all power reactors. Starting in March 2010, all nuclear power plants were required to be in compliance with 10 CFR part 73, Power Reactor Security Requirements; Final Rule.

An entity applying for a specific license to use nuclear material will also submit an application for a materials license to the NRC or an Agreement State. For materials licensees, the NRC's goal is to obtain detailed data on the materials possessed based on radioactivity thresholds. This information helps determine whether a licensee holds enough of a given isotope to cause harm as a result of accidental exposure or malicious use. This process will be discussed in more detail in later sections of this document.

The NRC's program and support offices employ technical staffs that are well versed in all aspects of facility operations, licensing, security, and nuclear material safety and safeguards. When licensees submit material for review, technical staff assesses the submittal, ensures that it addresses the correct safety, security, and regulatory issues, and either approves or rejects the request. This process often involves requests for additional information, meetings, and conference calls between the NRC staff and the licensee.

2.4 Updating Infrastructure Information

Information pertaining to specific activities, programs, issues, or concerns collected by Nuclear Sector partners is maintained and updated as appropriate. The Nuclear SSA, operating under guidance from the appropriate program management office, will coordinate efforts to update the IDW and will act as a conduit for future Nuclear Sector data calls initiated by other DHS components.

The NRC licensing and certification process ensures that any new assets coming into the sector are licensed and properly tracked. The NRC Headquarters Operations Center is staffed 24 hours per day and is able to receive information on changes in the status of assets. The NRC regularly provides facility and system information to the Nuclear SSA on request, and after the NSTS is populated, the NRC and DOE will use it to periodically update the quantities and types of risk-significant nuclear material held by their licensees.

3. Assess Risks

Figure 3-1: NIPP Risk Management Framework: Assess Risks

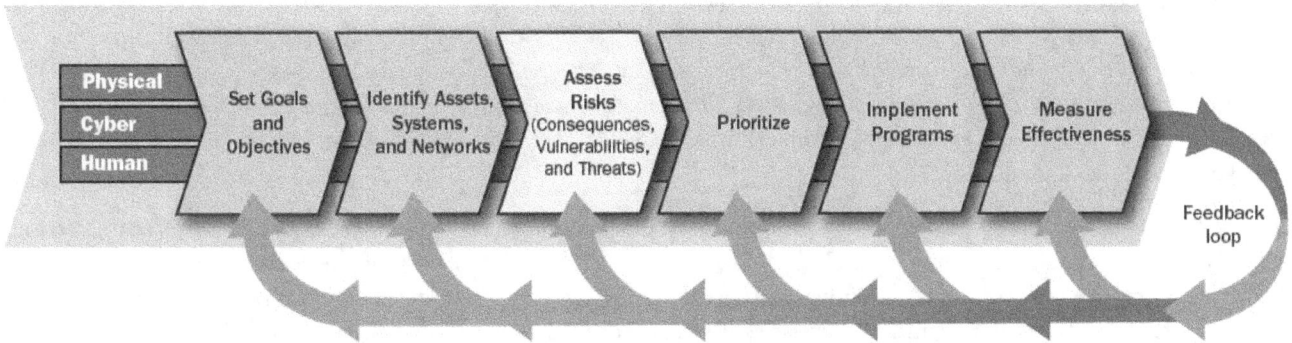

Continuous Improvement to enhance protection of CIKR

When compared to other CIKR sectors, the Nuclear Sector is unusual in that the NRC and Agreement States license civilian use of all risk-significant nuclear and radioactive facilities and materials in the United States. Thus, relative to other CIKR sectors, a large amount of information exists to inform the risk profile of Nuclear Sector assets, systems, and networks. In addition, significant domestic and international research has been done over the past 50 years on the risk characteristics of nuclear and radiological facilities and materials. This research has informed, and continues to inform, the determination by the NRC, DHS, DOE, and other partners of what facilities and materials are considered risk-significant and how best to mitigate those risks.

This chapter describes key Nuclear Sector risk assessment approaches, particularly those used since the September 11 attacks. Using a broad range of methodologies, Nuclear Sector partners conduct risk assessments to meet their own decision-making needs. In some cases, the risk assessment methodologies vary to fit the particular mission scope of the partner doing the assessment. In other cases, the methods may differ simply because of the availability of a wide range of effective tools for conducting risk assessments for nuclear and radiological facilities and materials. This chapter outlines some of the primary risk assessment methodologies and activities in the Nuclear Sector, including those applied to cybersecurity risks. Information pertaining to protective programs and resiliency strategies based upon these risk assessments is principally reserved for chapter 5.

In addition to the methodologies and activities described in this chapter, numerous interagency and public-private partnership activities are ongoing in the Nuclear Sector, for which risk assessment is an integral part. Federal, State, local, and private sector partners regularly and actively assess the risk environment in the Nuclear Sector in light of changes or potential changes to threats, vulnerabilities, and consequences. When necessary and appropriate, these partners also make recommendations for addressing the altered risk landscape. These activities are also described in chapter 5.

3.1 Risk Assessment in the Nuclear Sector

3.1.1 NRC Risk Assessment

Historically, NRC security regulations relied largely on deterministic analyses developed without benefit of quantitative or measurable estimates of risk. Most of these analyses focused on failures of engineered or administrative controls. The original regulatory requirements for nuclear reactors were developed in the early stages of reactor technology development, and thus were based on experience, testing programs, and expert judgment, in conjunction with conservative design margins and the defense-in-depth philosophy.[36] Security analyses complemented the deterministic analyses by introducing a new set of variables. As a result, the regulations have been updated over time to reflect the increased knowledge that comes with increased experience. The NRC has continued to regularly update and refine its analyses and analytic approaches. The deterministic approach asks two questions: "What can go wrong?" and "What are the consequences?" This approach assumes that adverse conditions can occur, and it requires that plant designs include safety systems capable of preventing or minimizing consequences.

The NRC has been conducting Probabilistic Risk Assessment (PRA) for more than 34 years to analyze risks to its licensees. PRA is a systematic process for examining how engineered systems, such as nuclear power plants, and human interactions with these systems work together to ensure plant safety and security. In 1995, the NRC adopted a PRA policy statement that directs that "the use of PRA technology should be increased in all regulatory matters to the extent supported by the state of the art in PRA methods and data, and in a manner that complements the NRC's deterministic approach and supports the NRC's traditional defense-in-depth philosophy."

In addition to the two deterministic approach questions, the PRA approach poses the additional question, "How likely is it that something will go wrong?" Applying this additional factor of likelihood to the threat and accident analysis process is known as risk-informing the process. By risk-informing the process, the NRC can focus its regulatory efforts on protecting the public from the events that (1) result in significant adverse consequences or (2) are most likely to occur.[37]

The NRC assesses risk to determine what regulatory measures are needed to ensure public health and safety. Since the September 11 attacks, the NRC conducts in-depth reviews of safeguards and security for the Nuclear Sector, which includes the following three-step process: (1) threat definition, (2) security assessments, and (3) regulatory improvements. The NRC regularly shares this information with other Federal agencies, including DHS.

3.1.2 DHS Risk Assessment

Consistent with the Homeland Security Act of 2002 and the 2009 NIPP, DHS evaluates risk on the basis of three main components: consequence, vulnerability, and threat:

- Consequence: Effect of an event, incident, or occurrence; reflects the level, duration, and nature of the loss resulting from the incident. For the purposes of the NIPP, consequences are divided into four main categories: public health and safety (e.g., loss of life and illness); economic (direct and indirect); psychological; and governance/mission impacts.

- Vulnerability: Physical feature or operational attribute that renders an entity open to exploitation or susceptible to a given hazard. In calculating the risk of an intentional hazard, a common measure of vulnerability is the likelihood that an attack is successful, if it is attempted.

---

[36] Defense-in-Depth Philosophy: A design and operational philosophy for nuclear facilities that calls for multiple layers of protection to prevent and mitigate accidents. It includes use of controls, multiple physical barriers to prevent release of radiation, redundant and diverse key safety functions, and emergency response measures.

[37] For more information on PRAs, see NRC publication NUREG/CR-6042, Perspective on Reactor Safety.

- Threat: Natural or manmade occurrence, individual, entity, or action that has or indicates the potential to harm life, information, operations, the environment, and/or property. Generally, to calculate risk, the threat of an intentional hazard is estimated as the likelihood of an attack being attempted by an adversary; for other hazards, threat is estimated as the likelihood that a hazard will manifest itself. In the case of terrorist attacks, the threat likelihood is estimated based on the intent and capability of the adversary.

For the purposes of the NIPP, consequences are divided into four main categories:

- Public Health and Safety: Effect on human life and physical well-being (e.g., fatalities, injuries, and illness);

- Economic: Direct and indirect economic losses (e.g., cost to rebuild asset, cost to respond to and recover from attack, downstream costs resulting from disruption of product or service, long-term costs due to environmental damage);

- Psychological: Effect on public morale and confidence in national economic and political institutions. This encompasses those changes in perceptions that emerge after a significant incident, which affect the public's sense of safety and well-being and can manifest in aberrant behavior; and

- Governance and Mission Impact: Effect on the ability of government or industry to maintain order, deliver minimum essential public services, ensure public health and safety, and carry out national security-related missions.

When possible, DHS seeks to use information from partners' risk assessments, which have been integrated into the NIPP framework, to contribute to an understanding of risks across sectors and throughout the Nation.

DHS Homeland Infrastructure Threat and Risk Analysis Center

The DHS HITRAC National Infrastructure Risk Analysis Program (NIRAP) conducts risk analyses for each of the 18 CIKR sectors, working in close collaboration with the SSAs, State and local authorities, and private sector owners and operators. Nuclear Sector partners from both the NSCC and the NGCC participate in the program through participation in the Strategic Homeland Infrastructure Risk Analysis (SHIRA) process, which is directed by HITRAC and updated annually. This process uses a NIPP-compliant methodology used by DHS to conduct cross-sector critical infrastructure risk analysis and to inform national and sector-specific CIKR risk profiles. With guidance from HITRAC and DHS NCSD, public and private sector representatives from the Nuclear Sector collaboratively determine the Nuclear Sector's SHIRA inputs. The SHIRA process has provided a mechanism for CIKR partners to assess threats and consequences—including those that are cyber-based—to Nuclear Sector assets, networks, and systems.

Chemical, Biological, Radiological, and Nuclear Risk Assessment

DHS is presently leading activities in support of an integrated CBRN risk assessment to address potential WMD threat scenarios, as required by HSPD-18. Together with current intelligence, this and other such assessments are intended to guide policy priorities and point to the greatest opportunities for risk abatement in relation to the various attack scenarios. A Radiological/Nuclear Terrorism Risk Assessment (RNTRA), led by DNDO, is presently addressing radiological and nuclear aspects in support of this assessment. This effort is leveraging the Bioterrorism and Chemical Terrorism Risk Assessments (BTRA & CTRA) required by HSPDs 8 and 22, respectively. Thus, the RNTRA is structured to be integrated with the BTRA and CTRA and attempts to use common consequence models and event tree structures where possible. RNTRA will also be used to support other risk analysis processes, as appropriate:

- Risk Analysis Process for Informed Decision making (RAPID);

- Homeland Security National Risk Assessment (HSNRA); and

- DNDO risk analysis of global nuclear detection architectures.

The RNTRA interagency working group anticipates completing its work by summer 2010.

3.1.3 DOE/National Nuclear Security Administration Risk Assessment

NNSA's GTRI is a vital part of the global efforts to combat nuclear terrorism. GTRI's unique mission to reduce and protect vulnerable nuclear and radiological material located at civilian sites in the United States and abroad directly addresses recommendations of the bipartisan 9/11 Commission. GTRI efforts are focused on the first line of defense, namely securing or removing vulnerable nuclear and radiological material at the source.

GTRI has developed a risk-based approach for focusing on the subset of radiological material that would cause the greatest damage, based on properties such as ease of dispersibility and high levels of radioactivity. GTRI uses the following definitions for an RDD and "significant" RDD:

- An RDD is any device (whether passive or active) with any amount of radioactive material used to maliciously contaminate people, equipment, and/or the environment without a nuclear explosion.

- A Significant RDD is a device with sufficient radioactive materials and a means (whether passive or active) that could be used to maliciously contaminate approximately 1 square kilometer (km2) (~250 acres, 0.386 square miles) or more to the EPA/ DHS PAG relocation guideline of 2 rem in the first year without a nuclear explosion.[38]

GTRI's process provides a systematic method to prioritize projects and assign resources. GTRI uses these prioritization criteria to guide funding and scheduling decisions to maximize program results and provide meaningful threat reduction to areas that present the greatest risk first. The prioritization criteria include the following factors:

- Nuclear and radiological material attractiveness; and

- Other prioritization factors (internal site security factors, country threat factors, locations factors).

The process methodology used by NNSA GTRI includes the following three principal steps:

Step 1: Determine GTRI Material Attractiveness Levels. Material attractiveness levels are a measure of risk based on the relative consequences if that type and quantity of material were used for an improvised nuclear device (IND) or RDD. Common potential consequences drive the need for common security upgrades on material of similar attractiveness levels. This graded security approach ensures the most attractive materials receive the most stringent protection.

Step 2: Determine Existing Site Security Condition and Location Factors. If two sites have identical materials, priority is given to the site that has the lesser existing security, greater external threat environment, and that is located in closer proximity to potential targets.

Step 3: Define Priority Level. Priority levels are a measure of overall risk based not only on the potential consequence of material, but also the current security and threat conditions that the material is under. Therefore, the GTRI priority levels are used to drive a project's urgency and to set resource allocations.

3.1.4 Industry Risk Assessment

Nuclear power plant owners and operators have generally supported risk-informed approaches to safety and security, both in fulfilling regulatory requirements, as well as voluntarily improving safety and security. Since the terrorist attacks on September 11, industry partners report having undertaken a number of relevant assessments, including conducting comprehensive reviews at all 65 of the Nation's commercial nuclear power plants. In addition, industry partners, including some members of the NSCC, are working with EPRI on programs intended to support technically sound design, maintenance, and operational decision making, while simultaneously contributing to safer, more secure, and more cost-effective plant operations.

---

[38] The U.S. Environmental Protection Agency/Department of Homeland Security (EPA/DHS) guidelines call for the relocation of people living in an area where the dose rate exceeds 2 rem/year. Federal Register. Preparedness Directorate; Protective Action Guides for Radiological Dispersal Device (RDD) and Improvised Nuclear Device (IND) Incidents. January 3, 2006. Vol. 1, No.1.

3.1.5 Cyber Security Risk Assessment

Regulatory Requirements to Protect Safety, Security, and Emergency Preparedness Functions from Cyber Attacks

In March 2007, the NRC updated the Design Basis Threat, defined in 10 CFR, Section 73.1 to include "cyber attacks" as an adversary characteristic that nuclear power reactors and Category I fuel facilities must protect against with high assurance. Then in March 2009, the NRC published 10 CFR Section 73.54, "Protection of Digital Computer and Communication Systems and Networks," which required nuclear power reactor licensees to provide high assurance that digital computer and communications systems and networks associated with the following categories of functions are protected from those cyber attacks:

- Safety-related and important-to-safety functions;

- Security functions;

- Emergency preparedness functions, including offsite communications; and

- Support systems and equipment which, if compromised, would adversely impact safety, security, or emergency preparedness functions.

By November 23, 2009, 10 CFR 73.54 required nuclear power licensees to submit their cybersecurity plans describing how they will comply with the above requirements to NRC for review and approval. The combined operating license applicants are also required to provide their cybersecurity plans for NRC's review and approval. To assist licensees, the NRC developed Regulatory Guide 5.71, Cyber Security Program for Nuclear Facilities, which provides a method to comply with the rule. The NRC developed this guide based on input from stakeholders, National Institute of Standards and Technology Special Publications, and cybersecurity recommendations from DHS. Regulatory Guide 5.71 was published in final form in January 2010, but the NRC provided licensees and applicants with a draft copy in July 2009 and an updated version on September 21, 2009, which they could use to meet the above requirements. In addition, sector stakeholders have been participating throughout the guidance development process.

Voluntary Cyber Risk Assessment Tools

DHS NCSD established the Control System Security Program (CSSP) to help industry and government improve the security of their control systems used in critical infrastructure throughout the United States. A key part of the CSSP mission is the assessment of these systems to identify vulnerabilities that could put critical infrastructure at risk for a cyber attack. After these vulnerabilities are identified, mitigation strategies are developed to enhance control system security. These assessments are available to facilities that use nuclear and radiological materials.

CSSP has established a collaborative process including vendors, owners and operators, industry partners, and other national laboratories to provide an assessment environment where control systems can be evaluated for security vulnerabilities. This controlled environment allows realistic assessments of systems and components without the adverse consequences resulting from potential system failures.

CSSP performs assessments to evaluate vendors' control systems software and assess security issues resulting from the interdependencies and network design of operational control systems installations. Operational control system assessments use nonintrusive methods, such as reviewing the production system network diagrams and firewall rules, and performing a hands-on assessment of a duplicate nonproduction installation of the system, when feasible. Assessment efforts focus on identifying and understanding the vulnerabilities in control systems that require access to the hardware and software that comprise these systems.

In addition, CSSP provides interested owners and operators with a Cyber Security Evaluation Tool (CSET). CSET replaces and builds on the Control Systems Cyber Security Self-Assessment Tool (CS2SAT). NCSD developed CSET using standards created by NIST and other standards organizations. This tool provides users with a systematic and repeatable approach to assess the security posture of their cyber systems and networks. CSET guides users through a step-by-step process to assess their control system and information technology network security practices against recognized industry standards. The output from CSET is a prioritized list of recommendations for improving the cybersecurity posture of the organization's enterprise and industrial control cyber systems. The tool derives the recommendations from a database of cybersecurity standards, guidelines, and practices. Each recommendation is linked to a set of actions that can be applied to enhance cybersecurity controls.

3.2 Securing Risk Assessment Information

When appropriate, risk assessment information is protected using one of the various methods available to CIKR partners. Some of these methods, described in more detail in chapter 8, include categorizing the information as PCII, SGI, or classified.

3.3 Infrastructure Screening

In the context of the NIPP, infrastructure screening is a high-level analysis that identifies whether a more detailed review of an infrastructure site should occur to more accurately determine its risk. If the infrastructure site is determined to be below a certain threshold of risk with this high-level analysis, then resources may be better spent analyzing other CIKR that are of greater risk.

3.3.1 DHS Screening

Nuclear Sector partners participate in DHS' NCIPP. In addition to helping provide the CIKR protection community with the information necessary to execute its mission, whether on a national, State, or local level, it also functions as a screening tool. It starts with the universe of risk-significant assets in the sector and enables sector partners to focus on the most critical.

3.3.2 NRC Screening

Security Screening

Similar to the NIPP method for risk analysis and management of critical asset protection, the NRC is using a security assessment decision-making framework that provides a process and criteria to evaluate results of security assessments for a broad range of activities subject to the NRC's regulatory authority. This framework serves as a tool to help determine where additional security and control measures or mitigating strategies were needed for Materials, Fuel Cycle, and RTR facilities.

Security assessments are performed on a range of threat scenarios for the transportation and licensed uses of IAEA Category 1 and Category 2 sources. Remote or speculative scenarios and scenarios with insignificant consequences are initially screened out, based on threat assessments and engineering evaluations. Asset attractiveness is evaluated using factors that consider the target iconic value, complexity of planning, resources needed, execution risk, and protective measures for the safety of the public. Attractiveness factors are valued and averaged to give overall ranking expressed as an Attractiveness Category. Effects are expressed, by order of magnitude, as a Consequence Category. The Attractiveness Category and the Consequence Category are then applied to a decision matrix to assess the need to develop additional mitigating strategies.

The NRC conducted security assessments, in conjunction with PRAs, across the range of sector assets to determine potential vulnerabilities and mitigation strategies for a range of threats against existing safety, safeguards, and security requirements, including security enhancements mandated since 9/11. The assessments allow NRC staff to confirm the adequacy of the existing regulatory framework, and can be used as a basis for addressing general and site-specific vulnerabilities identified through other NRC activities such as:

- Baseline security, including force-on-force [39] inspections at operating power reactors and Category I fuel cycle facilities to validate existing measures, or identify general or facility-specific vulnerabilities through testing of actual performance;

- Inspections to validate existing measures, or identify general or facility-specific vulnerabilities; and

- Tabletop drills [40] at operating power reactors and Category I fuel cycle facilities.

The general approach to conducting security assessments includes four basic elements that can be used for both screening and detailed analyses. These four elements are:

- Threat characterization and scenario definition;

- Barrier analysis;

- Systems response analysis; and

- Consequence analysis.

These elements are not necessarily sequential, and results in one element can reduce or obviate work in other elements. For example, if a threat scenario would result in little or no consequences (through consequence analysis screening), then further work on barrier analysis and system responses is unnecessary. Several of the NRC's major security assessment efforts use this concept. Efforts described in later sections of this chapter, with regard to assessing consequences, vulnerabilities, and threats, are also used in this screening process.

Results of these security assessments [41] are reported annually per the requirements of chapter 14, Section 170D of the Atomic Energy Act of 1954 (42 U.S.C. 2201 et seq.), as amended by the Energy Policy Act of 2005, which states that "not less often than once each year, the Commission shall submit to the Committee on Environment and Public Works of the Senate and the Committee on Energy and Commerce of the House of Representatives a report, in classified form and unclassified form, that describes the results of each security response evaluation conducted and any relevant corrective action taken by a licensee during the previous year." In addition to information on the security response evaluation program force-on-force (FOF) inspections, the NRC also provides additional information regarding the overall security performance of the commercial nuclear power industry and Category I fuel cycle facilities to keep Congress and the public informed of the NRC's efforts to protect the Nation's electric power infrastructure and strategic special nuclear material (SSNM) against terrorist attacks.

Screening During Licensing

Part of the initial nuclear power plant licensing process requires applicants to submit a safety analysis report that includes discussion of various hypothetical accident situations and their potential consequences. In addition, owners and operators apply a PRA to determine human interactions with plant systems. This process is quantitative in that probabilities of events with potential public health and safety consequences are calculated, as are the magnitudes of these consequences. The risk associated with such events is the product of the events' probabilities and their consequences. Information on this risk and on which failures contribute most to the risk are of great value to the NRC and the licensees in helping determine the acceptability of a licensed facility's overall design and operation, as well as in focusing the NRC's and the regulated industry's resources on those aspects of design and operation that are most risk-significant.

---

[39] Force-on-Force inspection: A two-phased, performance-based inspection designed to verify and assess the ability of the NRC licensees' physical protective systems and security organizations to provide high assurance that activities involving SNM are not inimical to the common defense and security of the facilities and do not constitute an unreasonable risk to public health and safety.

[40] Tabletop drills are analytical tools used to give participants insight into the licensee's protective strategies. These drills provide a strategic overview of the protective strategies, including the support of the command structure, physical barriers, and personnel.

[41] Results of these security assessments can be located at **http://www.nrc.gov/reading-rm/doc-collections/nuregs/staff/sr1885/**.

For materials and RTR licenses, the NRC uses a security assessment decision-making framework process to aid evaluation of the results of security assessments and their incorporation into future security measures for these licensees. This process helps identify the appropriate level of asset-specific mitigation strategies required for given scenarios. The framework considers the potential attractiveness of the asset, system, network, or function, and determines consequences for each scenario based solely on prompt fatalities from radiation exposure and chemical effects related to radioactive material processes.

To provide adequate protection of public health and safety, current NRC regulations are based on a conservative approach to design, construction, testing, operation, and maintenance of nuclear power plants. A defense-in-depth philosophy is pursued to prevent accidents and mitigate their consequences. Further, emergency response provisions are mandated to provide additional defense-in-depth protection to the surrounding population in the unlikely event of an accident or event resulting in release of radioactivity.

3.4 Assessing Consequences

Regardless of its initiator (e.g., terrorist act, human error, equipment malfunction, natural disaster), an event resulting in a significant off-site radioactive release will have several potential consequences. Some of these consequences, such as acute radiation dose from a plume released from a nuclear power plant, hazardous chemical release at a fuel facility, or panic induced in the local population following a report of a terrorist attack on a nuclear facility, are relatively prompt. Others, such as those resulting from contamination of food supplies, crops, local livestock and poultry, or economic effects, develop over a longer time. This section describes the processes that are used by sector partners to analyze the potential consequences of terrorist attacks across the Nuclear Sector.

3.4.1 DHS Consequence Assessment

As discussed in section 3.1.2, SHIRA is the principal tool used by DHS to analyze these impacts. In the SHIRA process, the public health and safety, economic, psychological, and governance and mission impact consequences are assessed for a range of relevant attack and disaster scenarios. DHS is also working to examine consequences to other CIKR through analysis of dependencies and interdependencies. One entity established in support of this effort is the National Infrastructure Simulation and Analysis Center (NISAC). Its charter is to develop advanced modeling, simulation, and analysis capabilities of the Nation's CIKR and their physical and cyber cross-sector dependencies and interdependencies in an all-hazards context (natural, accidental, and malevolent). Table 1-3 in section 1.1 of this document describes dependencies and interdependencies associated with the Nuclear Sector.

In addition, DHS works with CIKR partners to develop or improve consequence assessment methodologies that can be applied to various asset, system, or network types and to produce comparable quantitative consequence estimates. Many tools and methods can support the assessment of direct effects and consequences and are often sector-specific.

3.4.2 NRC Consequence Assessment

The NRC uses several methodologies to assess the potential consequences that would occur if one of the industry's assets, systems, networks, or functions is compromised. Security and safety assessments have been in use since the first civilian nuclear facilities were constructed in the 1960s. The NRC, with support from national laboratories, conducted extensive security assessments in the 1970s and 1980s. These assessments provided the foundation for the NRC's existing security requirements for power reactors and other facilities.

Following the September 11 attacks, NRC initiated a series of security assessments consisting of aircraft, land-based, water-borne, and cyber assessments to identify the potential vulnerabilities of nuclear power plant structures and systems, including reactor containments, spent-fuel pools, and dry fuel storage casks. Security assessments are also being performed to identify potential vulnerabilities associated with radioactive material use, storage, transportation, and waste activities. The results of the security assessments are used by the NRC to confirm and enhance, as necessary, the mitigating strategies put in place by its February 25, 2002 orders for a range of threats. These assessments support decisions by the NRC on whether existing security measures are sufficient to protect the public, and whether additional measures are necessary. The NRC incorporates the results of the assessments into any necessary regulatory improvements.

The NRC uses results from its ongoing security and mitigating measures assessments to assist in determining what, if any, additional preventive and mitigating actions may be needed to protect against threats that are likely to cause unacceptable consequences. Specific actions are required of nuclear power plant and Category I fuel cycle facility licensees to protect against threats within the DBT, or in pertinent threat scenarios in cases where an applicable DBT has not been established. The NRC uses the results as the technical basis for subsequent actions and decisions regarding design, operation, safety, and security of licensed facilities and activities. The results are also used to reevaluate physical protection, material control and accounting (MC&A), access authorization, safety and emergency preparedness controls, and related requirements needed for each category of facility and activity. Since September 11, the NRC has used these results to impose additional requirements on a wide range of licensees, as described elsewhere in this document. Examples of further improvements that the NRC may pursue after evaluating the results of additional security assessments include the following:

- Working with licensees to ensure well-implemented and well-executed mitigating or preventive measures;

- Requiring immediate action to maintain safety or enhance security;

- Modifying or eliminating current security measures;

- Modifying the NRC's regulations and policies;

- Issuing advisories, guidance, or other generic communications for significant, but not immediate, safety or security concerns; and

- Enhancing cybersecurity.

At the same time, it is recognized that some threats are beyond what is reasonable to expect CIKR owners and operators to protect against by themselves. DHS works closely with the NRC, the Federal community, State and local officials, and the private sector to address these threats.

To help address these threats at RTRs, for example, DHS in 2007 asked NNSA's GTRI to draw on its experience enhancing security of nuclear facilities abroad and provide voluntary security enhancements at domestic RTRs. Utilizing its protection methodology described elsewhere in this report, NNSA has implemented a program supported by DHS, NRC, and the Organization of TRTRs to provide voluntary security enhancements for the nation's 32 operating RTRs.

3.4.3 Assessing Emergency Planning in Determining Consequences

The intent of the NRC's emergency planning regulations is to reduce the impact of an accident on the public and environment, taking into consideration plant conditions, evacuation times, shelter factors, and other conditions that may exist at the time of an event. The concept of EPZs is discussed in detail in NRC Information Digest (NUREG)-0396, Planning Basis for the Development of State and Local Government Radiological Emergency Response Plans (RERPs) in Support of Light Water Nuclear Power Plants. In essence, EPZs are areas for which detailed planning is required to ensure that prompt and effective actions will be taken to protect the public against a radiological event. When considering the potential consequences of a radiological release, it is useful to consider the area required for planning as a means of distinguishing between the facilities. Appendix E to 10 CFR, part 50 addresses the content of emergency plans, including EPZs that are based on the general type of reactor and thus the potential impact postulated for the release of a radioactive plume on the population surrounding the facility. Appendix E provides EPZ criteria for the following reactor types:

- Nuclear power plants with an authorized power level greater than 250 thermal MW: 10-mile-radius EPZ for plume exposure, 50-mile radius EPZ for ingestion exposure;

- Gas-cooled nuclear reactors and nuclear reactors with an authorized power level less than 250 thermal MW: EPZ determined on a case-by-case basis (e.g., the now decommissioned Fort St. Vrain's EPZ for plume exposure was 5 miles); and

- RTRs: EPZ requirements determined using NRC Regulatory Guide[42] 2.6, Emergency Planning for Research Reactors. (Typically, the EPZ for plume exposure is less than 1 mile, usually far less.)

The NRC has concluded that the emergency planning basis for nuclear power plants remains valid in terms of timing and magnitude for the range of potential radiological consequences of a terrorist attack in the post-September 11 threat environment. Nuclear plant emergency plans in compliance with the emergency planning basis provide reasonable assurance that adequate protective actions can be implemented to protect public health and safety, regardless of whether a reactor accident is caused by equipment failure, human error, natural phenomena, or malevolent acts. This assessment is based on multiple studies (some preliminary) performed by the NRC staff and its contractors. Some fuel cycle facilities, manufacturers, and distributors have emergency plans. The planning basis is defined in NUREG-1140, A Regulatory Analysis on Emergency Preparedness for Fuel Cycle and Other Radioactive Material Licensees (1988) and the Emergency Planning and Community Right-to-Know Act.

3.4.4 Tools for Assessing Consequences of a Nuclear/Radiological Incident

Considerable insight into the consequences of a nuclear/radiological incident can be gained by using computer modeling software. Generally the software takes into account the source term, or amount of radiation associated with the release, and factors in the atmospheric conditions near the release to model the exposure to the surrounding public.

An example of a modeling program is the Radiological Assessment System for Consequence Analysis (RASCAL), which projects radiological consequences during accidents that can be compared with EPA protective action guidance and thresholds for acute health effects. The NRC is enhancing the code with a new RDD source-term library that incorporates results from research and development (R&D) testing of mock RDDs. The RASCAL-generated source terms are used by NARAC in atmospheric dispersion codes. Also, RASCAL-generated deposition patterns are used by the FRMAC for initial assessments of nuclides present and doses from deposited materials.

Under the revised Nuclear/Radiological Incident Annex (June 2008) to the NRF, Nuclear Sector response activities are supported by the Interagency Modeling and Atmospheric Assessment Center (IMAAC), an interagency center responsible for production, coordination, and dissemination of the Federal consequence predictions for an airborne hazardous material release. Through a partnership of the Departments of Homeland Security, Energy, Defense, and Commerce (through the National Oceanic and Atmospheric Administration (NOAA)), EPA, National Aeronautics and Space Administration (NASA), and the NRC, the IMAAC provides the single Federal atmospheric prediction of hazardous material concentration to all levels of the Incident Command.

3.4.5 Consequences of Malicious Use of Radioactive Sources

An RDD is any device used to deliberately disperse radioactive material to create terror or harm. The use of an RDD is widely recognized to have a greater likelihood of physical and social disruption than of lethal radiological consequences. In particular, the psychological and economic consequences of dispersal could be high. The consequences depend not only on the radioactive material involved (e.g., its isotopic composition and physical form), but also the dispersal mechanism (e.g., explosive or

---

[42] NRC Regulatory Guide: This series provides guidance to licensees and applicants on implementing specific parts of the NRC's regulations, techniques used by the NRC staff in evaluating specific problems or postulated accidents, and data needed by staff in its review of applications for permits or licenses.

non-explosive) and the environmental conditions under which it is released (e.g., urban, rural, weather). Thus, determining the absolute consequences of any potential dispersal in advance of its occurrence is impossible.[43]

A wide range of possible consequences may result from an RDD, depending on the type and size of the device and how dispersal is achieved. The consequences of an RDD may range from a small, localized area, such as a single building or city block, to large areas, conceivably many square miles. Most experts agree, however, that the likelihood of affecting a large area is very low. In most plausible scenarios, the radioactive material would not cause acutely harmful radiation doses, and the primary public health concern from those materials would be a small, more likely minute, increased chronic risk of cancer for those exposed.

To aid in the response to possible terrorist use of an RDD, DHS has issued Protective Action Guides for RDDs and INDs. This guidance was the result of an interagency process following the Top Officials Exercise 2 (TOPOFF-2) in 2005. Use of this guidance in subsequent exercises has significantly improved the ability of Federal and State governments to provide sound guidance to the public.

3.5 Assessing Vulnerabilities

Vulnerabilities are physical features or operational attributes that render an entity open to exploitation or susceptible to a given hazard. Vulnerabilities may be associated with physical (e.g., a broken fence), cyber (e.g., lack of a firewall), or human (e.g., untrained guards) factors. A vulnerability assessment can be a stand-alone process or part of a full risk assessment. Vulnerability assessments typically involve the evaluation of specific threats to the asset, system, or network under review to identify areas of weakness that could result in consequences of concern.

3.5.1 Engineering Analysis of Nuclear Facility Vulnerabilities

As previously described, the NRC uses a risk-informed approach to assessing vulnerabilities of licensed nuclear facilities and radioactive material. A security assessment is a systematic evaluation in which qualitative and quantitative techniques determine potential vulnerabilities to radiological sabotage, theft, or diversion of radioactive material. The NRC uses security assessments to identify effective countermeasures and mitigation measures to protect specific targets or materials. For example, the results are used by the NRC to confirm or enhance the mitigation measures implemented by power reactor licensees as a result of the February 25, 2002 NRC orders, and to assist national efforts to enhance infrastructure protection.

The NRC began conducting security assessments for operating power reactors, spent-fuel pools, nuclear fuel cycle facilities, transportation of nuclear material, and radioactive sources in the 1970s and 1980s. These initial assessments were used to establish the technical basis for security requirements for the facilities and materials. The potential impacts of terrorist attacks on power reactors have also routinely been evaluated as part of the FOF exercise program on a plant-by-plant basis since the 1980s and 1990s. FOF exercises are also conducted at Category I fuel cycle facilities in accordance with 10 CFR 73.46 (b)(9). After September 11, 2001, the NRC worked to strengthen its security programs while it reevaluated its DBT and improved its FOF inspections. In November 2004, NRC began implementation of its redesigned, full-scale FOF program that incorporates experience and lessons learned since September 11, 2001. The NRC has increased the frequency of FOF exercises so that each nuclear power plant site will conduct an NRC-evaluated exercise at least once every three years, with tactical response security drills in the intervening years. The current FOF program reflects the updated DBT and significantly increases the level of realism, while ensuring the safety of both plant employees and the public. The plants must also conduct their own annual

---

[43] U.S. Department of Energy and U.S. Nuclear Regulatory Commission, *Radiological Dispersal Devices: An Initial Study to Identify Radioactive Material of Greatest Concern and Approaches to Their Tracking, Tagging, and Disposition*, May 2003.

exercises. In addition, as a result of growing concerns about the threat and vulnerability of critical facilities to computer attacks, the NRC initiated cybersecurity assessments in 2002 and issued a final cyber rule in March 2009, as previously described.

Prior to the September 11 attacks, there were no security assessments of an intentional aircraft attack on a nuclear power plant, although some evaluations had been conducted to assess accidental crashes and the loss of large areas of the plant as a result of natural disasters, fires, or explosions. Following the September 11 attacks, the NRC promptly assessed the likelihood and potential consequences of terrorists targeting nuclear facilities for air attack, the physical effects of such a strike, and compounding factors such as meteorology, site layout, systems design, topographical features, and mitigation systems that would affect the impact of potential radioactive releases beyond the site boundary. Although the plants were not specifically designed to resist attack by aircraft, such as those that struck the World Trade Center and the Pentagon, nuclear power plant structures are robust and provide strong barriers that would help to limit the effects of an aircraft strike. The structures also have relatively low profiles, and many are shielded by natural or manmade obstacles such as hills, trees, power lines, and other buildings, reducing the likelihood of a successful hit by an aircraft. As a result of these preliminary evaluations, the NRC required that nuclear power plant licensees conduct interim enhancements to mitigate potential consequences in the unlikely event of a successful air attack on a nuclear power plant. In March 2009, the NRC published requirements under 10 CFR 50.54 (hh) to address potential aircraft threats and loss of large areas of a plant resulting from explosions or fire.

With regard to waterborne threats, the NRC has undertaken specific studies and identified the potential effects from attacks that included threats from bodies of water adjacent to NRC-licensed nuclear power plants. The NRC's April 2003 DBT orders require nuclear power plants to defend against waterborne assaults.

In January 2005, the NRC initiated implementation of a decision-making process for materials and RTR security assessments. This process enables the NRC to use security assessment information to determine the appropriate level of mitigation strategies required for a given threat scenario for specific materials or RTRs. The activity-specific description that was used as part of the security assessment input to the decision-making framework was provided to individual licensees for verification. Framework results, in conjunction with activity-specific security assessments and reviews, which focus on prompt fatalities, were used to determine that no further NRC actions were necessary at this time to enhance facility security or measures to mitigate consequences of an attack.

Further NRC security assessment efforts will be directed to confirm and extrapolate the results of existing studies. These efforts will focus on power reactor facilities and spent-fuel pools to identify consequences and risk mitigation measures for specific modes of attack. The NRC is developing security assessment methodologies to examine specific elements of the current threat environment.

During NNSA GTRI voluntary security enhancement visits, project teams assess the vulnerabilities at the site and evaluate the risk that nuclear or radiological materials at the site could be stolen or used in-place to sabotage the facility and/or resources in close proximity to the site. Project teams evaluate credible adversary pathways and probable scenarios to the target to ensure that the security systems function correctly. Decisions about upgrades are based on the performance of the present security system against postulated scenarios for theft or sabotage and the host's ability and commitment to sustain specific types of upgrade options. Analyses are based on expert judgment when specific information is not available. The analysis is used to identify site vulnerabilities that are then mitigated through appropriate security upgrades. Risk reduction can be estimated by comparing the upgraded system to the original or baseline system.

3.5.2 Radioactive Materials

Facility vulnerabilities are determined using a performance-based approach to assess physical security protection system effectiveness for preventing theft and sabotage of radioactive materials. Site visits to the representative facilities provide site-specific data, along with expert judgment in assessing physical protection system effectiveness. A conditional probability of a successful attack is calculated for various scenarios using an adversary threat matrix with increasing capabilities. Facilities are analyzed at the path and scenario levels. The relative probability of a successful attack is used to categorize the event threat scenarios. Risk is then evaluated qualitatively using a risk matrix by integrating the consequences for each scenario with the conditional probability of a successful attack. Risk rankings by facility, type of material, event, scenario, and threat are developed. The vulnerability of radioactive sources during transportation is discussed in the next section.

The materials security assessment also evaluates cyber systems and human element vulnerabilities. The human element is considered in both the physical protection system and in the adversary threat matrix (e.g., insider threat). Generally, IT and cyber system elements do not control chemical and physical processes involving risk-significant radioactive material, where failure would result in a consequence of concern. Rather, cyber system elements are assessed consistent with their importance to the physical protection system (e.g., access controls) and its effectiveness for preventing theft or sabotage.

Countermeasures for reducing the consequences and improving physical security protection system effectiveness are evaluated. Inventory reduction and limiting facilities to specific forms and quantities of isotopes are considered for reducing event consequences. Countermeasures to improve the probability that adversaries will be detected, interrupted, and successfully neutralized are assessed. General cost information is developed for countermeasures to examine the tradeoff between cost and the risk-reduction benefit.

3.5.3 Transportation of Risk-Significant Radioactive Sources

In the aftermath of September 11, NRC issued multiple safeguard advisories to enhance security of spent-fuel transportation and shipments of risk-significant radioactive material. These advisories recommended that licensees implement additional security measures during shipments. Licensees voluntarily complied with these advisories. The NRC also required security enhancements for spent-fuel shipments from power reactors and RTRs beginning in August 2002. The security measures for shipments have also been adjusted to reflect changes in the HSAS threat level.

In addition to the safeguard advisories, the NRC has used Regulatory Issue Summaries (RISs)[44] to clarify subjects such as the following:

- NRC Threat Advisory and Protective Measures System;

- Additional protective measures for transportation of greater than 100 grams of special nuclear fuel (SNF);

- Use of existing emergency plans and procedures for deployment of National Guard, State police, and other emergency responders in the owner-controlled area of a nuclear power plant; and

- Filing requirements for advance notification of SNF and SNM shipments.

The Homeland Security Act of 2002 amended the Federal hazardous materials transportation law (49 U.S.C. 5103) to include security in the Secretary of Transportation's mandate. The Act directed DOT to "prescribe regulations for the safe transportation, including security, of hazardous materials in intrastate, interstate, and foreign commerce." DOT's Pipeline and Hazardous Materials Safety Administration issued regulations requiring shippers and carriers of most hazardous materials, including certain radioactive material, to develop and implement security plans and ensure that their employee training includes a security component. The security plans are based on a structured analysis, such as DOT's Risk Management Self-Evaluation Framework, and cover personnel security, unauthorized access, and en route security. In addition, DOT's Federal Motor Carrier Safety Administration issued regulations requiring safety permits for all HRCQ of radioactive material, and requiring adequate security programs and related training. The NSTS also helps the NRC and its Agreement States track and regulate the medical, industrial, and academic uses of certain nuclear materials from the time they are manufactured or imported through the time of their disposal or exportation.

---

[44] The NRC issues Regulatory Issue Summaries to communicate with stakeholders on a broad range of matters that do not involve requests for action or information (unless strictly voluntary).

The radioactive material shipment process, by nature, is not particularly dependent on cyber system inputs and, therefore, is not susceptible to cyber intrusions. While generic route notifications are made to the NRC through normal telecommunications links for shipments of consequence, the information is time-sensitive, and shipping packages are well protected under NRC, DOE, and DOT regulations. Additional security measures have been implemented by NRC orders for notifications made by licensees regarding risk-significant radioactive material. Routes and times for spent-fuel shipments are protected as SGI and sent to the NRC through non-cyber-related media.

The NRC has also supported efforts by DHS CBP and USCG to implement advance electronic notification of dangerous goods crossing U.S. borders and to implement regulations on port and facility security. It ensured pre-notification of in-bond shipments (an import or export shipment that has not been cleared by CBP and is transported, stored, or handled with security to the government provided by indemnity bonds) for risk-significant material.

3.6 Assessing Threats

DHS provides its partners with Federal Government-coordinated unclassified assessments of potential terrorist threats and appropriate access to classified assessments when necessary and authorized. These threat assessments are derived from analyses of adversary intent and capability, and describe what is known about terrorist interest in particular CIKR sectors, as well as specific attack methods. Because international terrorists, in particular, have continually demonstrated flexibility and unpredictability, DHS and its partners in the IC also analyze known terrorist goals, objectives, and developing capabilities to provide CIKR owners and operators with a broad view of the potential threat and postulated terrorist attack methods.

The NRC requirements in 10 CFR 73.1 describe the DBT that applies to nuclear power reactors and Category I SNM. These DBTs were substantially supplemented following the attacks of September 11.[45] For the remainder of facilities that are not required to have a DBT, the NRC gathers and provides information on the spectrum of threats and ensures the continued adequacy of security measures to protect against these threats. This information provides a consistent basis for security assessments and measures.

The NRC, in concert with DHS, the IC, and law enforcement communities, evaluates the current threat environment—including cyber-based threats—affecting regulated activities and performs rapid assessments of the credibility of threats and security events. In addition, the NRC formally reviews the threat environment annually as part of a review of the adequacy of NRC's DBTs based on domestic and foreign events and intelligence. This process provides critical information that forms the basis for updates to the DBTs. After performing a peer review with DHS, Federal law enforcement, the IC, and other cleared partners, the NRC staff proposes updates to the DBTs to the Commission, if necessary. Participation in these assessments is important because partners can understand the risks to their facilities and make educated decisions on protective measures to be enacted. Also, information sharing will result in better identification of risks and vulnerabilities, which helps industry partner with others to protect its key assets, systems, networks, and functions.

3.6.1 DHS Homeland Infrastructure Threat and Risk Analysis Center

DHS HITRAC conducts integrated threat analysis for all CIKR sectors, including the Nuclear Sector. As called for in section 201 of the Homeland Security Act, HITRAC brings together intelligence and infrastructure specialists to ensure a complete and sophisticated understanding of the risks to U.S. CIKR. HITRAC works in partnership with the U.S. IC and national law

---

[45] On January 29, 2007, the NRC approved a final rule that enhances security regulations governing the DBT for radiological sabotage and the DBT for theft or diversion, imposing generically applicable security requirements similar to those previously imposed by the NRC's April 29, 2003 DBT Orders. The DBT Orders applied to existing licensees, and enhanced the level of security requirements necessary to ensure that public health, safety, common defense, and security are adequately protected. The rule modifies and enhances the DBT based on experience and insights gained by the Commission during implementation of the orders, and extensive consideration of the 12 factors specified in the Energy Policy Act of 2005. The guidance documents related to this rule are protected from public disclosure for security reasons; however, the rule generally describes modes of attack, weaponry, capabilities, and intentions of the adversary. Additional provisions are included in the rule that relate to multiple, coordinated groups of attackers, suicide attacks, and cyber threats.

enforcement to integrate and analyze threat information. It also works in partnership with the SSAs and owners and operators to ensure that their expertise on infrastructure operations is integrated into threat analysis.

HITRAC evaluates and monitors current incidents and threats to U.S. infrastructure and supports DHS decision makers and external customers with immediate analysis. HITRAC also maintains situational awareness of CIKR sectors and develops long-term strategic assessments of their risk factors. This is done by integrating threat information with the unique vulnerabilities and consequences of an attack associated with each sector. In addition, HITRAC analyzes the cross-sector implications of threats among all 18 CIKR sectors.

In close coordination with the NRC's Intelligence Liaison and Threat Assessment Branch (ILTAB), HITRAC briefs government and private sector partners on Nuclear Sector-specific threat information at the quarterly meetings of the NGCC and NSCC and on an as-needed basis. These briefs combine threat information from various classified and unclassified sources, with the goal of providing an overview of the particular risks facing the Nuclear Sector. HITRAC, in coordination with ILTAB, uses security incident data from the NRC protected Web server and National Infrastructure Coordinating Center (NICC) Patriot reports to conduct a monthly cross-sector analysis of suspicious activity, which is disseminated to the Nuclear Sector.

3.6.2 NRC Intelligence Liaison and Threat Assessment Branch

The ILTAB assesses the threat environment affecting regulated activities, performs rapid assessment of the credibility of threats and security events, coordinates with the intelligence and law enforcement communities, assesses illicit trafficking events, and reviews the adequacy of the DBTs based on domestic and foreign events and intelligence. ILTAB maintains the DBTs, threat attributes, and adversary characteristics. It also works with the NRC's Federal Security Coordinators on communicating threat information.

Compiling, evaluating, and protecting threat information is pivotal to the NRC's ability to assess and define the threat environment to the Nuclear Sector. In the wake of the September 11 attacks, NRC-licensed facilities have been reporting suspicious incidents to the NRC Headquarters Operations Center and regional offices daily. These reports comply with requests made by the NRC in a series of advisories following September 11. The NRC maintains this information in a protected Web server and security information database that are shared with authorized users. A descriptive report is filed each time a licensee reports a security-related event, along with information shared with other licensees and Federal, State, and local agencies. ILTAB can track, investigate, and evaluate the number and types of events, search for any adverse trends, and share security information with homeland security, law enforcement, and licensee officials who have a need to know. The nuclear industry may also provide inputs into threat scenarios and assessment through the NSCC. Access to the NRC protected Web server is available for official users on submission and approval of a request for an account.

3.6.3 Potential Threat Scenarios and Targets

Aircraft Attack at a Nuclear Power Plant

The NRC has entered into a MOU with the North American Aerospace Defense Command to ensure prompt notification of NRC power reactor licensees of imminent aircraft threats. All such licensees have put in place procedures for responding to potential aircraft threats that will allow them to place reactors in the safest possible configuration upon warning.

The NRC has conducted extensive analyses of the potential vulnerability of nuclear power plants to aircraft attacks. While these analyses are classified, the NRC remains convinced that nuclear power plants are among the most heavily protected civilian facilities in the United States. The private sector has also conducted an extensive analysis of aircraft impacts using different methodologies and has arrived at similar conclusions. The details are also classified.

The NRC published requirements under 10 CFR 50.54 (hh) for power reactor licensees to implement procedures for addressing potential aircraft threats and loss of large areas of a plant as a result of fires or explosions. Thus, the NRC maintains that nuclear power plant safety, security, and emergency planning programs continue to provide reasonable assurance of adequate protection of public health and safety. The NRC continues to perform additional analyses to look for potential vulnerabilities and identify any appropriate mitigating actions. For example, the NRC recently conducted structural analyses of two spent-fuel pools to provide added assurance of a spent-fuel pool safety margin.

Radiological Dispersal Device and Radiation Exposure Device

The NRC, DOE, and IAEA all use potential radiological consequences to set thresholds for categorizing radioactive material. In June 2002, the Secretary of Energy and the Chairman of the NRC convened an interagency working group on RDDs to address the Nation's concerns regarding use of radioactive material for a malevolent act. The working group's report used a systematic analysis to broadly assess radioactive materials and determine which are of greatest concern for use in an RDD. The report used input from an analysis prepared by Sandia National Laboratories[46] to provide a relative indication of risk-significant material. The report identified those radioactive materials of greatest concern, which were given first priority for consideration of increased security measures.

Concurrently, the IAEA, in revising the Code of Conduct for the Safety and Security of Radioactive Sources, assessed the relative risk of sources in Safety Guide No. RS-G-1.9.[47] This publication provides a categorization system for ranking radioactive sources based on their potential to cause harm to human health and for grouping the uses of these sources into discrete categories. The purpose of categorizing radioactive sources is to provide a fundamental and internationally harmonized basis for risk-informed decisions. It provides a categorization for radioactive sources used in industry, medicine, agriculture, research, and education.

A radiation exposure device (RED) is a device intended to expose people to radiation rather than to disperse radioactive material into the air, as would an RDD. An RED could be constructed from unshielded or partially shielded radioactive material in any form placed in any type of container. This type of device could be hidden in a structure or vehicle that does not significantly shield the radiation. It could be placed in a heavily populated area to expose many people before it is detected and removed. Depending on the physical properties, the same radioactive material could be used in an RDD or a RED. Radiation exposure devices can cause significant adverse health effects to humans, including injury, death, and latent stochastic effects. The degree to which an RED presents a human hazard is proportional to the amount of radioactive material used in the device, the nature of the radioisotope used, the amount of time a victim is exposed to the radiation, and the distance of a victim from the RED.

Improvised Nuclear Device

IND refers to quantities of high-purity (weapons-grade) uranium or plutonium that have been arranged with explosives to achieve a nuclear yield. INDs are not expected to create as great a yield as a military weapon using the same quantity of material, but they can still create explosions equal to many kilotons of TNT, which could create destruction on the same order of magnitude as that at Hiroshima and Nagasaki. Very few Nuclear Sector activities make use of this material; however, where it is used, protection from theft is a primary concern.

Potential Threats to Industrial and Medical Facilities That Use Risk-Significant Radioactive Sources

Consistent with the NRC's overall approach, security assessments were performed for licensed users who possess risk-significant quantities of radioactive material. Because of the great number and diversity among users, representative facilities with risk-significant radioactive material were assessed. Based on these assessments, the NRC determined that no additional security measures were required at the time.

---

[46] Sandia National Laboratories, An Initial Study to Identify Materials of Greatest Concern for Use in a Radiological Dispersal Device, November 15, 2002.

[47] International Atomic Energy Agency, Categorization of Radioactive Sources, Safety Guide No. RS-G-1.9, August 2005.

The NRC continues to support voluntary security enhancements for industrial and medical facilities. In an April 15, 2009 staff requirements memorandum (SECY-08-0184), the Commission stated that the "increased controls required by the NRC and Agreement States and implemented by licensees, along with voluntary additional facility and device hardening measures, have significantly improved the security of these sources." The Commission directed NRC staff to "continue to work with the NRC's Federal partners to implement the voluntary hardening program for certain blood and research irradiators and explore other possible federally funded voluntary initiatives to augment the safety and security for these essential components of our Nation's infrastructure." Also, they instructed the NRC staff to engage Federal partners in efforts to conduct research of alternative chemical forms for cesium-137.

Other facilities use radioactive material that is not categorized as risk-significant radioactive material. The form and quantity of material varies greatly, ranging from small amounts of radiochemicals used as tracers to large quantities of unsealed material used in radiopharmaceutical and radiochemical manufacturing, to risk-significant quantities of material used in sealed-source manufacturing. The licenses for these facilities may contain conditions, imposed by the NRC or the Agreement State and agreed to by the licensee, that take into account the emergency preparedness and response plans commensurate with the scope of operations and potential risk. Users of radioactive material that poses a greater risk to workers or the public are required to be analyzed in greater detail, and some may be required to have a formal emergency plan subject to approval by the NRC or the Agreement State.

Potential Threats to Radioactive Material Transportation and Radioactive Waste Storage

Significant protective measures continue to ensure the safe transport of such risk-significant nuclear material as SNM and high-level waste. Significant release of radioactivity from an accident involving transport of this type of material is unlikely; however, any material stolen or diverted from a shipment could be used in an RDD, with consequences similar to those described above.

The NRC has sponsored scientific studies to investigate the potential results of attacks on spent fuel storage and dry casks. The results of these studies are classified. The NRC responded to the terrorist attacks of September 11 by promptly developing and requiring security enhancements for both spent fuel storage and dry casks.

Potential Threats to Research and Test Reactors

The NRC completed a comprehensive decision-making process that uses security assessment information to determine the appropriate level of mitigation strategies to be implemented at RTRs. For these detailed security assessments, specific threshold scenarios, action sequences, and adversarial attributes were developed. The NRC has used the detailed security assessments to determine that no additional actions are required by the affected licensees. Previously, the NRC worked with licensees who own and operate RTRs to enhance security measures.

In 2007, DHS asked NNSA's GTRI to draw upon its experience enhancing security of nuclear facilities abroad and provide voluntary security enhancements at domestic RTRs, and then-NRC Chairman Dale Klein sent a letter to then-Energy Undersecretary Clay Sell affirming support for the voluntary enhancements. Utilizing its protection methodology described elsewhere in this report, NNSA has implemented a program supported by DHS, the NRC, and the Organization of TRTRs to provide voluntary security enhancements for the nation's 32 operating RTRs.

4. Prioritize Infrastructure

Figure 4-1: NIPP Risk Management Framework: Prioritize

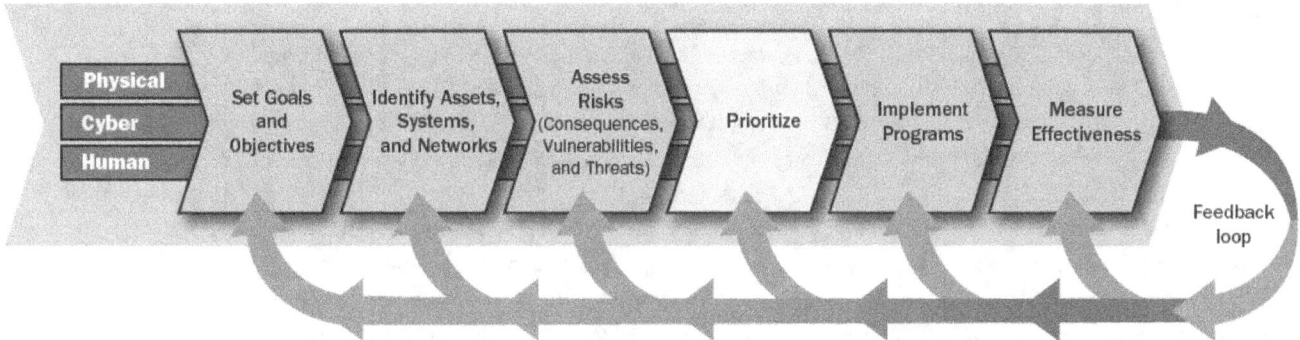

Continuous Improvement to enhance protection of CIKR

The NIPP risk management framework is informed by the fact that, under an all-hazards paradigm, it is neither possible nor necessary to protect every CIKR asset, system, and network equally against every possible CIKR threat. The Nation's CIKR protection programs must prioritize protection across and within sectors so that resources can be applied where they offer the most benefit for reducing risk by mitigating threats, reducing vulnerabilities, and minimizing consequences. Comparative analysis has consistently shown that nuclear power plants are among the most well-defended and robust commercial installations in the United States. They are built to maintain a high degree of safety and security in the event of natural disasters, such as hurricanes and tornadoes, and equipment malfunction or damage. In addition, nuclear power plants also have large and highly trained armed security forces providing high assurance that these critical facilities are secure from radiological sabotage or other external threats. Furthermore, the security of RTRs and risk-significant radioactive materials is assured by the effective application of regulatory requirements, and is supplemented by robust voluntary programs. It is generally agreed that no other CIKR sector attends to the security and protection of its assets, networks, systems, and functions as does the Nuclear Sector.

A systematic and consistent way of prioritizing assets provides transparency and increases the defensibility of decisions about government and private sector resource allocations. Prioritizing CIKR protection efforts within the Nuclear Sector maximizes value of expended resources. This chapter addresses the processes used to prioritize the Nuclear Sector's assets, systems, and networks.

4.1 DHS Efforts to Prioritize Infrastructure

Risk assessments are based on both science and technical evaluations, based in part on expert experience and judgment and, therefore, can have significant uncertainties. Definitive quantification of threat, vulnerability, and consequence is unrealistic. Many factors, including the mission, role, and liability of those performing the analysis, can result in different perspectives on the estimates of these components of risk. Judgments of importance can also vary, based on whether the analysis is conducted from a national or local point of view. DHS and its CIKR partners take these different perspectives into consideration when making prioritizations based on risk.

The Nuclear SSA, DHS/IP, along with the NGCC and NSCC partners, has responsibility to prioritize Nuclear Sector assets, systems, and networks for CIKR protection and resilience programs. As described in section 2.1, DHS executes this responsibility in collaboration with the SSAs through the NCIPP that includes the Level 1 and Level 2 program. Through this program, CIKR sector partners identify domestic infrastructure which, if disrupted, could critically impact the Nation's public health and safety, economic, and/or national security. These CIKR lists inform grant programs and are used during incidents as a tool for prioritizing Federal, State, and local response and recovery efforts. DHS also collaborates with international partners and the Department of State through the CFDI, which identifies similarly critical infrastructure outside the United States.

4.2 Other Nuclear Sector Efforts to Prioritize Infrastructure

4.2.1 NRC Prioritization Efforts

Following the attacks of September 11, the NRC prioritized nuclear infrastructure assets based on potential radiological consequences of a successful attack. Subsequent regulatory actions taken by the NRC reflect a higher set of priorities from a security perspective. For example, in March 2009, the NRC published a new rule to amend its security regulations and add new security requirements pertaining to nuclear power reactors. This rulemaking established generally applicable security requirements similar to those required by Commission orders issued after September 11. The rulemaking also added several new requirements developed as a result of insights gained from licensee implementation of the security orders, and NRC review of site security plans, implementation of the enhanced baseline inspection program, and NRC evaluation of FOF exercises. This rulemaking also enhances the NRC's security regulatory framework for the protection of new nuclear power plants. This set of higher priorities is reflected in the NRC's implementation of the HSAS. The NRC used the results of the security assessments to develop and issue Regulatory Issue Summaries (RISs) to each of the categories of licensees for which it has required security enhancements. These RISs contain security measures corresponding to each of the five color-coded levels contained in the HSAS that licensees can consider for implementation.

The NRC also used the security assessment results and, in coordination with licensees, the Nuclear SSA, and other Federal and State agencies, developed necessary enhancements to security measures to ensure public safety. These additional enhancements applied to areas such as transportation of risk-significant radioactive materials (other than spent fuel and Category I quantities of SSNM) and commercial or medical use of radioactive material having significant risk.

In March 2009, the NRC published a new rule that nuclear power plants will be required to provide high assurance that digital computer and communication systems and networks are protected adequately against cyber attacks. To facilitate rule compliance, the NRC published a regulatory guide and security plan template in January 2010, which describes in detail what systems and functions need to be protected. The new cybersecurity rule and inspection program are described more fully in chapter 5.

4.2.2 Radioactive Materials

The IAEA categorization of radioactive material is based on a definition of a dangerous source. That is, such a source that could, if not under control, give rise to exposure sufficient to cause severe deterministic effects (i.e., fatal or life threatening) or a permanent injury.[48] Five categories are defined by the IAEA (see Table 4-1):[49]

---

[48] The IAEA Safety Guide No. RS-G-1.9, "Categorization of Radioactive Sources," details the underlying methodology for the categorization. The IAEA publication EPR-D-Values 2006, "Dangerous quantities of radioactive material (D-values)" provides the basis for the radioactivity levels corresponding to the D-values for all radionuclides. The Category 3 threshold corresponds to this activity level.

[49] Text from Radiation Sources Protection and Security Task Force 2006 Report to Congress and to the President.

Table 4-1: IAEA Categories of Radioactive Materials

Category	Risk in being close to an individual source	Risk in the event that the radioactive material in the source is dispersed by fire or explosion
1	**Extremely dangerous to the person:** This source, if not safely managed or securely protected, would be likely to cause permanent injury to a person who handled it or who was otherwise in contact with it for more than a few minutes. It would probably be fatal to be close to this amount of unshielded radioactive material for a period in the range of a few minutes to an hour.	This amount of radioactive material, if dispersed, could possibly—although it would be unlikely—permanently injure or be life threatening to people in the immediate vicinity. There would be little or no risk of immediate health effects to people beyond a few hundred meters away, but contaminated areas would need to be cleaned up in accordance with international standards. For large sources, the area to be cleaned up could be km² or more.
2	**Very dangerous to the person:** This source, if not safely managed or securely protected, could cause permanent injury to a person who handled it or who was otherwise in contact with it for a short time (minutes to hours). It could possibly be fatal to be close to this amount of unshielded radioactive material for a period of hours to days.	This amount of radioactive material, if dispersed, could possibly—although it would be very unlikely—permanently injure or be life threatening to people in the immediate vicinity. There would be little or no risk of immediate health effects to people beyond a hundred meters or so away, but contaminated areas would need to be cleaned up in accordance with international standards. The area to be cleaned up would probably not exceed a km².[a]
3	**Dangerous to the person:** This source, if not safely managed or securely protected, could cause permanent injury to a person who handled it or who was otherwise in contact with it for some hours. It could possibly—although it would be unlikely—be fatal to be close to this amount of unshielded radioactive material for a period of days to weeks.	This amount of radioactive material, if dispersed, could possibly—although it would be extremely unlikely—permanently injure or be life threatening to people in the immediate vicinity. There would be little or no risk of immediate health effects to people beyond a few meters away, but contaminated areas would need to be cleaned up in accordance with international standards. The area to be cleaned up would probably not exceed a small fraction of a km².
4	**Unlikely to be dangerous to the person:** It is very unlikely that anyone would be permanently injured by this source; however, this amount of unshielded radioactive material, if not safely managed or securely protected, could possibly—although it would be unlikely—temporarily injure someone who handled it or who was otherwise in contact with it for many hours, or who was close to it for a period of many weeks.	This amount of radioactive material, if dispersed, could not permanently injure people
5	**Most unlikely to be dangerous to the person:** No one could be permanently injured by this source.[b]	This amount of radioactive material, if dispersed, could not permanently injure anyone.

[a] The size of the area to be cleaned up would depend on many factors (including the activity, the radionuclide, how it was dispersed, and the weather).

[b] Possible delayed health effects are not taken into account in this statement (see para. II.2 [of the Safety Guide]).

Source: IAEA Safety Guide No. RS-G-1.9, "Categorization of Radioactive Sources," Appendix II, Table 3.

Using this categorization, the NSCC-R has developed an inventory of applications of these materials used beyond the scope of nuclear power, fuel cycle, non-power reactors, and waste facilities. The list of applications was compiled from information available from NEI, industry groups, and representatives of companies or users from this vast community. The inventory serves as the basis of a matrix that, for each category of use, provides a description of use, form of materials used, typical radionuclides, and maximum quantity. The matrix was developed to ensure that the wide range of radioactive material applications in the Nuclear Sector—beyond the scope of nuclear power, fuel cycle, non-power reactors, and waste facilities—were considered for additional controls based on risk. While not all applications involve use of risk-significant radioactive material, those that do have been highlighted in accordance with the IAEA categorized approach and given priority status on this basis of risk. The matrix was provided to the NRC and was found to be consistent with its risk assessment, also based on the IAEA Code of Conduct categorization.

Furthermore, the Radiation Source Protection and Security Task Force ("Task Force") created in accordance with the Energy Policy Act of 2005 (more fully described in chapter 5), was tasked with evaluating available information on lists of radioactive sources that government agencies have established for security or safety-related purposes to determine whether agencies are being consistent in their approaches to protecting these sources and recommending changes, if appropriate. One area the report was to cover was a list of additional radiation sources that should be required to be secured under the Energy Policy Act. In the August 2006 Task Force Report, the Task Force concluded that the responsible agencies were protecting the appropriate radioactive sources (i.e., those sources requiring security based on the potential attractiveness of the source to terrorists and the extent of the threat to public health and safety) and recommended that no additional radionuclides be added to the list of risk-significant sources. The Task Force Report also indicated that the Code of Conduct serves as an appropriate framework for considering which sources warrant additional protection. The Task Force recommended that the U.S. Government periodically reevaluate the list of radionuclides that warrant enhanced security and protection to assess their adequacy in light of the evolving threat environment.[50] The next Task Force Report is due in 2010.

In 2007, the Task Force tasked the Radiation Sources Subgroup (the subgroup) to integrate with current NIPP actions to do the following:

1. Provide the mechanism to obtain Federal agency agreement on what constitutes a significant RDD and RED;

2. Reevaluate the list of radioactive sources that warrant enhanced security and protection, with consideration of radionuclides available worldwide; and

3. Obtain Federal agency concurrence on the quantities of radioactive material (e.g., identify consequences of concern) sufficient to create a significant RDD and a significant RED, with consideration of social, economic, and psychological consequences.

The subgroup's report will be reflected in the next Task Force Report to the President and Congress, which is due in 2010.

4.2.3 Nuclear Materials

In the administration of its voluntary security enhancement programs, NNSA/GTRI considers the primary materials of concern to be nuclear materials that could be used by terrorists to fabricate a crude nuclear weapon and radioactive isotopes that would be most effective for an RDD. While experts agree that the most difficult step for terrorists seeking to make a crude nuclear weapon is the acquisition of fissile materials, these materials are used in some commercial, medical, and scientific endeavors such as research reactors, medical isotope production and scientific analysis of materials, education, and training. The IAEA published guidelines in INFCIRC/225/Rev. 4 to assist governments in protecting against the unauthorized removal of HEU and plutonium (Pu), which could lead to the construction of an improvised nuclear explosive device or the sabotage of facilities containing such materials.

---

[50] Report of the Radiation Source Protection and Security Task Force (August 15, 2006).

4.2.4 Radioactive Material Shipments

Federal regulations define the requirements for shipping radioactive material. Shipments are categorized and prioritized based on the level of radioactivity for each isotope contained in the shipment. Any shipment of amounts above a given threshold is reported to the NRC Headquarters Operations Center. This includes transshipment of in-bond shipments of radioactive material not licensed in the United States. The shipper must provide the amount and type of material shipped, departure and arrival dates and locations, and the route and mode of travel for each leg of the shipment. Consistent with the NRC's orders on risk-significant radioactive material shipments, other security precautions are also taken, such as pre-notification of the States through which shipments are made.

Spent fuel and SSNM shipments are given a higher priority than other radioactive material due to the serious potential consequences of a shipment being compromised. Shipment times and routes are sent to the NRC Headquarters Operations Center. Certain information related to the shipments is protected from disclosure or controlled as SGI. Extra precautions include obtaining NRC approval for a shipping plan, minimizing time in transit, avoiding intermediate stops, using armed escorts and immobilization devices, and notifying State governors' representatives of the shipments. Shipments of risk-significant radioactive material or radionuclides are also reported and tracked to maintain situational awareness and coordinate actions in response to threat information and security plans.

4.2.5 Radioactive Waste Facilities

Spent fuel storage facilities, along with nuclear power reactors and other facilities that possess risk-significant radioactive material, are prioritized based on the size and type of material. Other types of radioactive waste facilities (e.g., low-level waste storage and disposal and uranium mills) are not expected to pose significant off-site consequences in the event of an attack.

4.2.6 The National Nuclear Security Administration's Global Threat Reduction Initiative Prioritization Efforts

GTRI does not prioritize its efforts based on facility type; instead, it uses the risk-based approach described in chapter 3 to prioritize its work. GTRI's prioritization criteria consider factors such as the material attractiveness levels, existing site security conditions, and locations in Urban Area Security Initiative Tier 1 and Tier 2 metropolitan areas, as defined by DHS.

5. Develop and Implement Protective Programs and Resiliency Strategies

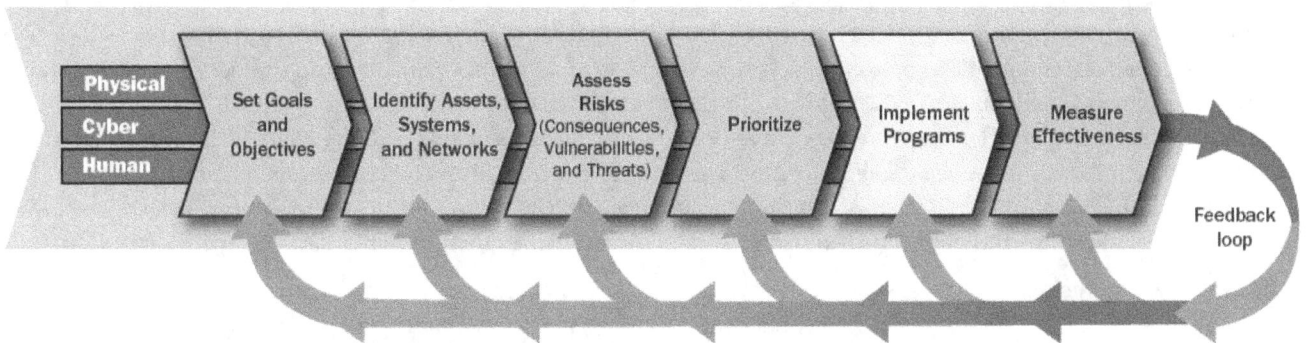

Continuous Improvement to enhance protection of CIKR

5.1 Overview of Sector Protective Programs and Resiliency Strategies

While historically the Nuclear Sector has shown strong efforts in developing protection and resiliency strategies, sector partners must continue to sustain the level of progress made in developing and implementing these strategies intended primarily to prevent the malicious use of Nuclear Sector assets to harm the Nation's public health, safety, morale, or economic well-being. Nuclear CIKR partners also have sought to advance, as appropriate, the continued secure operation of Nuclear Sector CIKR and to prevent their disruption. Nuclear Sector partners continue to cooperate to reinforce defense capabilities for nuclear facilities; to ensure that radiological materials are transported, used, and disposed of in secure settings; to better control sensitive information; and to enhance emergency preparedness and response. The objective of these efforts is to ensure all reasonable steps are taken to prevent the use of Nuclear Sector CIKR in a manner that is hostile to the United States and to execute planning and coordination necessary to ensure the resilience of the Nuclear Sector and the ability of Nuclear Sector partners to manage the response and recovery from all hazards in a way that is consistent with national policy and other relevant authorities.

Nuclear Sector protective programs and resiliency strategies, therefore, play a crucial role in the Nuclear Sector's overall risk management approach. The overall approach for protecting assets in the Nuclear Sector is founded on four fundamental, equally important security functions:

- **Prevent or Delay an Incident.** Nuclear facilities vary in the degree to which they are required to provide fixed security measures, based on the risk that the facility or activity presents to the public. Security programs for nuclear power plants and certain fuel cycle facilities include protective layers (e.g., owner-controlled area, protected area, and vital area or materials access area), physical barriers (e.g., personnel, vehicle, and watercraft), intrusion detection devices, alarm stations, redundant communications systems, armed security organizations with response officers specifically trained and detailed to those functions, comprehensive background checks for personnel with access to protected areas, fitness-for-duty programs for the workforce, and procedures to integrate State and local resources into the response plan for attacks on the facilities. Other Nuclear Sector CIKR are subject to risk-informed[51] regulatory requirements. Voluntary programs, such as the Voluntary Security Enhancement Programs described in chapter 6, provide a cost-effective means to further enhance security and thus strengthen the Nuclear Sector's preventive posture.

- **Detect a Potential Incident.** Many nuclear facilities have programmatic detection elements that are part of a mandated security program. Nationally, DNDO is responsible for developing the Global Nuclear Detection Architecture (GNDA), the underlying strategy that guides the U.S. Government's nuclear detection efforts.

- **Mitigate or Respond to an Incident.** Highest risk Nuclear Sector facilities have contingency plans that include integration of site security forces with resources provided by State and local government agencies. These plans require the facility to maintain an armed security organization, with response officers specifically trained and detailed to protect nuclear assets. Other facilities housing lesser amounts of radioactive material onsite, such as RTRs, and sites containing radioactive material subject to the NRC increased controls, may not be required to post armed guards; these facilities generally rely on such measures as staff background screening, access controls, vehicle and package searches, and coordination with appropriate local, State, and Federal response organizations. The NRF, particularly its Nuclear/Radiological Incident Annex, establishes a comprehensive, national, all-hazards approach to domestic incident response in the Nuclear Sector. In addition, the NRC Incident Response Plan, NUREG-0728, was developed to reflect the NRC's response to radiological and other incidents and emergencies, especially incidents involving NRC licensees. The plan assigns internal NRC responsibilities for responding to any potentially threatening incident involving NRC-regulated activities and for assuring that the NRC fulfills its statutory mission.

- **Recover from an Incident.** Highest-risk Nuclear Sector facilities' contingency plans include steps to recover control of a facility, resume operation, and/or render the facility safe. These facilities have plans in place for coordinating these efforts with Federal, State, and local governments and local law enforcement agencies.

5.2 Determining the Need for Protective Programs and Resiliency Strategies

As indicated in section 5.1, protective programs and resiliency strategies in the Nuclear Sector may be regulatory or voluntary. In either case, the substance of these programs is driven by the need for a comprehensive approach to the protection and resilience of the Nation's Nuclear CIKR, including all appropriate measures to prepare for and respond to incidents which may affect these assets. The specific content of these programs, and the details of their implementation, are determined by CIKR partners based on each partner organization's specific mission, authorities, and decision-making procedures. DHS IP, as the Nuclear SSA, works with each of these partners within the context of the NIPP partnership framework to coordinate and integrate these activities and to identify areas where additional attention may be warranted.

The partnership framework established by the NIPP facilitates coordination of protective activities across the Nuclear Sector and with other CIKR sectors. Quarterly meetings of the NGCC, which includes representatives from State radiation control offices and the State, Local, Tribal, and Territorial Government Coordinating Council (SLTTGCC), enable Nuclear Sector government partners to share information, coordinate, and seek appropriate assistance in the development of protective programs. Similarly, quarterly meetings between the NGCC and the private sector NSCC provide a mechanism by which private sector partners may provide input to government CIKR protection deliberations and seek appropriate support for protective programs originated by industry, as well as provide government partners with a venue to obtain private sector expertise, contribution, and cooperation.

---

[51] Risk-informed is defined by the 2009 National Infrastructure Protection Plan (NIPP) as, "The determination of a course of action predicated on the assessment of risk, the expected impact of that course of action on that risk, and other relevant factors."

> **Cybersecurity in the Nuclear Sector**
>
> Protecting the cyber elements of the Nuclear Sector is a critical part of overall protection of the sector. Part of achieving protection requires implementation of NRC-mandated cybersecurity programs at all commercial nuclear power plants. The nuclear industry should also maintain awareness of the latest cybersecurity measures developed or recommended by NCSD, United States Computer Emergency Readiness Team (US-CERT), and other government and industry bodies concerned with cybersecurity.

The NSCC and the NGCC may also establish working groups to identify and audit programs and strategies already in place or to execute other functions as directed.

For the Nuclear Sector, Congress has provided certain Federal departments and agencies with statutory authority to promote the public interest through the promulgation, implementation, and enforcement of rules and regulations. These regulations are developed and amended through rulemakings conducted according to legally prescribed procedures, which enable the participation of interested stakeholders in the rulemaking process. The resulting regulations carry the force of law. In the Nuclear Sector, parties subject to the regulations must develop programs to ensure that regulatory requirements are satisfied. Similarly, the government agencies charged by Congress with implementing and enforcing these regulations have in place rulemaking, inspection, enforcement, and other programs that support their regulatory duties.

The NRC is the principal U.S. authority responsible for licensing and regulating the civilian use of nuclear and radiological materials to protect public health and safety, promote the common defense and security, and protect the environment. The Atomic Energy Act of 1954, as amended, requires that civilian uses of nuclear materials and facilities be licensed, and it empowers the NRC to establish such standards to govern these uses as "the Commission may deem necessary or desirable in order to protect health and safety and minimize danger to life or property." NRC rules and orders constitute the minimum acceptable security conditions under which nuclear and radioactive material may be stored, used, or disposed. NRC regulations also contain reporting and other requirements intended to provide the NRC with reasonable assurance that these materials, and the facilities that use them, are adequately protected.

The minimum risk posture for commercial nuclear power plants and Category I fuel cycle facilities is defined by the DBT rule, which describes the general adversary characteristics against which these facilities' security forces must defend. DBT elements and characteristics represent the largest spectrum of threats—including cyber-based threats—against which the NRC has determined private sector facilities must be able to defend with high assurance.

Recognizing that DBT characteristics for commercial nuclear power plants and Category I fuel cycle facilities necessarily impact DHS' area of responsibility—as described in HSPD-7 and the NIPP—for the identification, prioritization, and coordination of Nuclear Sector CIKR and associated protection activities, measures, and strategies to prevent, deter, and mitigate the effects of threats to the Nuclear Sector CIKR, when possible, the NRC will continue to seek the views of CIKR partners regarding the impacts of the proposed changes in either DBT. [52] The NRC considers input from DHS and other sector partners as part of its independent decision-making process consistent with its statutory responsibilities and authorities. Conformance with the DBT rulemaking is tested through baseline security inspections, including FOF, and various other NRC programs intended to pro-

---

[52] Though neither HSPD-7 nor the NIPP alters, or impedes the ability to carry out, the authorities of Federal departments and agencies to perform their responsibilities under law and consistent with applicable legal authorities and presidential guidance, the NIPP is applicable to all partners with CIKR protection responsibilities and includes explicit roles and responsibilities for the Federal Government's effort to protect all CIKR, including that which is under the control of independent regulatory agencies. Some regulatory agencies play an important supporting role in developing and implementing this Nuclear SSP and for implementing related protective activities within the Nuclear Sector. For additional information on the relationship of the NIPP and SSPs to other CIKR plans and programs, see section 5.3 (p. 76) of the 2009 NIPP.

vide assurance that security forces employed at nuclear power plant and major fuel-cycle facilities are, at a minimum, capable of defeating the threat specified in the appropriate DBT.

Regulatory standards and requirements for materials and RTRs are likewise based upon the NRC's determination of what constitutes the minimum standards necessary to promote the common defense and security, or protect public health and safety, or the environment.

Other regulators with authorities in the Nuclear Sector, such as the EPA and the DOT, implement regulatory programs in support of their respective congressional mandates. MOUs and similar agreements between regulatory agencies play a crucial role in the application of these regulations, helping to avoid duplication and to streamline administration and compliance.

While Nuclear Sector regulations establish a robust baseline for safety and security, partners recognize the potential for continuous improvement. Sector partners work collaboratively to identify and execute voluntary or incentive-based activities, such as those addressed in chapter 6, to further strengthen security. The NNSA/GTRI voluntary security enhancement program is supported by the DHS, NRC, the Organization of Agreement States (OAS), and other Federal, State, and private organizations. The enhancements are consistent with and complementary to the NRC and OAS increased controls requirements.

The NGCC assists with identifying and coordinating non-regulatory CIKR programs in the Nuclear Sector. These activities are intended to supplement—not replace—existing regulatory requirements. When evaluating the need for non-regulatory protective programs and resiliency strategies and similar initiatives, members of the NGCC may solicit additional risk analyses and other input as necessary to inform their decisions. The success of any protective program, whether new or existing, is based in large part on the input and cooperation of sector CIKR partners, particularly the NSCC, and on the availability and commitment of the necessary resources. The NGCC remains aware of protective program implementation, seeking to ensure these activities are both effective and supported by Nuclear Sector partners. Further, the NGCC is the principal mechanism by which the Nuclear Sector coordinates with other CIKR sectors and with other DHS elements to implement cross-sector protective actions and mitigate dependencies. Through NGCC-Cyber participation in the Nuclear Sector Joint Cybersecurity Subcouncil, which includes industry partners and remains abreast of evolving, sector-specific cybersecurity considerations, threats, and potential consequences, the NGCC is able to assess the implementation and maintenance of existing cybersecurity programs, identify cyber-related program needs, and develop long-term protective plans for cyber assets. The Nuclear Sector Joint Cybersecurity Subcouncil, in addition, serves as the focal point for Nuclear Sector participation in national efforts to deter, respond, and recover from cyber attacks, for example, through its involvement in the development of the National Cybersecurity Response Plan.

The 12-agency Radiation Source Protection and Security Task Force ("Task Force"), created according to Section 651(d) of the Energy Policy Act of 2005, is charged with consulting relevant Federal, State, and local partners to evaluate and provide recommendations on protecting radioactive sources in the United States from potential terrorist threats. The initial Task Force report was submitted to President George W. Bush on August 15, 2006. The 2006 report included 10 recommendations and 18 "actions," which did not rise to the level of a recommendation. The Task Force will submit a 2010 Report to Congress and the President.

As part of its activities, the Task Force establishes subgroups to address specific radioactive source-security issues. These subgroups provide an additional forum in which Federal agencies may identify the need for specific protective programs and resiliency strategies. Operating through consensus whenever possible, subgroup members develop findings and recommendations that are provided to the full Task Force. If subgroup members cannot achieve consensus, areas of disagreement are brought to the full Task Force for resolution. Disagreements that cannot be resolved by Task Force members are noted in its reports.

5.3 Protective Program and Resiliency Strategy Implementation

As indicated in section 5.2, the implementation of Nuclear Sector protective programs is the responsibility of individual sector partners as required by their unique missions and relying primarily on their own resources. Interagency coordination of these programs is achieved through the NGCC, the principal Federal interagency body responsible for coordinating domestic civilian nuclear and radiological security strategies, activities, policies, and communications, including those activities conducted in partnership with State and local partners, and those between government and industry. Voluntary Nuclear Sector protective and resiliency programs in many cases intersect with existing regulatory requirements. These programs are, therefore, implemented in close coordination with relevant regulatory authorities.

If the NRC determines an activity is not appropriate for implementation voluntarily by its licensees, it may require action through rulemaking, orders, or license amendments. Each of those regulatory processes includes sector partner interactions to review and comment on the proposed requirements. Interaction is consistent with the sensitivity of the proposed requirement. In some cases, such as work-hour controls for security force personnel, broad public interaction is undertaken. In most circumstances, the sensitivity of the requirements permits only cleared CIKR partners to participate in the process. Based on partner input, the NRC may revise the proposed requirements prior to final issuance. For security orders issued by the NRC, regional meetings are conducted with the specific categories of licensees and Agreement State regulators to discuss proposed actions and obtain comments on implementation guidance. Where practical, industry representative groups may propose industry-specific implementation guidance that could be endorsed by the NRC. Ultimately, any enhanced protective measures implemented by order or license condition will be codified in the NRC's regulations.

5.3.1 CIKR Partner Roles and Responsibilities in Program Implementation

CIKR partner responsibilities for program implementation depend on the role the partner plays in the sector and, when appropriate, their statutory authorities. CIKR partners, and their corresponding roles and responsibilities within the sector partnership framework, are detailed in the ensuing sections.

5.3.1.1 U.S. Department of Homeland Security

As both the Nuclear SSA and the national coordinator for the protection of CIKR, DHS has substantial responsibilities in the Nuclear Sector. DHS leads national coordination efforts to reduce risks to the Nation's CIKR, and to strengthen national preparedness, timely response, and rapid recovery of these assets in the event of an attack, natural disaster, or other emergency. DHS has charged IP with implementing these responsibilities.

Within IP, the SSA EMO coordinates, develops, and implements programs that help achieve security by effectively reducing vulnerabilities and consequences of attack using risk-based assessments, industry best practices, protective measures, and comprehensive information sharing between the private sector and all levels of government. The mission of SSA EMO is to build, sustain, align, and leverage relationships with sector partners to effectively coordinate the identification, prioritization, and protection within the Nuclear Sector, as well as in the other five CIKR sectors for which IP is the lead Federal coordinator. This entails, among other responsibilities, maintaining this Nuclear Sector-Specific Plan and submitting the corresponding Nuclear Sector CIKR Protection Annual Report, assessing sector-level performance to enable protection program gap assessment, identifying protection priorities, coordinating and supporting risk assessment and management programs for high-risk CIKR, and supplying sector-specific CIKR information for incident response. During the execution of these responsibilities, the SSA EMO works closely with the NRC and, as appropriate, DOE to ensure the necessary protection and resilience of the Nuclear Sector.

The Nuclear SSA chairs the NGCC, through which, in partnership with the NSCC, as appropriate, the Nuclear SSA coordinates with existing emergency management and public health and safety communities regarding response and recovery issues associated with a terrorist act or other disasters. Both independently and in coordination with CIKR partners, as appropriate, the Nuclear SSA supports DHS and SSA responsibilities, as described in the NRF and its relevant Support Annexes, most prominent of which are the CIKR, the Private-Sector Coordination, and the Public Affairs Support Annexes.[53] Other DHS components provide crucial support to the Nuclear Sector as well.

DNDO, established by HSPD-14, serves as the primary Federal Government entity responsible for furthering the development, acquisition, and support for deployment of an enhanced domestic system to detect and report on unauthorized attempts to import, possess, store, transport, develop, or use a unauthorized nuclear explosive device, fissile material, or radiological material in the United States, and to improve that system over time.

The responsibilities of the FEMA Radiological Emergency Preparedness (REP) Program include leading off-site emergency planning, review, and evaluation of RERPs and procedures developed by State and local governments, and determining whether State and local governments can implement such plans and procedures. The NRC considers FEMA's findings on off-site emergency preparedness and plans when considering the adequacy of the on-site emergency planning program and determining the overall state of reasonable assurance for nuclear power plants.

FEMA chairs the Federal Radiological Preparedness Coordinating Committee (FRPCC), the interagency body that coordinates Federal peacetime radiological emergency planning and preparedness assistance to State and local governments. Representatives from 20 Federal departments, agencies, and offices presently sit on the FRPCC. FEMA also chairs the Regional Assistance Committees (RACs), which help State and local governments develop RERPs and periodically review and update plans and observe exercises to evaluate plan effectiveness. RACs help coordinate regional Federal response planning and preparedness activities.

FEMA and other DHS elements also support the department's responsibilities under the Nuclear/Radiological Incident Annex to the NRF, which assigns DHS responsibility for all deliberate attacks involving nuclear and radiological facilities or materials, including RDDs and INDs.

Other DHS elements, including TSA, CBP, USCG, and NCSD also support Nuclear Sector security and resiliency as part of their broader mission areas.

5.3.1.2 Nuclear Regulatory Commission

HSPD-7 directs the Secretary of Homeland Security to "continue to work with the NRC and, as appropriate, DOE in order to ensure the necessary protection" of the Nuclear Sector.

The NRC began operations in 1975 and derives its fundamental authorities from the Atomic Energy Act of 1954, as amended, and the Energy Reorganization Act of 1974. The NRC was established to regulate the civilian use of nuclear materials for commercial, industrial, academic, and medical uses to protect public health and safety and the environment, and promote the common defense and security.

The NRC's scope of responsibility includes regulation of commercial nuclear power plants; RTRs; nuclear fuel cycle facilities; medical, academic, and industrial uses of radioactive materials; the decommissioning of these facilities and sites; and the

---

[53] These documents may be found online, at www.fema.gov/emergency/nrf.

transport, storage, and disposal of radioactive materials and wastes. The NRC has designed its regulations to protect both the public and occupational workers from radiation hazards.

The NRC issues licenses and oversees licensees for 104 commercial nuclear power reactors; 32 RTRs; approximately 4,500 licensed reactor operators; 3 early site permits; 4 reactor design certifications; 40 uranium recovery sites; 9 major fuel cycle facilities; approximately 4,400 research, medical, industrial, government, and academic materials licensees; and an increasing number of independent spent-fuel storage installations (currently 46 licensees). The NRC also consults with the DOE regarding disposal options for waste incidental to reprocessing and monitors DOE disposal actions for these incidental wastes.

The NRC is responsible for regulating domestic activities related to radiation protection and nuclear safety for nuclear facilities and for promoting the common defense and security related to uses of radioactive materials. The NRC also licenses the import and export of radioactive materials; participates in international nuclear activities, including multilateral and bilateral safety and security activities; and works closely with its international counterparts to enhance nuclear safety and security worldwide.

In addition, 37 States have signed agreements with the NRC under which they assume regulatory responsibility for the use of certain quantities of radioactive materials for civilian purposes in their respective States. These Agreement States implement State regulations that are compatible with NRC regulations. In all, they issue about 80 percent of radioactive materials licenses in the United States. The NRC works closely with Agreement States to ensure a consistent regulatory framework nationwide.

The NRC inspects and reviews the security program at each nuclear plant to ensure safety, security, and continued compliance with NRC regulations. It also has a regulatory program specifying the requirements for physical protection of licensed materials at fuel cycle facilities and spent fuel stored at ISFSI. It also regulates some security measures that protect transport of SNF and other high-activity shipments. More discussion about the NRC role in regulating prevention, protection, response, and recovery requirements is available in the NRC Information Digest (NUREG-1350). Details of these security requirements, as well as specific security plans, strategies, and measures used to defend commercial nuclear power plants and Category I fuel cycle facilities, are sensitive and are not available to the public.

Because of its expertise in the Nuclear Sector and its protection, the NRC also supports DHS in the transition from steady-state protection activities governed by the NIPP and this plan to the incident management activities governed by the NRF. The Nuclear/Radiological Response Incident Annex to the NRF identifies DHS as the coordinating agency "for all deliberate attacks involving nuclear/radiological facilities or materials, including RDDs and INDs." The NRC coordinates incident response activities for all other incidents involving NRC-licensed facilities and activities that are not of national significance. The NRC has updated its incident response program documents and procedures in accordance with the NRF.

5.3.1.3 Department of Energy/National Nuclear Security Administration

The mission of DOE/NNSA's GTRI is to reduce and protect vulnerable nuclear and radiological materials at civilian sites world-wide. These efforts focus on the first line of defense, namely securing or removing vulnerable nuclear and radiological materials at their source. GTRI has three goals that provide a comprehensive approach to achieving its mission and denying terrorist access to nuclear and radiological materials:

1. Convert research reactors and isotope production facilities from the use of HEU to LEU;

2. Remove and dispose of excess nuclear and radiological materials; and

3. Protect at-risk WMD-usable nuclear and radiological materials worldwide against theft and sabotage until a more permanent threat reduction solution can be implemented.

To achieve its mission, GTRI is working in more than 100 countries. In 2008, GTRI launched a voluntary security program to enhance the protection of nuclear and radiological materials at domestic facilities. Under the program, security experts from DOE's national laboratories, led by NNSA headquarters staff, provide security assessments, share observations, and make recommendations for enhancing security. When appropriate, GTRI pays for the installation of agreed-upon security enhancements. Typical security enhancements include automated access control, motion sensors, radiation sensors, electronic seals, alarm control and display systems, remote monitoring to off-site response locations, enhanced guard force communications and protection equipment, delay elements, and transportation security enhancements, when appropriate.

The NNSA's GTRI is increasingly applying its convert, remove, and protect framework domestically to better secure domestic nuclear and radiological material. GTRI is pursuing this framework through its domestic radiological material removal, material protection, and reactor-conversion programs. The latter effort entails supporting the conversion of U.S. RTRs that rely on HEU fuel to the use of less proliferation-prone LEU.

The NNSA Office of Emergency Response provides a responsive, flexible, efficient, and effective radiological emergency response capability, applying NNSA's unique technical expertise resident within the DOE complex. As a result, the appropriate infrastructure is in place to provide command, control, communications, and properly organized, trained, and equipped response personnel to successfully resolve an emergency event. The DOE NEST program provides NNSA with technical assistance to a lead coordinating agency in response to incidents, including terrorist threats that involve the use of nuclear materials. Additional NNSA assets that may be deployed domestically include: the AMS, which detects and maps radioactive material at an emergency scene to determine contamination levels using fixed-wing and rotary aircraft; Atmospheric Release Advisory Capability (ARAC), which develops and disseminates predictive dose and deposition plots generated by sophisticated computer models; FRMAC, which provides the technical capabilities focused on radiological consequence management to assist and coordinate Federal radiological monitoring and assessment activities and effects; and REAC/TS, which provides advice and medical consultation for injuries resulting from radiation exposure and contamination and serves as a training facility.

Along with the Department of State, NNSA also serves as a key liaison with several international partners concerned with nuclear and radiological security, the most prominent of which is IAEA. In addition to the IAEA, NNSA collaborates routinely with other international partners as part of its national security mission.

5.3.1.4 U.S. Department of Justice

The Department of Justice (DOJ) provides investigative and prosecutorial support to other Federal CIKR partners, including those in the Nuclear Sector, for the enforcement of Federal laws and regulations. As mandated in HSPD-5, HSPD-7, the NRF, and current interagency agreements, the U.S. Attorney General, generally acting through the FBI and in cooperation with relevant Federal departments and agencies, is primarily responsible for coordinating Federal activities of other members of the law enforcement community to detect, prevent, preempt, and disrupt terrorist attacks against the United States.

5.3.1.5 Other Federal Agencies

Several additional Federal agencies provide key, specialized support to Nuclear Sector CIKR prevention, protection, response, and recovery mission areas. These include the following, which in some cases respond specifically to mitigate the cross-sector consequences arising from an incident affecting or utilizing Nuclear Sector CIKR:

· Department of Commerce;	· Department of Transportation;
· Department of Defense;	· Department of Veterans Affairs;
· Department of Health and Human Services;	· Environmental Protection Agency;
· Department of the Interior;	· National Aeronautics and Space Administration; and
· Department of Justice;	· Intelligence Community.
· Department of State;	

Some of these agencies (e.g., DOT and EPA) have regulatory responsibilities for particular aspects of the Nuclear Sector.

5.3.1.6 State, Local, Tribal, and Territorial Agencies

Consistent with existing law and policy, State, local, tribal, and territorial governments are also responsible for implementing the homeland security mission, protecting public safety and welfare, and ensuring the provision of essential services to communities and industries within their jurisdictions. As noted in section 2.2.4 of the 2009 NIPP and elsewhere in this Nuclear SSP, these governments also play an important role supporting CIKR protection and resilience in the Nuclear Sector.

State, local, tribal, and territorial law enforcement, emergency response, and other executive agencies develop protective measures and strategies to deter, detect, and prevent terrorist attacks on nuclear facilities and other Nuclear Sector assets within or near their areas of jurisdiction. As described in the NRF and its Nuclear/Radiological Incident Annex, and consistent with existing authorities, these entities serve as a conduit to their Federal partners, passing appropriate threat and other information to Federal agencies as warranted. Moreover, non-Federal government partners interface with the Federal Government in instances when an incident exceeds or is anticipated to exceed State, local, tribal, or territorial resources.

Additionally, as described in chapter 1 of the SSP, the NRC has transferred some responsibility for the control of SNM, source material, and byproduct material to certain Agreement States, pursuant to Section 274b of the Atomic Energy Act of 1954, as amended.

5.3.1.7 CIKR Owners and Operators

Nuclear Sector CIKR owners and operators are required to protect public health and safety and implement common defense and security by managing risks associated with the material under their control, and by applying security measures and complying with regulations and other requirements as established by the NRC and other regulatory authorities. While State and local governments, and in certain situations Federal agencies, may be called upon to augment private on-site security forces deployed at Nuclear Sector facilities, or to respond to threats of radiological theft or sabotage, the owners and operators of Nuclear Sector CIKR are principally responsible for the security and resilience of their assets.

In addition to ensuring safety and security, NRC licensees operating large nuclear facilities are responsible for on-site emergency response to radiological emergencies. These facilities are required to maintain an emergency plan that describes provisions for the initial facility accident response, timely augmentation of response capabilities, adequate training of emergency response personnel to better interface with various on-site and off-site supports, and response activities.

Additional responsibilities and expectations for CIKR owners and operators, including those in the Nuclear Sector, are addressed in section 2.2.5 of the 2009 NIPP. Robust participation by Nuclear Sector owners and operators, as members of the NSCC, in the NIPP sector partnership model is one such expectation. Common functions for all CIKR SCCs are described in section 4.1.2.3 of the 2009 NIPP. These responsibilities include, among other things, serving as a strategic communications and coordination mechanism between CIKR owners, operators, and suppliers, and, as appropriate, with the NGCC.

5.3.1.8 International Partners

Several international and Federal efforts also relate to the security of radioactive and nuclear material. The international strategy for controlling radioactive sources includes creation of international safety and security standards and import and export controls. Nuclear Sector partners coordinate with the Department of State, as appropriate, in the exercise of these international partnerships. For example, to reduce the risk of nuclear and radioactive materials being obtained overseas for malicious use against the United States or its overseas assets, NNSA has bilateral cooperative programs with more than 100 countries.

Since 2002, the NRC has had an active program for assisting its international counterparts to enhance national nuclear safety and security regulatory oversight of civilian radioactive materials. Areas where the NRC is providing assistance include: development of national registries of radioactive sources; development and implementation of laws, rules, and regulations and enhancing day-to-day regulatory oversight; and workshops on how the NRC approaches the physical protection of radioactive sources.

The IAEA, established in 1957, is an independent, inter-governmental, science and technology-based organization in the United Nations family that serves as a global focal point for nuclear cooperation. The IAEA assists its member states, in the context of social and economic goals, to plan and use nuclear science and technology for various peaceful purposes, such as generating electricity, and facilitates transfer of technology and knowledge in a sustainable manner to developing member states.

Part of the IAEA's mission involves developing nuclear safety standards and, based on these standards, promoting achievement and maintenance of high levels of safety in applications of nuclear energy, as well as protection of human health and the environment against radiation. The IAEA also verifies, through its inspection system, that member states comply with their commitments, under the Non-Proliferation Treaty and other agreements,[54] to use nuclear material and facilities only for peaceful purposes.

The IAEA helps member states identify the best means to strengthen their nuclear security, and it has initiated several types of missions to evaluate and assess nuclear security arrangements in member states: International Nuclear Security Advisory Service (INSAS), International Physical Protection Advisory Service (IPPAS), Integrated Regulatory Review Service (IRRS), International Team of Experts (ITE), and State System of Accounting for and Control of Nuclear Material Advisory Service (SSACAS) missions. When requested by a member State, International Nuclear Security Advisory Service (INSServ) missions identify overall needs for additional or improved security measures for the member's nuclear-related activities, whether involving nuclear material and facilities or other radioactive material, such as radioactive sources, and relevant facilities. The INSServ makes recommendations that provide the platform for subsequent, more specific nuclear security assistance, either through IAEA programs or bilateral support programs.

With the help of IPPAS missions, IAEA assists member states in strengthening and enhancing the effectiveness of the physical protection of their nuclear material and facilities. An IPPAS mission may be nationwide or facility-specific. During a mission, the member's physical protection system is reviewed and compared with the international guidelines and internationally recognized best practices. Based on this review, recommendations for improvements are provided, including follow-up activities and assistance. Following the recommendations from IPPAS missions, several member states have initiated upgrades of their physical protection systems through bilateral support programs.

Based on information collected during various missions, the IAEA develops an Integrated Nuclear Security Support Plan (INSSP) that consolidates the nuclear security needs of a member state into one plan for nuclear security improvements and assistance. The IAEA also has missions to help countries without nuclear programs develop safety and security measures for sources and radioactive material. For example, the IAEA conducts IRRS and advisory missions that cover radiation, waste, and transport safety. The Agency also provides Regulatory Authority Information Service (RAIS) software to provide countries with a comprehensive management system for the safety and security of radioactive sources.

5.4 Monitoring Program Implementation

As noted elsewhere in this chapter, Nuclear Sector risks, assets, and protective programs and resiliency strategies are continuously monitored and assessed, and remedial measures are taken as necessary to ensure relevant risks are adequately addressed. Nuclear Sector partners responsible for the implementation of specific protective programs and resiliency strategies are also principally responsible for monitoring the effectiveness of these programs. Robust regulations and inspection programs, in addition to continuous coordination and information sharing among all partners through the NGCC and in other forums, enables decision makers in the Nuclear Sector to identify protective programs and resiliency strategies that are successful and merit continued support, and to determine where and how additional benefits may be obtained. Where a technological solution may be warranted, Nuclear Sector partners consider various options, including partnership with the DHS S&T Directorate. Additional information relating to the status of specific protective programs and resiliency strategies may be found in chapter 6.

---

[54] Legally binding agreements between signatories to work against the spread of WMD.

6. Measure Effectiveness

Figure 6-1: NIPP Risk Management Framework: Measure Effectiveness

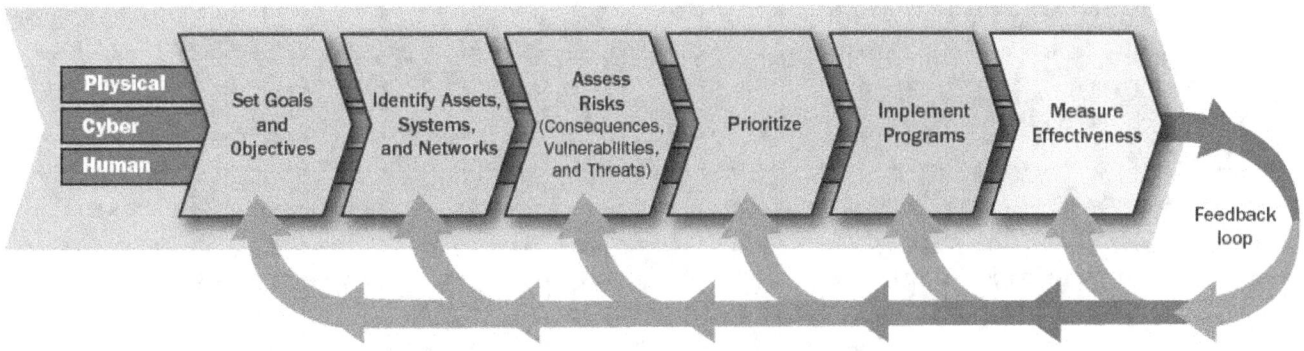

Continuous Improvement to enhance protection of CIKR

The use of performance metrics is a critical step in the NIPP risk management process "to enable DHS and the SSAs to objectively and quantitatively assess improvements in CIKR protection and resiliency at the sector and national levels."[55] Performance metrics allow NIPP partners to track progress on sector priorities and provide "a basis for DHS and the SSAs to establish accountability, document actual performance, facilitate diagnoses, promote effective management, and provide a feedback mechanism to decision makers."[56] Since the initial publication of the Nuclear SSP in May 2007, the Nuclear SSA has continued to formalize and refine its ability to measure the performance of risk mitigation activities (RMAs) in the sector. This development process has been coordinated with and conducted in reliance upon guidance provided by the appropriate DHS components with overall responsibility for CIKR metrics and reporting. Performance metrics for many of the sector's most important CIKR protection and resilience programs will be identified and reported in the Nuclear Sector Annual Report (SAR).

The focus of the NIPP metrics program is to track progress toward a strategic goal by measuring beneficial results or outcomes of RMAs; however, the key to NIPP performance management is to align outcome metrics to sector priorities.

---

[55] Department of Homeland Security, National Infrastructure Protection Plan: Partnering to Enhance Protection and Resiliency (2009).
[56] Ibid.

6.1 Risk Mitigation Activities

This section lists key RMAs underway within the Nuclear Sector, as well as additional RMAs that are important elements of the nuclear CIKR protection and resilience efforts. The list is not meant to be all-inclusive, but is risk-informed. This list is meant to highlight the breadth of activities reducing risk in the Nuclear Sector and the means by which sector partners are achieving the sector's mission and goals. The list includes the regulatory programs that provide the security baseline for many elements of the sector, as well as key voluntary programs that help ensure that the breadth of sector asset, system, and network types—including nuclear power reactors, research and test reactors, nuclear materials, and cyber systems—are secure and resilient.

For each RMA included below, descriptive metrics have been developed, as well as output metrics and outcome metrics when possible, and will be provided as part of the Nuclear SAR.

6.1.1 Security Requirements for Nuclear Power Plants and Other Nuclear Facilities

The Nation's nuclear power plants had implemented strong physical protection programs decades before September 11, 2001. The plants were already surrounded by fences with continuously monitored perimeter detection and surveillance systems, and they were guarded by well-trained and well-armed security forces. The plants also had redundant and diverse safety equipment so that if any active component became unavailable, another component or system would satisfy its function. A similar layered, defense-in-depth approach is applied to securing these assets. In addition, plant operators were trained to respond to unusual events and emergencies, and each plant had carefully designed emergency plans in place.

Following the attacks of September 11, the NRC issued new requirements for security enhancements at nuclear facilities. These included measures to provide additional protection against vehicle-borne improvised explosive devices, as well as water- and land-based assaults. The NRC also required nuclear facility licensees to assess the potential impact of a terrorist-initiated event on site emergency plans. In addition to these efforts, the NRC evaluates key emergency response and security interface elements to ensure effective integration of the security plan, emergency plan, and operational mitigating actions.

NRC Baseline Inspection Program

The NRC continues to implement the Reactor Oversight Process (ROP), which is the agency's key program for ensuring plant and radiological safety, security, and emergency preparedness at operating nuclear power plants. The basic principles and philosophy of the ROP, which includes the security-focused Baseline Inspection Program, are to ensure that a defined, repeatable, and objective process is applied to identify findings, determine their significance, and document results in accordance with ROP program guidance. Program instructions and inspection procedures help ensure that licensee actions and regulatory responses are commensurate with the safety or security significance of the particular event, deficiency, or weakness.

Within each ROP cornerstone (see Figure 6-2), NRC resident inspectors, headquarters, and regional security inspectors follow detailed inspection procedures to conduct NRC inspections. In the aggregate, the results of these inspections contribute to an overall assessment of licensee performance. The Security Cornerstones Baseline Inspection Program comprises 11 inspectable areas that are reviewed periodically at each power reactor facility: access control; access authorization; contingency response; equipment performance; security personnel training; personnel fitness-for-duty; owner-controlled area oversight; protective strategy; material control and accounting; protection and control of SGI; and irradiated fuel transportation.

Figure 6-2: Cornerstones of the ROP[57]

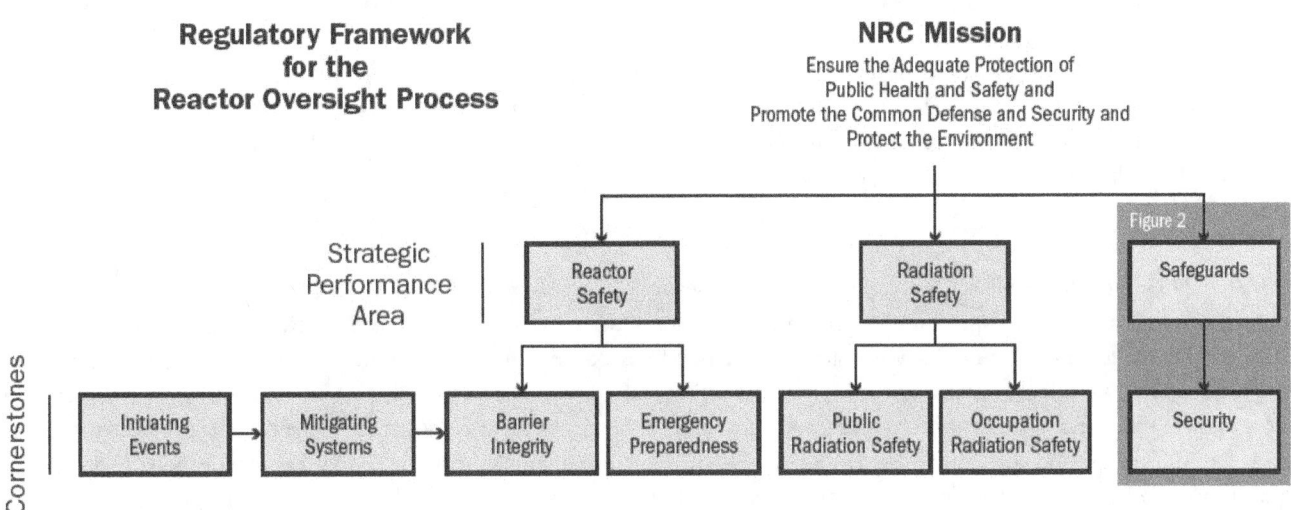

NRC Resident Inspector Program

NRC Resident Inspectors are assigned to every existing U.S. nuclear power facility. The number of inspectors at a site typically equals the number of nuclear reactor units located at the site; however, at least two resident inspectors are assigned to each site. Resident Inspectors maintain inspection programs for the various areas defined in the seven cornerstones of safety, including security, and are supported by Specialist Inspectors from the NRC's regional offices to identify potential safety or security concerns. Specialist Inspectors provide the in-depth, expert knowledge necessary to comprehensively review specific areas associated with the NRC's safety and security missions. Collectively, the Resident and Specialist Inspectors perform indepth inspections in areas such as engineering design, radiation controls, security, emergency preparedness, and fire protection. Both Resident and Specialist Inspectors play a key role in the risk-informed Baseline Inspection Program.

NRC Force-on-Force Inspections

The NRC initiated the FOF exercise program in the early 1980s as a means to confirm the adequacy of nuclear power plant and risk-significant fuel cycle facility security programs. The purpose is to evaluate the effectiveness of NRC licensees' security plans against a series of attack scenarios by a simulated commando-style mock adversary force seeking to exploit potential deficiencies in the plants' defensive strategies. The capabilities of the mock adversary are predicated on DBT elements and characteristics. DBTs provide a general description of the attributes of potential adversaries that might attempt to commit radiological sabotage or theft or diversion against which NRC licensees' physical protection systems must defend with high assurance. The DBTs have been part of the NRC regulations in 10 CFR, Section 73.1 since 1979. DBTs are regularly reviewed and, when appropriate, revised to reflect changes in the threat environment.

During the nuclear power plant FOF exercises, the adversary force attempts to reach and destroy enough safety equipment to set in motion an event that would damage the reactor's core or spent-fuel pool and potentially cause a release of radioactive material to the environment. The nuclear power plant's security forces, in turn, seek to interdict the adversary force and prevent it from reaching the safety equipment. After September 11, 2001, the NRC issued supplemental requirements related to the DBT, which required licensees to enhance security. As a result, the agency expanded its FOF program to reflect these

---

[57] Nuclear Regulatory Commission, Report to Congress on the Security Inspection Program for Commercial Power Reactor and Category I Fuel Cycle Facilities: Results and Status Update: Annual Report for Calendar Year 2008 (2008).

changes and make the exercises more realistic, while also ensuring the safety of both plant employees and the public. These changes have significantly increased the level of complexity for each exercise in terms of planning, preparation, and logistical support. In addition, to improve the realism of FOF exercises, the NRC has incorporated the use of Multiple Integrated Laser Engagement System (MILES) equipment (mock weaponry) into the exercises. When used properly and with sufficient training, MILES equipment provides a much greater degree of realism and reduces many artificialities of simulated combat. The FOF program tests and evaluates licensees' equipment and their conduct and control of the exercises. NRC-graded FOF inspections are conducted at least once every three years at each site.

Cybersecurity Rule

In March 2009, the NRC published a comprehensive cybersecurity rule that requires nuclear power plant licensees to provide high assurance that digital computer and communication systems and networks are adequately protected against cyber attacks. The digital computer and communication systems and networks associated with safety, security, and emergency preparedness functions, as well as support systems and equipment, if compromised, would adversely impact safety, security, or emergency preparedness functions. The new cybersecurity rule requires each nuclear power plant licensee to submit its cybersecurity plans for NRC review and approval by November 23, 2009. Each submittal includes a proposed schedule for implementing its cybersecurity plan. The plans describe how criteria set forth in the new cybersecurity rule will be implemented. Applications for new reactors received on or after November 23, 2009, must also include a cybersecurity plan.

To facilitate rule compliance, the NRC developed Regulatory Guide 5.71, *Cyber Security Programs for Nuclear Facilities*, based on NIST Special Publications, to provide a method to comply with the cybersecurity rule. This regulatory guide also includes a cyber-security plan template that licensees can use to develop their cybersecurity plan. The NRC published this regulatory guide in January 2010, but had previously provided a draft copy to all power reactor licensees (as well as combined operating license applicants) in July 2009 and an updated version on September 21, 2009, which license applicants could use to meet the above requirements. In addition, stakeholders have been participating in the guidance development process since its inception. The industry also developed NEI 08-09, "Cyber Security Plan for Nuclear Power Reactors," which includes a template licensees and applicants can use when developing their plan submission.

In addition to these programmatic cybersecurity tasks, NRC reviews digital (I&C) system security as part of the regulatory review process for new reactors and digital upgrades included in license amendment requests. The intent is to ensure that cybersecurity engineering life-cycle activities are an integral part of the digital I&C system design and development processes, consistent with the "build security in" principle.

6.1.2 Research and Test Reactors

The NRC requires RTRs to maintain security and emergency plans in accordance with regulations established in 10 CFR 73. Because of the relatively small source terms (i.e., quantity and enrichment of special nuclear material), thermal power output, and physical design for RTRs, the more extensive security preparations required of power reactors are not required of RTR facilities. However, the NRC also imposes varying RTR security requirements based on its evaluation of each RTR's site-specific considerations, such as source-term, thermal power output, and physical design. The NRC refers to this method as a "graded approach" to RTR security.

After the September 11 attacks, the NRC reviewed the adequacy of security policies and practices at licensed nuclear facilities, including RTRs, many of which use SNM of moderate and low strategic significance and other source material. Following reviews and assessments of security at all nuclear facilities, the NRC determined that additional security precautions were prudent at RTRs. During the remainder of 2001 and in 2002, RTR facilities implemented additional security precautions based on NRC advisories and onsite evaluations. Between 2002 and 2004, NRC gained commitments from the RTR facilities with nuclear fuel to implement additional security measures (ASMs), which enhanced protection against radiological sabotage or theft. The

NRC also worked with Congress to gain additional statutory authority for fingerprint-based FBI criminal history records checks. This additional authority for fingerprinting was granted through the Energy Policy Act of 2005, which made changes to the Atomic Energy Act, as amended. These requirements were mandated through orders for access to Safeguards Information and unescorted access to RTRs. The NRC is currently using the rulemaking process to codify these requirements in the U.S. CFR.

Following reviews and assessments of security, the NRC staff used a graded approach with increasing requirements, depending on the type of fuel or amount of radiological materials (i.e., higher licensed power level).

The specifics of any post-September 11 security enhancements at individual RTRs cannot be made publicly available; however, general examples of the enhancements include:

- Enhanced background screening of staff;

- Improved access controls to key areas within the facilities;

- Augmented observation of activities within controlled areas;

- Improved internal and external communication systems;

- Additional vehicle and package searches; and

- Enhanced coordination with appropriate Federal, State, and local response organizations.

Through on-site inspections, the NRC has verified that all RTRs have measures in place to protect their nuclear material and limit the radiological consequences following potential acts of sabotage. Nonetheless, the NRC continues to evaluate the effectiveness of these security measures and will take additional steps if necessary.

6.1.3 Security Requirements for the Use and Transport of Radiological Materials

Increased Controls for NRC Licensees That Possess Sources Containing Radioactive Material Quantities of Concern

In 2005, the NRC and Agreement States determined that certain additional controls were necessary for licensees that have risk-significant radioactive materials to supplement existing regulatory requirements in 10 CFR 20.1801 and 10 CFR 20.1802. The controls applied to radioactive materials licensees who possess, or have near-term plans to possess, radionuclides of concern at or above threshold limits. These measures include access controls; measures to detect, assess, and respond to unauthorized access; coordinating shipments of these materials with the NRC; physical barriers to prevent theft or diversion; and protecting information regarding the use and handling of the high-risk radioactive materials.

National Source Tracking System

The NRC's NSTS is a secure, Web-based database designed to enhance the accountability of risk-significant radioactive sources. The NSTS meets the U.S. Government's commitment to implement a national source registry, as described in the Code of Conduct on the Safety and Security of Radioactive Sources, which IAEA issued in January 2004. NSTS helps the NRC and Agreement States track and regulate the medical, industrial, and academic uses of certain nuclear materials from the time that they are manufactured to disposal or exportation. In so doing, the NSTS enhances the ability of the NRC and Agreement States to conduct inspections and investigations, communicate information to other government agencies, and verify legitimate ownership and use of nationally tracked sources.

Transportation Regulations

Following the attacks of September 11, the U.S. DOT Pipeline and Hazardous Materials Safety Administration issued regulations that require shippers and carriers of most hazardous materials, including certain radioactive materials, to develop and implement security plans and ensure that their employee training includes a security component. The security plans are based on a structured analysis, such as DOT's Risk Management Self-Evaluation Framework, and cover personnel security, unauthorized access, and en route security. The DOT Federal Motor Carrier Safety Administration also issued regulations requiring safety permits for HRCQ of radioactive material, as well as requiring adequate security programs and related training.

6.1.4 Voluntary Programs to Enhance Nuclear Sector Security and Preparedness

Hostile Action-Based Emergency Preparedness Drills

To enhance emergency responders' preparedness to deal with a security emergency situation at commercial nuclear power plants, the nuclear industry is sponsoring a voluntary initiative to conduct emergency preparedness (EP) drills using hostile action-based (HAB) scenarios as initiating events. These HAB EP drills demonstrate the licensee's ability under a postulated hostile environment to coordinate event response of on-site security, operations, and emergency response personnel with off-site organizations, such as State and local emergency management, fire fighting, medical response, and law enforcement.

The NRC has worked with NEI and licensees to proceed on schedule to complete this voluntary, non-evaluated drill phase by the end of Calendar Year 2009 (CY 2009). Significant lessons learned have been captured and are available to industry through the NEI members' Web site and to off-site response organizations on the DHS Lessons Learned and Information Sharing Web site (LLIS.gov). The HAB EP scenarios are being incorporated into the existing EP drill and exercise program as part of proposed NRC rulemaking. The NRC and FEMA observe the drills to inform proposed changes to EP regulations and guidance.

Research and Test Reactors Voluntary Security Enhancement Program

In coordination with the RTR Subcouncil to the NGCC and NSCC, NNSA/GTRI is implementing voluntary security enhancements at RTR facilities nationwide. Under the program, NNSA/GTRI conducts a site visit and makes recommendations for voluntary security enhancements. Security enhancements are jointly determined by NNSA/GTRI and the facility owner and operator and are funded by NNSA/GTRI. The voluntary enhancements improve security beyond what is required by law and are consistent with RTR security regulations. Typical security enhancements include automated access control, motion sensors, radiation sensors, electronic seals, alarm control and display systems, remote monitoring to off-site response locations, enhanced guard force communications and protection equipment, delay elements, and transportation security enhancements, when appropriate. The project was piloted in January 2008 at two university facilities and uses a prioritized ranking methodology developed by NNSA, NRC, and DHS for additional RTR volunteers.

Radiological Voluntary Security Enhancements

Under this program, security experts from DOE's national laboratories, led by NNSA/GTRI headquarters staff, provide security assessments, share observations, and make recommendations for enhancing security at facilities that house high-risk radioactive sources. When appropriate, NNSA pays for the installation of agreed-upon security enhancements. The security upgrades are aimed at improving deterrence, control, detection, delay, response, and sustainability. Typical security enhancements include: automated access control; motion sensors; radiation sensors; electronic seals; alarm control and display systems; remote monitoring to off-site response locations; enhanced guard force communications and protection equipment; delay elements; and transportation security enhancements, when appropriate.

Responder Training and Tabletop Exercises

Another component of the GTRI Radiological Voluntary Security Enhancements is alarm response force training and tabletop exercises. The Response Force Training Program assists law enforcement develop and execute response procedures and devise ways to protect themselves and the public during events involving radiological materials. NNSA and the FBI also administer a tabletop exercise program that designs, develops, and facilitates exercises for first responders and other officials who would be involved in the early stages of a terrorist event involving nuclear or radiological materials. The objective of these programs is to promote coordinated planning, communications, cooperation, and team building among local first responders in a dynamic threat environment.

Cesium Chloride In-device Delay

An integral part of GTRI's voluntary security enhancements for radiological facilities is its in-device delay (IDD) for cesium chloride irradiators. As part of the voluntary security enhancements program, NNSA is collaborating with the private sector to enhance the security of blood and research irradiators that use cesium chloride sources (Cs-137). Best Theratronics Ltd (formerly MDS Nordion), J.L. Shepherd & Associates (JLSA), and Pharmalucence, Inc. (formerly CIS-US) are the three major domestic manufacturers and vendors of self-contained irradiators containing Cs-137. The purpose of the program is to install upgrade kits on existing irradiators to significantly increase the time needed for unauthorized source removal and to modify existing product lines so that new devices incorporate the upgrades. Vulnerability analyses were conducted on the products, and engineering upgrade kits were fabricated to increase the delay time for removal of the radioactive sources. Irradiators currently in use are being upgraded on a voluntary, risk-based determination basis, and the irradiator manufacturers have agreed to include the delay features on all future product lines.

Off-Site Source Recovery Project

The Off-Site Source Recovery Project (OSRP) is a U.S. Government activity sponsored by the NNSA's GTRI. Its mission is to remove excess, unwanted, abandoned, or orphan radioactive sealed sources that pose a potential risk to health, safety, and national security. Sealed source recovery was initially considered a waste management activity, as evidenced by its initial organization under the DOE's Environmental Management (EM) program. After the terrorist attacks of 2001, however, the interagency community began to recognize the threat posed by excess and unwanted radiological materials, particularly those that could not be disposed at the end of their useful life. After being transferred to the NNSA to be part of GTRI, OSRP's mission was expanded to include not only material that would be classified as GTCC when it became waste, but also any other sealed sources that pose a potential risk to public health, safety, and/or national security.

GTRI prioritizes the recovery of registered disused radioactive sealed sources based on threat reduction criteria developed in coordination with the NRC. GTRI source recovery activities are implemented by Los Alamos National Laboratory, Idaho National Laboratory, and the CRCPD. As of October 2009, GTRI/OSRP has been able to recover more than 24,000 sources from more than 700 domestic sites.

6.2 Process for Measuring Effectiveness

6.2.1 Measuring Sector Progress

NIPP metrics measure the progress of CIKR protection efforts and provide CIKR partners with feedback to inform the continuous improvement of risk mitigation activities. The NIPP Metrics Program provides the basis for establishing accountability, documenting performance, identifying issues, promoting effective management, and reassessing CIKR goals and objectives. The importance of measuring progress is underscored by executive and legislative requirements that provide the foundation for NIPP metrics. The executive and legislative requirements are derived from the following:

- HSPD-7 mandates the collection of metrics to assess protection programs and activities and requires SSAs to report annually on their efforts to identify, prioritize, and coordinate CIKR protection activities.

- The Homeland Security Act of 2002 (PL 107-296) requires DHS to conduct comprehensive assessments of CIKR vulnerabilities, analyze the data, and subsequently identify CIKR protection priorities across DHS and SSAs.

- Implementing Recommendations of the 9/11 Commission Act of 2007 (PL 110-53) mandates that DHS provide Congress with a report on the comprehensive assessments it conducts in accordance with the Homeland Security Act of 2002.

- The Consolidated Appropriations Act of 2008 (PL 110-161) requires the Assistant Secretary for Infrastructure Protection to brief Congress semi-annually on progress in implementing the NIPP.

These authorities provide DHS the bases to collect relevant programmatic information from Federal partners on interagency CIKR protection and resiliency activities, and to work with State and local partners, and with the private sector, to assess progress in pursuing the Nation's homeland security objectives.

NIPP metrics are reported in two ways: (1) National Coordinator Progress Indicators; and (2) Sector Progress Indicators:

- The National Coordinator Progress Indicators describe DHS Office of Infrastructure Protection efforts to support NIPP and Sector-Specific Plan activities.

- Sector Progress Indicators collectively describe the progress made by each sector and the effectiveness of activities within the CIKR sectors.

The National Coordinator Progress Indicators are reported in the NAR. Metrics discussed in this document are used to assess the value or progress associated with RMAs, and they are included in the SAR. The types of data collected to assess the progress of RMAs include:

- Descriptive Data communicate RMA progress or explain the beneficial value of an RMA during the reporting period.

- Output Data gauge whether specific activities were performed as planned; track the progression of a task; or report on the output of a process. Output data show progress in performing the activities necessary to achieve CIKR protection goals and can serve as leading indicators for outcome measures. They also help build a comprehensive picture of the sector's CIKR protection status and activities.

- Outcome Data indicate progress, value, or beneficial results toward achieving a strategic goal and associated target rather than a level of activity. A high-level metric may demonstrate national achievement of risk mitigation as a result of implementation of a particular CIKR protection initiative.

The NIPP provides the framework for DHS to work with the SSAs and sector CIKR partners to gather the information necessary to assess CIKR protection and resilience program performance. This data collection process also helps DHS respond to frequent information requests from Congress, the Government Accountability Office (GAO), and OMB. In the Nuclear Sector, the Nuclear SSA has responsibility for collecting data on sector RMAs and works with its sector partners to determine proper measures and reporting for each RMA.

6.2.2 Information Collection and Verification

Because the quantity of risk-significant materials and the number of facilities in the Nuclear Sector are relatively small and licensed by the Federal Government, a relatively large amount of information is available for assessing the success of RMAs underway, as well as identifying areas where additional RMAs may be warranted. The Nuclear SSA obtains metrics data from Nuclear Sector partners throughout the year as a regular part of the CIKR protection and resilience coordination and communications processes, as well as annually for inclusion in the Nuclear SAR and the NIPP metrics portal.

As noted in chapter 5, the primary CIKR protection and resilience coordination and communication mechanism across the Nuclear Sector is the CIPAC partnership, which includes the NGCC and the NSCC and the respective subcouncils, as well as working groups or focus groups that are chartered for specific deliverables. In addition, the Nuclear SSA participates in additional interagency forums through which CIKR protection and resilience information is shared, such as the Radiation Source Protection and Security Task Force, which provides Federal and State partners in the sector with a forum for assessing the security of radioactive sources, and the quarterly NRC-DHS-DOE Tri-Lateral information sharing and coordination meeting. The

Nuclear SSA does not generally request data from owners and operators for metrics purposes beyond what is already required by law.

6.2.3 Reporting

The primary means of reporting metrics information to the NIPP Measurement and Reporting Office (MRO) is through the Nuclear SAR and the NIPP metrics portal. The SAR, which is written in coordination with public and private Nuclear Sector partners, also provides an opportunity to share with those partners the Nuclear Sector's metrics results each year.

6.3 Using Metrics for Continuous Improvement

Practical, current, and relevant metrics are central to continuous improvement of the Nuclear Sector's protective posture. Identifying and implementing programs to improve the Nuclear Sector's risk posture involves reassessing risk in a changing security environment and taking action on those items that address areas of greatest risk or provide the greatest risk reduction for the investment available. If the SSA, NGCC, or NSCC determines that sufficient progress is not being made toward a particular goal or in response to a particular threat, vulnerability, or consequence type, sector partners may be able to redirect resources accordingly.

In addition to quantitative measures, qualitative feedback received from partners can be applied to improve the effectiveness and efficiency of public and private sector CIKR protective programs and resiliency strategies. The SSA works with sector partners to identify and share lessons learned and best practices. This feedback loop is a critical step in continuously improving CIKR protection and will be used in ongoing modifications of the Nuclear Sector risk posture.

7. CIKR Protection Research and Development

7.1 Overview of Sector Research & Development (R&D)

By facilitating technological advances to enhance Nuclear Sector security and resilience, R&D programs can provide a cost-effective and efficient means of using limited resources. A coordinated Nuclear Sector-level R&D plan promotes risk mitigation in the sector, efficient resource allocation, and the application of appropriate technological solutions across sectors and subsectors.

Several members of the NGCC and the NSCC maintain relevant R&D programs, as do private-sector associations, such as EPRI and international partners such as the IAEA. This chapter describes how the Nuclear Sector may strengthen appropriate collaboration among these and other agency- or organization-level R&D programs, as well as how they may be linked more closely with sector-specific and national R&D planning efforts, technology requirements, current and candidate R&D initiatives, and gaps. The Nuclear SSA, with support from members of the NGCC and the NSCC, maintains overall responsibility for coordinating these R&D activities.

7.2 Sector R&D Requirements

To a large extent, Nuclear Sector partners benefit from the same technology as other CIKR sectors. The national R&D planning process is designed to address common issues faced by partners across sectors and to ensure a coordinated R&D program that yields the greatest value across a broad range of interests and requirements. Cross-sector R&D collaboration, therefore, will remain a primary means of identifying effective practices and assessing Nuclear Sector R&D requirements. The sector will continue to actively support R&D efforts addressing widely recognized CIKR needs, such as:

- Communications interoperability;
- Personal identity verification and authentication;
- Technical surveillance, monitoring, and detection capabilities; and
- Cybersecurity.

In some cases, an R&D mission need may be unique to the Nuclear Sector. This is particularly the case for modeling, simulation, and analysis products intended to support security and decision-making in the sector. Nuclear Sector-specific R&D requirements are identified over the course of intensive interagency coordination through the NGCC and other interagency, as well as public-private, forums.

7.3 Sector R&D Plan

7.3.1 New R&D Initiatives

As noted in section 7.2, Nuclear Sector partners will continue to work closely with partners in other CIKR sectors to leverage advances in relevant technologies and to promote low-cost refinements to existing technologies and projects to maximize their potential value for Nuclear Sector stakeholders. This cross-sector exchange will be coordinated through full Nuclear Sector participation in the NIPP R&D Requirements Generation Process. As a result, the Nuclear SSA will continue to support applicable technologies through participation in entities such as the NIPP Requirements Steering Group, DHS S&T Directorate Integrated Product Teams (IPTs), DHS CIKR Cross-Sector R&D Working Group, and other forums. The Nuclear SSA and other sector partners will, in addition, continue to support and engage in R&D projects external to the NIPP framework.

If the NGCC and NSCC recognize a need, a Nuclear Sector R&D Working Group may be constituted to develop a detailed R&D plan specific to the Nuclear Sector. Until such time, members of the NGCC and the NSCC can continue to identify requirements—either collectively or independently—that, after consultation with the Nuclear SSA, may be transmitted for consideration to S&T and the Office of Science and Technology Policy (OSTP) by means of the Nuclear SAR and the National Critical Infrastructure Protection (NCIP) R&D Plan. Requirements that address mission needs unique to the Nuclear Sector that cannot be satisfied more efficiently by adapting existing technologies developed through the S&Ts IPTs will be prioritized for action. Other considerations will include consistency with Nuclear Sector goals, as defined in section 1.3 of this plan; potential impact of reducing risk, which could result from R&D; cost effectiveness; likelihood of success of the R&D effort; and amount of time needed from the start of the R&D effort to implementation of the technology into protective measures.

The Nuclear SSA retains responsibility for communicating these R&D requirements to DHS S&T and OSTP, and will continue to coordinate with the NRC, DOE, DNDO, and other NGCC sector partner agencies. The Nuclear SSA will formally communicate the sector's R&D needs annually, if not more frequently. It also will coordinate appropriate Nuclear Sector input to support S&T planning.

Through the mechanisms described above and other processes as appropriate, the Nuclear SSA will continue to explore potential solutions to identified Nuclear Sector R&D needs, including:

- Secure methodologies and assessments to advance state-of-the-art reactor consequence analyses, particularly approaches that incorporate offsite health and economic consequences and may be used to support cross-sector comparisons;

- Secure supply-chain analysis for radiological byproduct material (e.g., sealed sources and radioisotopes), considering both security and continuity-of-supply aspects;

- Secure hardware and systems to support real-time tracking of individual high-risk radioactive sources to enable timely detection and response to the theft or diversion of such source(s); and

- Secure hardware and systems to support surveillance, detection, and monitoring of multiple threats in the owner-controlled area of a commercial nuclear power plant.

The Nuclear SSA will continue to maintain awareness of measures to resolve these and other identified Nuclear Sector R&D needs, and support the identification of additional requirements as appropriate. The Nuclear SSA will request and continuously integrate input on existing Nuclear Sector R&D from members of the NGCC, as well as from other sector partners. Before the Nuclear SSA engages these agencies, it first will solicit information relative to the themes that S&T and OSTP have identified for integration across sectors. Supporting agencies will identify requirements relative to these themes. The Nuclear SSA will thus work with partners to collect and prioritize capability requirements that can be supported by technology development. This information may then be used to determine whether current R&D programs meet requirements or if new programs are needed.

NGCC members are encouraged to maintain agency or department-level R&D planning processes, as needs identified through such mechanisms will inform any decision by the NGCC and NSCC to establish and maintain a sector-specific NIPP R&D working group. The Nuclear SSA will regularly solicit information on these plans from all sector partners to form the basis for the Nuclear Sector's NCIP R&D Plan inputs, to share innovations with the widest audience of potential stakeholders, and for other purposes consistent with the NIPP.

Cybersecurity R&D needs will continue to be considered along with non-cyber R&D needs; however, such needs will be identified by the existing Joint Nuclear Cybersecurity Subcouncil and developed in consultation with NCSD and other members of CSCSWG, as appropriate. Furthermore, Nuclear Sector partners are developing a cybersecurity roadmap for the Nuclear Sector, through which cybersecurity R&D needs may be identified. Using these existing structures will enable the Nuclear Sector to react more quickly to the highly dynamic nature of cybersecurity risks.

7.3.2 Existing R&D Initiatives

The Nuclear SSA will continue to regularly provide partner agencies with information on relevant ongoing Federal R&D initiatives. As noted in section 7.3.1, the Nuclear SSA will coordinate an annual review of sector challenges, technology requirements, and current Federal R&D initiatives with the SSAs, S&T, and OSTP. Appropriate action, in coordination with S&T and OSTP, will be taken to support existing R&D initiatives judged to be of particularly high priority.

Salient aspects of R&D programs of the primary NGCC members (e.g., DOE, DHS, the NRC, and EPA) with ongoing efforts relevant to Nuclear Sector CIKR protection and resiliency R&D are outlined below.

7.3.2.1 *Department of Energy Activities*

The NNSA/GTRI is leading several R&D initiatives to enhance the security and resiliency of the Nuclear Sector, including:

- A pilot transportation project to assess various commercial tracking and radio frequency identification (RFID) applications for its source recovery shipments;

- Assessing alternative technologies to replace those using certain high-risk radioactive sources; and

- Assessment of options and potential alternatives to enhance the resiliency of the North American supply of the radiopharmaceutical molybdenum-99.

7.3.2.2 *DHS Activities*

Two DHS components—DNDO and S&T—maintain R&D programs of relevance to Nuclear Sector CIKR protection and resilience.

DNDO research efforts focus on developing tools and systems for detecting nuclear materials that might enable terrorist activities. DNDO has conducted, and continues to conduct, long-range research and development in the areas of new detector materials, active interrogation, passive systems, sensor readout approaches, forensics, and integrated systems. Specific successes exist in all areas and include progress on "contactless" readout approaches, several new promising detector materials, advancement of passive imaging systems to Advanced Technology Demonstrations (ATDs), progress on mono-energetic x-ray sources, and progress on integrated data and detector systems. Another important long-range R&D area in which significant progress has been made is detection of highly shielded SNM. Success in various exploratory research efforts were such that DNDO has launched another ATD to produce devices capable of finding highly shielded SNM. This ATD is currently in the proposal solicitation phase. Another effort with a similar goal is the Cargo Advanced Automated Radiography System (CAARS), which uses advanced radiographic techniques to automatically detect the presence of shielded SNM. CAARS is described more fully below. Finally, long-range R&D has been conducted in the area of improved hand-held detectors using advanced detector materials and capabilities. This program, called the Intelligent Personal Radiation Locator (IPRL), has units with high sensitivity, directionality, and wireless capabilities.

Near-term development includes the next generation of passive radiation portal monitors through the Advanced Spectroscopic Portal (ASP) Program. ASP systems address a substantial capability gap in currently deployed systems by increasing the probability of detecting a smuggled nuclear device, while decreasing the probability of false alarms for naturally occurring radioactive material or innocent radioactive material (such as granite tiles, ceramics, and cat litter) or incorrectly dismissing nuclear material.

Joint Integrated Non-Intrusive Inspection Program

Through the Joint Integrated Non-Intrusive Inspection (JINNI) program, DNDO and CBP are coordinating efforts to develop, test, and acquire Non-Intrusive Inspection (NII) systems that perform the traditional contraband mission (i.e., drugs, explosives, money) as well as, or better than, current systems and perform the shielded nuclear material mission with little or no impact on CBP operations. The JINII program has two main components. First, a test and evaluation campaign will be performed with currently deployed and soon to be deployed NII systems. These tests will fully characterize the ability of each system to manually detect shielded nuclear material. Simultaneously, a rapid research campaign is being performed to determine if simple methods are available to upgrade the currently deployed and soon to be deployed NII systems to incrementally improve shielded nuclear material detection performance. Second, the JINII program will continue its development of CAARS that is specifically designed to automatically detect shielded nuclear material at a high throughput rate. CAARS units will also be capable of the detection of traditional contraband, such as high explosives and drugs, but not with the same level of automation.

Human Portable Radiation Detection Systems Program

DNDO also has an on-going program called the Human Portable Radiation Detection Systems (HPRDS) program. HPRDS addresses operational issues for DHS assets performing radiation detection functions as part of their law enforcement duties by acquiring and deploying next-generation hand-held and wearable radioisotope detection and identification systems. HRPDS specifically addresses device form-factor and human interface issues, system ruggedness, and interoperability and communicability for hand-held and wearable systems with advanced threat identification algorithms. Because systems developed under the HPRDS program are complementary to a wide variety of law enforcement operational environments, performance information will be shared with State, territorial, and local governments that are participants in the domestic portion of the global nuclear detection architecture. With this performance information, State, territorial, and local partners will be able to make informed grant requests and purchasing decisions.

Intelligent Personal Radiation Locator Program

Another relevant DNDO program is an ATD of the IPRL. This program is pushing technology to ultimately replace the existing generation of radiation pagers with a radioisotope identifier that will wirelessly communicate with similar devices in the vicinity, automatically combining data to increase sensitivity and determine source location. IPRL systems will be pocket-sized radiation detectors with the capability of determining the direction, energy, and isotope of the detected radiation, and its own location and orientation, thus having the ability to locate the source of the alarm. The systems will function autonomously and provide the user with alarms, but have a significantly low false alarm rate so that large numbers of these detectors can be used routinely without significantly impacting the day-to-day duties of the personnel carrying them. IPRL is a technology investigation and demonstration program that will produce performance test units for government characterization and evaluation. The results of the government assessments will feed into the HPRDS program for development and, if warranted, acquisition.

Preventive Radiological/Nuclear Detection

DNDO recognizes the important role of State and local agencies in detecting and interdicting illicit radiological and nuclear materials. To support their efforts, DNDO seeks to identify security partner needs and develop programs and products to enhance their preventive radiological/nuclear detection (PRND) capabilities. To accomplish this, DNDO conducts targeted outreach to raise awareness of the threat posed by terrorists armed with radiological or nuclear devices and has created the Joint Analysis Center (JAC) to provide secondary reach-back to State and local agencies to quickly adjudicate alarms. DNDO works with FEMA's National Preparedness Directorate to include PRND-specific language in the annual DHS grant guidance to encourage States and urban areas to build PRND capabilities within their communities. To supplement the equipment purchased using DHS grant funds, DNDO continues to develop programs and products to assist States and urban areas in planning, organizing, equipping, training, and exercising PRND capabilities. Many of the programs and products offered by DNDO are the result of efforts by the DNDO State and Local Stakeholder Working Group.

Specific programs and products developed by DNDO include a series of PRND training courses for State and local agencies, sample concepts of operation, protocols, and procedures, and results from PRND equipment test campaigns that have been posted on the Responder Knowledge Base. DNDO has led the Southeast Transportation Corridor Pilot program, which has resulted in the inclusion of PRND capability in the commercial vehicle inspection programs of nine States and the District of Columbia and has provided lessons learned that are currently being applied by other States. Finally, DNDO has developed the PRND Program Management Handbook and associated modules. With the assistance of DNDO facilitators, the State of Florida and five of its major cities are using the handbook to develop a statewide PRND implementation plan. Other States have requested the facilitated delivery, and it is expected that the Handbook and products currently available from DNDO will significantly improve the ability of State and local agencies to detect and interdict illicit radiological and nuclear material.

DNDO also leads an effort to identify key vulnerabilities and threats associated with WMDs, specifically with regard to radioactive and nuclear items. DNDO, together with CBP and TSA, is working to facilitate international general aviation operations, while enhancing security for these operations and for the nation as a whole.

In April 2007, then-DHS Secretary Chertoff directed CBP and DNDO to implement full radiological and nuclear scanning of all arriving international general aviation aircraft. DHS achieved this goal at the end of 2007. Today, all international general aviation aircraft are scanned upon arrival in the United States by CBP officers using hand-held radiation isotope identification devices (RIIDs). DNDO and CBP have also conducted a testing program at Andrews Air Force Base to identify improved operating procedures using these handheld detectors and to determine requirements for improved next-generation technologies. These measures are part of a much larger initiative to create a Global Nuclear Detection Architecture to protect our country from radiological and nuclear threats, whether they come by land, air, or sea.

S&T ensures DHS and the homeland security community have the science, technical information, and capabilities needed to more effectively and efficiently prevent, protect against, respond to, and recover from all-hazards or homeland security threats. A key focus is on developing state-of-the-art systems to protect the Nation's people and critical infrastructure from chemical, biological, explosive, and cyber attacks. S&T accomplishes its mission through customer-focused and output-oriented research, development, testing and evaluation (RDT&E) programs that balance risk, cost, impact, and time to delivery. These RDT&E programs support the needs of the operational components of DHS and the first responder community and address cross-cutting areas such as standards and interoperability.

This work is deliverable-focused and driven by the requirements of S&T customers that play an integral role in identifying mission-capability relevant technologies that they need to support their homeland security missions. Through customer-led IPTs, the S&T Directorate builds a mutual understanding of what capabilities customers need, working to develop and transition them into the field through Federal, State, local, tribal, territorial, and private partners.

S&T has six divisions and four key offices, each of which has an important role in implementing RDT&E activities. These divisions are: Borders and Maritime; Chemical and Biological; Command, Control, and Interoperability; Explosives; Human Factors/Behavioral Sciences; and Infrastructure and Geophysical. Crosscutting the six divisions are the following key offices: Innovation; Test & Evaluation and Standards; Transition; and Research, which includes Laboratory Facilities and University Programs.

Through the Nuclear SSA, the Nuclear Sector has to date initiated close working relationships with a number of these S&T divisions including:

- Infrastructure and Geophysical Division: Nuclear Sector partners are considering the potential application of DHS-sponsored advanced surveillance technologies in the Nuclear Sector;

- Borders and Maritime Division: The Nuclear Sector is seeking to leverage ongoing DHS research on tracking, monitoring, and sensing technologies; and

- Command, Control and Interoperability Division: Partners are seeking to improve interoperable communications for emergency responders, among other initiatives.

The Nuclear SSA anticipates continuing collaboration with these and other S&T elements to address newly identified sector mission needs.

7.3.2.3 Nuclear Regulatory Commission Activities

The NRC has a well-established process, through its Office of Nuclear Regulatory Research, for identifying and funding research projects that will support its mandate to protect public health and safety. The projects identified through this process will also advance the R&D goals enumerated in this SSP.

The NRC process for planning and budgeting research activities is consistent with the strategies and measures in its most recent Strategic Plan. Where key uncertainties in analyses that influence the agency's ability to make sound decisions are identified, research is proposed to address those gaps. These candidate research programs are prioritized according to their contribution to meeting strategic goals. For example, one of the NRC's strategic goals is to enable use and management of radioactive material and nuclear fuels for beneficial civilian purposes in a manner that: (1) protects public health, safety, and the environment; (2) promotes the security of our Nation; and (3) provides for regulatory actions that are effective, efficient, realistic, timely, and open. A research activity is rated "high" if it is a significant contributor to the strategies being used to accomplish a goal. An activity is classified as a "medium" priority if it directly contributes (e.g., if accomplishing the activity supports being able to implement the strategies to accomplish the goal), and classified as "low" if it has a less substantial contribution. The expected outcomes of NRC activities associated with this strategic goal include: (1) no nuclear reactor accidents, (2) no releases of radioactive material that result in significant radiation exposures, (3) no acute radiation exposures resulting in fatalities, and (4) no releases of radioactive material that cause significant adverse environmental impacts.

Research activities are prioritized along with other NRC activities, and a research budget is established. Activities with relatively low-ranking scores are dropped or delayed if the NRC's budget cannot support those research activities. The NRC will coordinate through the SSA to communicate identified R&D needs to S&T and OSTP annually.

The NRC also coordinates interagency R&D planning and activities through the Counter-Terrorism Technical Support Office, Technical Support Working Group, and the DoD Physical Security Advisory Group.

The NRC's Office of Nuclear Regulatory Research (RES) provides technical advice, tools, and information to identify and resolve safety issues, make regulatory decisions, and promulgate regulations and guidance. This includes conducting confirmatory experiments and analyses; developing technical bases that support the NRC's safety decisions; and preparing the agency for the future by evaluating the safety aspects of new technologies and designs for nuclear reactors, materials, waste, and security. The NRC RES is addressing challenges as the industry matures, including the availability of new technologies.

NRC RES focuses its research primarily on near-term needs related to oversight of operating light-water reactors, the technology currently used in the United States; however, recent applications for advanced light-water reactors and pre-application activity regarding nonlight-water reactor vendors have prompted the agency to consider longer-term research needs.

The NRC ensures protection of public health, safety, and the environment through research programs that do the following:

- Examine technical issues, including:
  - Material degradation issues (e.g., stress-corrosion cracking and boric acid corrosion);
  - New and evolving technologies (e.g., new reactor technology, mixed oxide fuel performance);
  - Experience gained from operating reactors; and
  - Probabilistic risk assessment (PRA) methods.
- Examine human factor issues including safety culture and human interaction with computers, such as simulator training.
- Develop and improve computer codes as computational abilities expand and additional experimental and operational data allow for simulation that is more realistic. These computer codes analyze a wide spectrum of technical areas, including the following:
  - Severe accidents;
  - Radionuclide transport through the environment;
  - Health effects of radioactive releases;
  - Nuclear criticality;
  - Fire conditions in nuclear facilities;
  - Thermal-hydraulic performance of reactors;
  - Reactor fuel performance; and
  - PRA of each nuclear power reactor.
- Ensure the secure use and management of nuclear facilities and radioactive materials by investigating potential security vulnerabilities and possible compensatory actions.

Radioactive waste programs and security are additional focus areas for research, as is infrastructure support, which includes information technology and human resources.

The NRC also has cooperative agreements with universities and nonprofit organizations to research specific areas of interest to the agency. These cooperative agreements and grants include the following organizations:

- EPRI for work on fire risk and advancing probabilistic risk assessments;
- Pennsylvania State University for research on spacer grid thermal hydraulics and nuclear fuel cladding behavior;
- University of Tennessee for work on sparse radiation survey data;
- Ohio State University for research on the risk importance of digital systems;
- Massachusetts Institute of Technology for work on advanced nuclear technologies;
- University of Maryland for work on fire risk and uncertainties; and
- NIST for work on mathematical fire modeling.

The NRC collaborates with the international research community on nonlight-water reactor technologies. This collaboration helps the agency initiate activities focused on new technologies using minimal resources. Collaboration is aided by the agency's leadership role in the standing committees and senior advisory groups of international organizations, such as IAEA and AEA.

The NRC also has research agreements with foreign governments for international cooperative research that include the following projects:

- Halden Reactor Project in Norway for research and development of fuel, reactor internals, plant control and monitoring, and human factors;

- Phebus International Source Term Program (Phebus-ISTP);

- Studsvik Cladding Integrity Project in Sweden for nuclear fuels research; and

- Integral high burnup fuel/loss-of-coolant accident tests at Studsvik in Sweden.

7.3.2.4 EPA Activities

Since 2001, EPA's Office of Radiation and Indoor Air (ORIA) has been pursuing a voluntary program initiative known as alternative technology initiative (ATI). It is a comprehensive effort that included collaboration with an expert panel comprising representatives from Federal and State governments to provide recommendations to strengthen technology, identify barriers to implementation, offer insights into regulations, and identify technologies and applications.

The ATI identified several potential non-nuclear alternatives to radioisotopic technologies for category 2, 3 and 4 sources used in industrial applications. To enhance the likelihood of acceptance, ORIA is collaborating with the EPA Environmental Technology Evaluation (ETV) Program for an independent testing, evaluation, and validation of each technology's capabilities and operational parameters. For each technology, the ETV Program will issue a validation report that would provide credible, objective, quality-assured data needed to allow purchasers and users of these alternatives to make informed purchase and application decisions. The validation reports will be posted on the ETV Web site.

7.4 Sector R&D Management Processes

The Nuclear SSA will continue to monitor the progress of R&D, assess its impact on sector goals, and update its R&D strategy as needed. To accomplish this, the SSA will continue to coordinate with the NGCC, NSCC, and other partners, as described in preceding sections. Furthermore, as noted in sections 7.2 and 7.3 of this plan, the Nuclear SSA will remain apprised of non-Nuclear Sector-specific R&D efforts that could have benefits to the sector through information provided by S&T, OSTP, and others.

8. Managing and Coordinating SSA Responsibilities

This chapter of the SSP provides additional information on the programs and processes through which the Nuclear SSA, as one of the six sector-specific branches within the SSA EMO, administers its responsibilities as the sector lead for coordinating protective programs and resilience strategies in partnership with CIKR partners; how the Nuclear SSA manages SSP development, maintenance, and implementation; the processes used for identifying and managing budgetary and resource needs for CIKR protection and resilience; and the processes used for establishing and tracking SSP implementation milestones.

8.1 Program Management Approach

It is vital that CIKR partners develop and implement a coordinated and unified security strategy to mitigate risk, increase resilience, and protect against all hazards, whether naturally occurring or man-made. DHS is the SSA for 11 of the 18 CIKR sectors. The Secretary of Homeland Security has designated the DHS Office of Infrastructure Protection to carry out the SSA mission for six of those CIKR sectors: the Chemical, Commercial Facilities, Critical Manufacturing, Dams, Emergency Services, and Nuclear Sectors.

IP executes SSA functions for these six CIKR sectors through the SSA Management Project, which is managed by the SSA EMO. SSA EMO is one of seven divisions within IP, and contains six branches. Each of the six SSA EMO branches is responsible for implementing the SSA mission for one of the six CIKR sectors.

As a component of the DHS National Protection and Programs Directorate, IP is responsible for managing the coordinated national program to reduce all-hazards risk to the nation's CIKR and for strengthening national preparedness, timely response, and rapid recovery in the event of an incident or emergency. IP manages this mission through three program areas:

- Identifying and analyzing threats and vulnerabilities;

- Coordinating nationally and locally through partnerships with both government and private sector entities; and

- Mitigating risk and effects (encompassing both readiness and incident response).

IP Divisions	Infrastructure Information Collection Division (IICD)	Infrastructure Analysis & Strategy Division (IASD)	Protective Security Coordination Division (PSCD)	Infrastructure Security Compliance Division (ISCD)	Contingency Planning and Incident Management Division (CPIMD)	Sector-Specific Agency Executive Management Office (SSA EMO)	Partnership and Outreach Division (POD)
IP Projects	Infrastructure Information Collection Infrastructure Visualisation Infrastructure Data Management	Infrastructure Sector Analysis	Vulnerability Assessments Protective Security Advisors Bombing Prevention	Infrastructure Security Compliance	Infrastructure Coordination & Incident Management	SSA Management	CIKR Partnerships NIPP Management

Mission Areas

▨ Identification and Analysis	▨ Mitigation Programs	▨ Coordination and Information Sharing

IP created the SSA EMO to oversee the SSA mission of leading the unified public-private sector effort to coordinate, develop, and implement a comprehensive security strategy for the six CIKR sectors for which it is responsible. Each SSA ultimately relies on strong public-private partnership and coordination for the implementation of meaningful programs to reduce all-hazards risk across the six CIKR sectors. To execute its mission, SSA EMO established five primary program areas to support implementation of the SSPs and NIPP risk management framework and build and mature SSA functionality: Planning and Project Integration, Education and Training, Partnership and Information Sharing, Exercises and Incident Management, and Assessment and Mitigation.

These program areas contain cross-sector and sector-specific initiatives that allow SSA EMO to manage the overall process for building CIKR protection partnerships and for implementing the SSP by leveraging CIKR security expertise, relationships, and resource investments, prioritized as a result of effective risk management:

Planning and Project Integration: Effective planning and project integration enables the Nuclear SSA, through SSA EMO, to build and sustain partnerships both internal and external to DHS; to synchronize and communicate common objectives, responsibilities, and initiatives across the six DHS/IP SSAs; to readily share relevant cross-sector information; and to better understand the security needs and requirements of sector partners.

While CIKR sectors exhibit unique characteristics and maintain different security priorities and needs, SSAs share certain common requirements (e.g., SSPs, SHIRA, the NCIPP, participation in national-level exercises, and metrics development), which they can execute efficiently under a single organizational structure. The incorporation of common SSA functions under one organizational umbrella within IP facilitates cohesive and coordinated budgetary, acquisition, personnel, and programmatic planning that provides significant benefits to CIKR sector partners.

Education and Training: To raise CIKR awareness and increase the cadre of trained individuals across SSA EMO sectors, SSA EMO has developed and collaborated with sector partners to develop a wide range of training and security awareness initiatives. These programs help raise the security bar within CIKR sectors and provide easy-to-use, accessible tools that enable sector partners to share best security practices across the entire range of CIKR protection activities.

Partnership and Information Sharing: The cornerstone of effective CIKR protection and resilience planning and program implementation is the voluntary public-private partnership established under the CIPAC. Each SSA works closely with government and private sector partners to ensure a comprehensive critical infrastructure protection and resiliency strategy is developed that reflects sector needs and priorities. Strong and inclusive partnership is also vital to efficient information sharing across government, as well as between government and the private sector. Timely, accurate, and actionable information sustains educated decision-making for the implementation of programs and initiatives across the entire spectrum of critical infrastructure protection activity. Effective information sharing is particularly important in a fluid risk environment, such as during incident conditions and with respect to cybersecurity, where new vulnerabilities and mitigation strategies evolve daily. For cybersecurity initiatives in critical infrastructure, the SSA works most closely with the DHS Office of Cybersecurity and Communications (CS&C) in conjunction with the Nuclear Cyber Subcouncil to support the broad sharing cybersecurity information, to bring awareness to issues of concern, to share leading cybersecurity practices and to participate in cyber-related exercises.

Exercises and Incident Management: The SSAs are responsible for providing DHS, other government decision-makers, and private sector partners, with a clear and accurate picture of the potential or real impact of an incident to the sector and of the potential cross-sector, regional, and international consequences resulting from the incident. SSA EMO is responsible for carrying out the following core incident management functions for its six sectors:

• Situational Awareness: Monitor information flow and threats to gain and maintain awareness of an incident or potential incident. This includes awareness of events specific to SSA EMO sectors, as well as events across all 18 CIKR sectors that may affect SSA EMO sectors.

• Analyses and Assessments: Analyze and assess incoming situational and tactical information, and place it in a proper sector-specific context for DHS and other key decision-makers to support greater understanding of sector risks. The SSAs also provide guidance to senior leadership for prioritization, protection, resiliency, and recovery activities associated with an incident.

• Information Sharing: Participate in robust multi-directional incident information sharing with government and private sector partners to ensure timely, clear, and pertinent information is provided to support decision-making.

• Requests for Information (RFIs): Provide sector-specific information to the IP Contingency Planning and Incident Management Division incident management cell and NICC in response to RFIs from CIKR partners.

• Assessment and Mitigation: Each CIKR sector contains its own unique characteristics and risk landscape. Accordingly, each SSA works with partners to develop sector-specific security improvements designed to deter, mitigate, or neutralize potential attacks. Where possible, the SSA leverages the SSA EMO's integration functions to develop and pilot cost-effective tools and programs that can be replicated across CIKR sectors. As the risk landscape changes, the SSA works with Federal, State, local, tribal, and territorial governments, and private sector partners, to develop and implement security practices that build resilience within its sector and exploits SSA EMO's cross-sector capabilities to drive risk downward.

The five program areas outlined above enable SSA EMO to manage SSA responsibilities and achieve the greatest possible efficiencies across the IP SSAs; these program areas directly support SSP implementation and the NIPP risk management framework (see Figure 8-1).

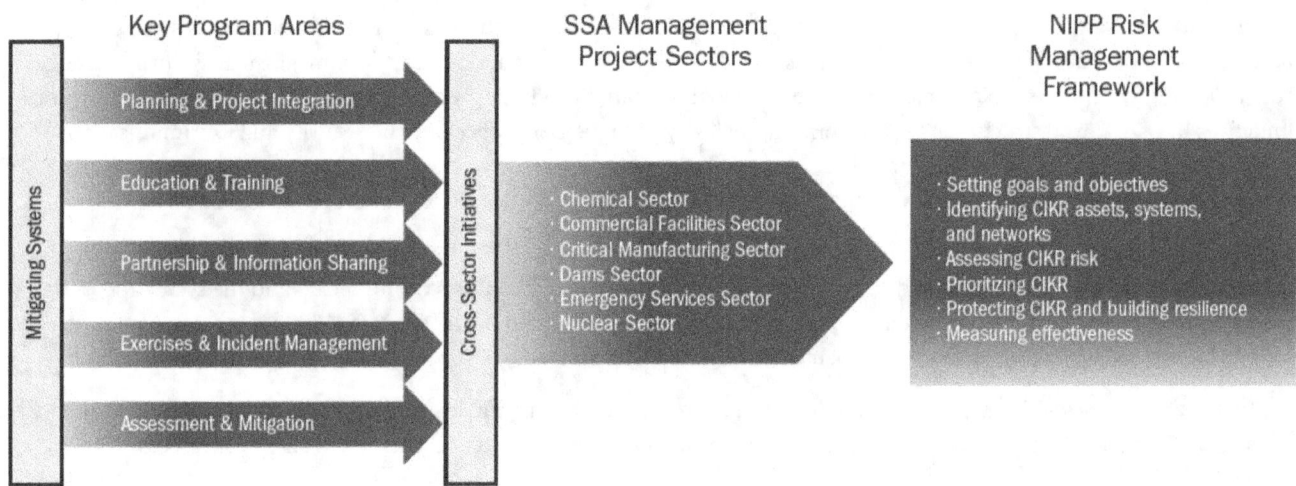

SSA Management Project

Support for Core Mission Processes

The efficiencies created by housing the six SSAs under one organizational structure ensure that each SSA is able to carry out its responsibilities to lead, coordinate, and implement its SSP in partnership with its public and private sector stakeholders, and that the SSA can provide sector-specific input for the ongoing implementation of the overarching national cross-sector CIKR strategy.

Section 6.1 of this plan describes key Nuclear Sector risk reduction activities undertaken by public and private sector partners and coordinated through the CIPAC structure. These activities correlate to one or more of the goals identified by Nuclear Sector partners (described in section 1.3), and contribute to achieving the sector's vision to "promote the protection and resiliency of the Nuclear Sector against natural and manmade disasters, and to lead by example to improve the Nation's overall critical infrastructure readiness."

8.2 Processes and Responsibilities

8.2.1 SSP Maintenance and Update

Because the SSP is the primary planning document for each CIKR sector, it is essential that the plan is kept current and that it reflects substantive changes to sector priorities, goals, dynamics, and programs. As one of its core competencies, the SSA is accountable for coordinating the development and maintenance of the sector's SSP.

The Nuclear SSA works with NGCC and NSCC partners, State representatives, subject matter experts, and others as appropriate—often through dedicated working groups—to assess requirements for updating and amending the Nuclear SSP (based on changes to sector priorities, NIPP Program Management Office (PMO) guidance, and other sector-specific factors) and to agree on SSP revisions. The Nuclear SSA strives to ensure that the Nuclear SSP remains a comprehensive security planning document that accurately captures the sector landscape, sets forth commonly agreed-upon sector goals and priorities, accurately describes sector resilience initiatives and protective programs, and outlines criteria for measuring progress toward risk reduction. The SSA coordinates all comments and maintains full version control over the document. The current triennial revision process will also include final review by the Homeland Security Council's Interagency Policy Committee.

In the production of the 2010 Nuclear SSP, the Nuclear SSA assembled an SSP Working Group comprising public and private sector partners to draft and review chapters of the document. These draft chapters were then submitted to the NGCC and NSCC for review and comment. The product is a collaborative plan that describes how public and private sector partners cooperate to ensure that Nuclear CIKR are protected and resilient.

8.2.2 Sector-Specific Plan Implementation Milestones

The NIPP risk management framework provides a logical basis for describing the broad activities that the Nuclear SSA and its partners will take in implementing the Nuclear SSP. The implementation milestones shown in Table 8-1 enable sector partners, the SSA, and DHS to gauge progress toward verifying, validating, and realizing the goals and objectives, as defined in chapter 1. The milestones described in this section are complementary to the progress reported each year through the SAR.

Table 8-1: SSP Implementation Milestones

	NIPP Activity	Milestones
1	Set Sector Goals and Objectives	• Review sector goals and objectives annually to ensure they continue to reflect the Sector's CIKR protection and resilience priorities
2	Identify Sector Assets, Systems, and Networks	• Continue to support the development of Level 1, Level 2, and Sector Lists • Continue to support CFDI
3	Assess Risks	• Support DHS and interagency risk assessment projects as appropriate for nuclear and radiological materials, including the HITRAC National Risk Estimate and the interagency Radiological/Nuclear Terrorism Risk Assessment (RNTRA) led by DHS
4	Prioritize Infrastructure	• Use HITRAC and other risk assessments to ensure that protective programs and resiliency strategies continue to reflect relative risk in the sector
5	Implement Protective Programs and Resiliency Strategies	• Complete implementation of the Research and Test Reactor voluntary security enhancement program • Complete implementation of the Radiological Devices voluntary security enhancement program • Complete implementation of the In-Device Delay program for irradiator facilities • Update the Sealed Source Matrix quarterly, which tracks Federal programs and initiatives to improve the security of sealed sources • Develop an integrated exercise program for power reactors modeled on the 2008 and 2010 Integrated Pilot Comprehensive Exercises • Complete implementation of cybersecurity plans at all of the Nation's nuclear power plants in accordance with the NRC cybersecurity rule published in 2009
6	Measure Progress	• Develop a streamlined process for identifying appropriate metrics for sector protective programs and resiliency strategies and collecting metrics data
7	Coordinate Research and Development	• Work with NISAC or other research and development resources to obtain a supply chain analysis for radioisotopes • Participate in the Critical Infrastructure Capstone IPT
8	Coordinate and Manage SSA Responsibilities	• Develop a Cyber Security Roadmap for the Nuclear Sector • Complete all reporting requirements, including the Sector Annual Report, annual metrics reporting, SSP Updates, and SSP Rewrites

Milestones for the specific programs and activities that are the responsibility of the six SSAs within the SSA EMO are tracked and managed through the SSA Management Project Management Plan (PMP). The PMP is a comprehensive business planning document that describes how IP will administer and resource SSA activities within its six sectors, and how it will gauge the progress of internal business processes and SSA programmatic activities.

SSA EMO leadership meets regularly with IP and DHS senior leadership to discuss the status of various SSA initiatives, which includes formal IP quarterly reports that track budget, acquisition, personnel, and SSA Management Project execution. These internal reporting and management mechanisms better enable SSA EMO to plan for and meet the needs of the SSA and of the sector, and to address DHS, congressional, and White House reporting requirements.

8.2.3 Resources and Budgets

The SSA is responsible for leading the effort to coordinate protection and resiliency initiatives and strategy across the sector; however, it is important to note that the private sector and numerous Federal, State, local, tribal, and territorial governments carry out critically important programs in support of the greater critical infrastructure protection mission, based on assessed risk and priorities. Accordingly, it is beyond the SSA's capability and scope of mission to account for all resources devoted to CIKR protection in the sector or to direct allocation of resources beyond its control.

SSA EMO manages resourcing and budget for the six SSAs under the authority of IP. The SSA EMO's budget is dedicated exclusively to supporting the mission and functions of the six SSAs under its purview.

As described in section 8.1, SSA EMO has developed the SSA PMP, a comprehensive five-year planning document, to describe budget, personnel, acquisition, and programmatic strategies for the six IP SSAs and the Interagency Security Committee PMO. The PMP directly supports the sector-specific partnership, information sharing, and risk management efforts that each SSA has prioritized in coordination with its sector partners. The PMP is a living document and will be amended and adapted to accommodate changing SSA and sector requirements.

Using the PMP to guide and prioritize its business processes, SSA EMO works within the IP budget process to submit personnel and program requirements in accordance with the needs of each of the IP SSAs for which it is responsible. Each SSA within SSA EMO is responsible for outlining SSA personnel needs, sector-specific programmatic priorities, and associated cost estimates in alignment with overarching SSA EMO and sector goals, objectives, and priorities. The SSA's budget is managed at the SSA EMO Office level and budget allocation decisions are made based on the stated priorities of each SSA EMO SSA and through a consultative process among SSA EMO and IP leadership.

SSA requests are submitted as part of the IP budget, which is incorporated as a component of the DHS annual budget submission to the Office of Management and Budget.

8.2.4 Training and Education

Training and education are a key focus of IP's SSAs. One of the core goals of the SSAs is to enhance sector-specific critical infrastructure protection capabilities through the coordinated development of education and training programs. Training and education initiatives are critical to ensuring the continual improvement of CIKR preparedness efforts across both government and the private sector.

To support broad situational awareness across CIKR sectors, SSA EMO is currently developing a voluntary, Web-based, interactive training program designed to assist CIKR sector employees across sectors in identifying suspicious activities at their facilities. This voluntary training is appropriate for any CIKR employee and will be available on-online. Based on cross-sector industry best practices, the interactive program augments an organization's existing security training. As described throughout this document, the Nuclear SSA also leverages the expertise of government and private sector stakeholders to develop and participate in sector-specific exercise training and education initiatives, including the development of leading physical and cybersecurity practices to complement existing private sector security, preparedness and resiliency training programs.

To foster preparedness and increase effective response during an incident, the Nuclear SSA works within the sector to develop and participate in sector-specific, as well as national level, cross-sector exercises. These initiatives provide critically important measures for the state of preparedness, information sharing, and incident management procedures and protocols. These initiatives complement the suite of radiological and security exercises facilitated by the DHS, NRC, and the FEMA Radiological Emergency Preparedness Program. Examples of cross-sector exercises in which the Nuclear SSA and its partners have participated include: TOPOFF-4, the 2009 National Level Exercise, and Cyberstorm II. In addition, as described in chapter 6, DOE/NNSA provides law enforcement personnel that may respond to an event at a radiological facility with security and awareness training. DOE/NNSA also provides online security awareness training to radiological facility owners and operators.

Furthermore, as described in chapter 6 of this plan, nuclear power plants will be implementing the cybersecurity rule recently published by the NRC. These partners have expressed a need for cybersecurity training to facilitate rule compliance. The joint Nuclear Cyber Subcouncil, which includes the DHS/NCSD, is collaborating to identify training opportunities to meet this need.

8.3 Implementing the Sector Partnership Model

Chapter 1 of the Nuclear SSP describes the specific organizations and participants involved in the coordinated development and implementation of a robust and comprehensive CIKR protection and resiliency strategy for the Nuclear Sector. The Nuclear SSA works with these partners to support more focused initiatives targeting specific subsectors or issues of concern as well as broader initiatives and strategies that foster partnership, coordination, information sharing, and risk management activities across the sector. In addition, the Nuclear SSA works with public and private sector partners to ensure that international physical and cybersecurity issues with implications for the sector are properly addressed and coordinated. The NIPP sector partnership model is the overarching framework within which the broad CIKR partnership operates.

8.4 Information Sharing and Protection

8.4.1 Information Sharing

Development and maintenance of a robust public-private partnership requires routine and comprehensive information sharing among all sector partners. The ability to efficiently share information with government and owners and operators within the sector and across sectors is vital to efficient steady-state infrastructure protection activity and to effective incident management. Timely information provides broad situational and specific tactical awareness and enables risk-informed decision making for the implementation of programs and initiatives during normal and incident management operations. The Nuclear SSA has made information sharing, including sharing of threat information, open source data, and bi-annual classified briefings to appropriate stakeholders, a core component of its critical infrastructure protection strategy. In addtion to the information sharing and coordination mechanisms described in chapter 1, as well as ad hoc means of partner communications (e.g., e-mails, teleconferences), the Nuclear SSA uses various information-sharing mechanisms supported by IP and other DHS components to communciate and coordiante with its partners. Some of these are descibed below.

8.4.1.1 Homeland Security Information Network—Critical Sectors (HSIN-CS)

The Nuclear SSA supports the development of the Homeland Security Information Network-Critical Sectors (HSIN-CS) to facilitate information sharing within and across critical infrastructure sectors and actively encourages all sector partners to use HSIN to share practices and coordinate through sector portals. HSIN-CS is designed to enable communication within a given sector, between multiple sectors, and between a sector and government entities. HSIN-CS offers four major components to network participants:

- Alerts Broadcasting and Narrowcasting from DHS: A secure medium for DHS and sector leaders to transmit actionable alerts and warnings about threats to critical infrastructure to a vetted audience;

- HSIN-CS Portal: A capability of storing sensitive documents, including sophisticated imaging and maps. The portal also enables real-time analysis of data and reporting tasks. The portal will provide a knowledge base enabling planning and coordination within and across all CIKR sectors;

- Collaboration Tools: A peer-to-peer collaboration space for members to engage in real-time dialogue. Members can create their own private groups to discuss defined topics and collaborate on common documents; and

- HSIN-CS Infrastructure: An underlying technology platform and network that can support additional infrastructure can be added.

Examples of information posted include notes from the monthly suspicious activity calls, redacted Patriot reports, incident updates, workshop notifications, and other important documents.

8.4.1.2 National Infrastructure Coordinating Center

The National Infrastructure Coordinating Center (NICC) serves as IP's focal point for coordination across the 18 CIKR sectors during normal operations and incident management activities. The NICC is both an operational component of IP and a watch operations element of the DHS National Operations Center (NOC). The NICC operates 24 hours a day, 7 days a week, 365 days a year to facilitate coordination and information sharing with CIKR sectors. The NICC produces consolidated CIKR reports for incorporation into the Federal Interagency DHS Common Operating Picture. During an incident, the NICC provides situation reports to the SSAs through the Executive Notification Service (ENS); the SSAs, in turn, contact their respective CIKR owners and operators and related government agencies to develop impact assessments.

8.4.1.3 Cybersecurity Information Sharing

The United States Computer Emergency Readiness Team (US-CERT) operates on a 24/7 basis and is a single point of contact for cyberspace analysis, warning, information sharing, and incident response and recovery for CIKR partners. It is a partnership between DHS and the public and private sectors designed to enable protection of cyber infrastructure and to coordinate the prevention of and response to cyber attacks across the Nation.

US-CERT coordinates with CIKR partners to disseminate reasoned and actionable cybersecurity information through a Web site, accessible through the HSIN and mailing lists. Among the products that it provides are:

- Cybersecurity Bulletins: Weekly bulletins written for systems administrators and other technical users that summarize published information concerning new security issues and vulnerabilities;

- Technical Cybersecurity Alerts: Written for system administrators and experienced users, technical alerts provide timely information on current security issues, vulnerabilities, and exploits;

- Cybersecurity Alerts: Written in a language for home, corporate, and new users, these alerts are published in conjunction with technical alerts when security issues affect the general public;

- Cybersecurity Tips: Tips provide information and advice on various common security topics. They are published biweekly and are primarily intended for home, corporate, and new users; and

- National Web Cast Initiative: DHS, through US-CERT and the Multi-State Information Sharing and Analysis Center (MS-ISAC), has initiated a joint partnership to develop a series of national Web casts that will examine critical and timely cybersecurity issues. The purpose of the initiative is to strengthen the Nation's cyber readiness and resilience.

US-CERT also provides a method for citizens, businesses, and other important institutions to communicate and coordinate directly with the Federal Government on matters of cybersecurity. The private sector can use the protections afforded by the Critical Infrastructure Information Act to electronically submit proprietary data to US-CERT.

Industrial Control Systems Computer Emergency Readiness Team (ICS-CERT) is the Nation's first dedicated response center aimed at reducing the frequency and effect of cyber attacks on industrial control systems. The ICS-CERT was created in 2009 to coordinate global efforts and respond to cyber vulnerabilities and threats affecting the industrial control systems that operate critical infrastructure and key resources. Industrial control systems include supervisory control and data acquisition, process control, distributed control and other digital devices that monitor and manage critical operations within chemical facilities, oil and gas refineries, power plants, transportation systems, and many more. The ICS-CERT addresses security threats to control systems and provides a means to share information across all sectors. ICS-CERT is also one of the principal components of the Strategy to Secure Control Systems, providing a central mechanism for coordinating incident response and stakeholder efforts to effectively manage cybersecurity risk. Located at Idaho National Laboratory (INL) and managed by the DHS CSSP, the response team will monitor, collect, and analyze cyber incidents reported by industrial control systems stakeholders across all sectors of the nation's critical infrastructure.

Cross-Sector Cyber Security Working Group (CSCSWG) provides a forum to bring government and the private sector together to collaboratively address risk across all CIKR sectors under CIPAC. The CSCSWG addresses a wide variety of cybersecurity issues and enables comprehensive planning and sharing of information across the community of interested partners.

The Joint NGCC/NSCC Cyber Subcouncil, established within the NIPP framework, comprises public and private sector partners with primary responsibility for cybersecurity in the Nuclear Sector, including DHS, FBI, NRC, and private-sector representatives. A key objective of the subcouncil is to share information, within the CIPAC framework, with regard to cybersecurity risks.

8.4.1.4 Sharing of Threat Information

The Nuclear SSA hosts classified threat briefings quarterly with appropriately cleared public and private sector partners in conjunction with meetings of the NSCC and NGCC. The Nuclear SSA holds additional classified and unclassified threat briefings as appropriate and warranted by circumstances. In addition, the joint Nuclear Cyber Subcouncil hosts classified and unclassified cyber-specific threat briefings as necessary and appropriate with cleared members of the joint Cyber Subcouncil. All of these briefings are closely coordinated with the IC and are primarily facilitated by HITRAC.

8.4.2 Operations Centers

During an emergency, the following operations centers will work together to address the situation by performing situation assessments and information-sharing functions. For example, the NRC will provide staffing to the NOC and Strategic Information and Operations Center (SIOC) during incident response operations, and the DOE Emergency Operations Center (EOC) will work with both DHS and NRC to monitor and direct DOE emergency response assets during radiological incidents. In addition, DHS has an operating mechanism in place that allows the NOC to notify the NICC.

National Operations Center (NOC). The DHS NOC is the primary national hub for situational awareness and operations coordination across the Federal Government for incident management. It provides the Secretary of Homeland Security and other principals with information necessary to make critical national-level incident management decisions.

The NOC is a continuously operating multi-agency operations center. The NOC's staff monitors many sources of threat and hazard information from across the United States and abroad. It is supported by a 24/7 watch officer contingent, including: (1) NOC managers; (2) selected Federal interagency, State, and local law enforcement representatives; (3) IC liaison officers provided by the DHS Chief Intelligence Officer; (4) analysts from the Operations Division's interagency planning element; and (5) watch standers representing dozens of organizations and disciplines from the Federal Government and others from the private sector.

The NOC facilitates homeland security information sharing and operations coordination with other Federal, State, tribal, local, and nongovernmental partners. During a response to a significant incident, the NOC meets its information-fusion and information-sharing responsibilities by providing spot reports, situation reports, and other information-sharing tools, all supported by and distributed through its common operating picture. The continued development and rapid integration at the Federal, State, tribal, and local levels of electronic reporting and information-sharing tools supporting the NOC's common operating picture is a very high priority.

NOC Operational Components. The following components of the NOC provide integrated mission support:

- National Response Coordination Center (NRCC). The NRCC is FEMA's primary operations management center, as well as the focal point for national resource coordination. As a 24/7 operations center, the NRCC monitors potential or developing incidents and supports the efforts of regional and field components.

  The NRCC also has the capacity to increase staffing immediately in anticipation of or in response to an incident by activating the full range of Emergency Support Functions (ESFs) and other personnel as needed to provide resources and policy guidance to a Joint Field Office (JFO) or other local incident management structures. The NRCC provides overall emergency management coordination, conducts operational planning, deploys national-level entities, and collects and disseminates incident information as it builds and maintains a common operating picture. Representatives of nonprofit organizations within the private sector may participate in the NRCC to enhance information exchange and cooperation between these entities and the Federal Government.

- National Infrastructure Coordinating Center (NICC). The NICC continuously monitors the Nation's critical infrastructure and key resources. During an incident, the NICC provides a coordinating forum to share information across infrastructure and key resources sectors through appropriate information-sharing entities such as the Information Sharing and Analysis Centers and the Sector Coordinating Councils.

DNDO Joint Analysis Center. Staffed with personnel from the DoD, DOE, DHS, FBI, and NRC, the Joint Analysis Center (JAC) will provide status tracking for the United States Government Global Nuclear Detection Architecture. With a direct conduit from the alarm source to national assets for spectrum analysis, JAC will provide 24/7 response for radiological alarm resolution and the capability to marry intelligence, illicit activity, and threats with a known radiological architecture that will provide total situational awareness to decision-makers. The JAC facilitates the U.S. Government Interagency Nuclear Decision Protocols to adjudicate nuclear detection events by providing:

- Situational Awareness: The JAC achieves situational awareness through visibility into deployed components, access to information, and historical data. Information is received from deployed radiological/nuclear detection assets, radiological/nuclear related events, the global nuclear detection architecture, the NRC and Agreement State material licensing data, and historical data on all detection events, illicit and legitimate.

- Alarm Adjudication: JAC provides State, local, and/or tribal organizations with a direct link to technical reachback for alarm adjudication. Technical reachback is performed by the DOE National Laboratories.

- Information & Analysis: JAC consolidates intelligence reports, law enforcement information, and technical data across the interagency to facilitate an understanding of the Global Nuclear Detection Architecture and its performance. Data mining and analysis of nuclear detection assets, events, and the operating environment facilitate after-action reviews of events and allow for the implementation of lessons learned.

- Information Sharing: JAC facilitates the information flow on radiological detection events between the interagency and State and local entities. Passing information both up to the Federal level and down to the local level, the JAC ensures that appropriate action is taken to resolve alarms.

- Operations Support Directorate: The Operations Support Directorate within the Domestic Nuclear Detection Office is responsible for establishing and operating a real-time situational awareness and support capability by monitoring the status of, and collecting information from, both overseas and domestic detection systems through the JAC and other programs. Operational support services include the development of protocols and standards, as well as a technical support infrastructure, or reachback, to ensure appropriate expertise is in place to support prompt alarm resolution.

NRC Headquarters Operations Center. The NRC operations center is staffed 24/7 to serve as the focal point for communications, analysis, and response in support of State and local agencies during an emergency involving a U.S. commercial nuclear power plant; research, training, or test reactor; fuel cycle facility; or nuclear material licensee. The NRC Headquarters Operations Officer (HOO) receives event reports and emergency declaration notifications. The HOO performs an initial assessment of the safety significance of each report based on extensive technical training, experience, agency guidance, and procedures. These reports may come from NRC licensees, State agencies that regulate Agreement State licensees, security and law enforcement personnel, contractors, military facilities, other government agencies (U.S. or foreign), or private citizens. Event and routine reports are maintained in databases and posted daily to the NRC Web site. Security reports are also maintained in a database, but are shared with only select personnel at the NRC, the licensees, and other Federal and State agencies. Significant events occurring at nuclear facilities that could affect the public require activation of the NRC's Incident Response Plan and prompt notification of other Federal agencies, including DHS. These events could be related to a plant accident involving equipment malfunction or operator error that could lead to a radioactive release. They could also be caused by an increase in the licensee's security posture because of some real or perceived threat to the facility. In addition to reporting actual events, facilities routinely contact the HOO to conduct communications testing.

FBI Strategic Information and Operations Center (SIOC). The FBI SIOC is the focal point and operational control center for all Federal intelligence, law enforcement, and investigative law enforcement activities related to domestic terrorist incidents or credible threats, including leading attribution investigations. The SIOC serves as an information clearinghouse to help collect, process, vet, and disseminate information relevant to law enforcement and criminal investigation efforts in a timely manner. The SIOC maintains direct connectivity with the NOC. The SIOC, located at FBI Headquarters, supports the FBI's mission in leading efforts of the law enforcement community to detect, prevent, preempt, and disrupt terrorist attacks against the United States.

The SIOC maintains liaison with the National Joint Terrorism Task Force (NJTTF). The mission of the NJTTF is to enhance communications, coordination, and cooperation among Federal, State, tribal, and local agencies representing the intelligence, law enforcement, defense, diplomatic, public safety, and homeland security communities by providing a point of fusion for terrorism intelligence and by supporting Joint Terrorism Task Forces throughout the United States.

DOE Emergency Operations Center. The EOC functions as the DOE focal point for collecting, receiving, and disseminating essential information about emergencies, situations, incidents, or events affecting departmental facilities, sites, programs, operations, and activities. It coordinates requests for departmental national emergency response assets and capabilities. In addition, it supports classified and unclassified emergency response operations and requirements and facilitates inter- and intra-departmental interfaces related to emergency response operations, coordination, and information exchange. EOC is staffed 24/7 year-round, with access to various secure and non-secure IT and physical resources, equipment, and communications systems and networks.

National Response Center. The primary function of the National Response Center is to serve as a national point of contact for reporting all radiological, chemical, biological, oil, and etiological discharges into the environment anywhere in the United States and its Territories. The center is staffed 24/7 year-round by USCG personnel. In addition to gathering and distributing spill data for Federal On-Scene Coordinators[58] and serving as the communications and operations center for the National Response Team, the center maintains agreements with various Federal entities to make additional notifications about incidents meeting established trigger criteria. The center notifies the NRC and DOE by telephone regarding all incidents involving radioactive material releases to the environment.

The National Response Center also takes Terrorist/Suspicious Activity Reports and Maritime Security Breach Reports. It established the Domestic Preparedness Chemical/Biological Hotline in conjunction with DOD and DOJ. The center takes reports through toll-free numbers (1–877–24–WATCH or 1–800–424–8802) on any incident related to potential or actual domestic terrorism, and coordinates notification and response with the FBI and the U.S. Army's 20th Support Command, which is the Army's command and control headquarters responsible for providing CBRNE forces to respond, assess, exploit, and eliminate CBRNE hazards worldwide.

National Cybersecurity and Communications Integration Center (NCCIC). The DHS NCCIC is a 24/7 coordinated, cybersecurity watch, warning, and incident response center. The mission of the NCCIC is to mitigate risks that could disrupt or degrade critical information technology functions and services, while allowing for flexibility in handling traditional voice and more modern data networks. The new unified operations center combines two DHS operational organizations: US-CERT, which leads a public-private partnership to protect and defend the nation's cyber infrastructure, and the National Coordinating Center for Telecommunications (NCC), the operational arm of the National Communications System. In addition, the NCCIC will integrate the efforts of the National Cybersecurity Center (NCSC), which coordinates operations among the six largest Federal cyber centers; the DHS Office of Intelligence and Analysis, and private sector partners.

8.4.3 Protecting Information

Often, the information used by DHS and its CIKR partners to effectively manage risk and protect the Nation's critical infrastructure may contain sensitive security information and/or sensitive business and proprietary information. As a result, information protection is a significant concern for the SSA and for CIKR partners that provide this sensitive information.

8.4.3.1 Sensitive but Unclassified Information and Classified Information

Information held by the SSA and by sector partners is designated as classified, sensitive but unclassified, or open according to corresponding distribution conditions and classification guidelines. Although the Federal Government maintains a preference for full transparency, the security sensitive nature of much of the information obtained by the SSA and its government partners may require classified or restricted access and protection from general public disclosure.

8.4.3.2 Protected Critical Infrastructure Information

The PCII Program, created by the Critical Infrastructure Information Act (CIIA) of 2002, is an information-protection mechanism to facilitate information sharing between the private sector and the government. DHS and other Federal, State, and local analysts use PCII to:

- Analyze and secure critical infrastructure and protected systems;

- Identify vulnerabilities and develop risk assessments; and

- Enhance preparedness measures.

If submitted information satisfies the requirements of the CIIA, it will be protected from public disclosure to the maximum extent permitted by law. The PCII Program is managed by the Infrastructure Information Collection Division within IP.

---

[58] The Federal official predesignated by the EPA or USCG to coordinate responses under subpart D of the National Contingency Plan, or the government official designated to coordinate removal actions under subpart E of the plan.

The rules governing the PCII Program are located in 6 CFR, part 29. General information on the PCII Program, including instructions on how to submit information in compliance with the program, can be found on the DHS Web site at **http://www.dhs.gov/pcii**.

8.4.3.3 Critical Infrastructure Partnership Advisory Council

DHS has exercised its authority under section 871 of the Homeland Security Act to exempt CIPAC from the Federal Advisory Committee Act.[59] This ensures that the CIPAC members can discuss sensitive security issues without the risk that these discussions could become public and jeopardize security. The CIPAC can meet as a whole, or in the form of joint committees specific to a particular sector.

8.4.3.4 Safeguards Information

Safeguards Information (SGI) is a special category of sensitive unclassified information authorized by Section 147 of the Atomic Energy Act. SGI concerns the physical protection of operating power reactors, spent fuel shipments, strategic special nuclear material, or other radioactive material. While SGI is considered to be sensitive unclassified information, its handling and protection more closely resemble the handling of classified confidential information. The categories of individuals who are permitted access to SGI are listed in 10 CFR 73.22(b) and 10 CFR 73.59. This type of information is shared with partners as necessary and appropriate.

---

[59] Federal Register (FR) 14930 (March 24, 2006).

Appendix 1: Acronyms and Abbreviations

ACI	American Concrete Institute
AEA	Atomic Energy Act
AMS	Aerial Measuring System
ANS	American Nuclear Society
ANSI	American National Standards Institute
AP	Additional Protocol
ARAC	Atmospheric Release Advisory Capability
ARG	Accident Response Group
ASCE	American Society of Civil Engineers
ASM	Additional Security Measures
ASME	American Society of Mechanical Engineers
ASNT	American Society for Nondestructive Testing
ASP	Advanced Spectroscopic Portal
ATD	Advanced Technology Demonstrations
ATI	Alternative Technology Initiative
BTRA	Bioterrorism Risk Assessment
BWR	Boiling Water Reactor
BZPP	Buffer Zone Protection Program
CAARS	Cargo Advanced Automated Radiography System
CBP	Customs and Border Protection
CBRN	Chemical, Biological, Radiological or Nuclear
CERFP	Nuclear and Explosive Enhanced Response Force Packages
CFATS	Chemical Facility Anti-Terrorism Standards
CFDI	Critical Foreign Dependencies Initiative
CFR	Code of Federal Regulations

CII Act	Critical Infrastructure Information Act
CIKR	Critical Infrastructure and Key Resources
CIP	Critical Infrastructure Protection
CIPAC	Critical Infrastructure Partnership Advisory Council
CNPPD	Chemical and Nuclear Preparedness and Protection Division
CPIMD	Contingency Planning and Incident Management Division
CR	Comprehensive Review
CRCPD	Conference of Radiation Control Program Directors
CROWN	Comprehensive Review Outcomes Working Network
CS&C	Office of Cyber Security and Communications
CS2SAT	Control Systems Cyber Security Self-Assessment Tool
CSCSWG	Cross-Sector Cyber Security Working Group
CSET	Cyber Security Evaluation Tool
CSSP	Control System Security Program
CST	Civil Support Team
CTRA	Chemical Terrorism Risk Assessment
CY	Calendar Year
DBT	Design Basis Threat
DHS	Department of Homeland Security
DNDO	Domestic Nuclear Detection Office
DOC	Department of Commerce
DoD	Department of Defense
DOE	Department of Energy
DOJ	Department of Justice
DOS	Department of State
DOT	Department of Transportation
EM	Emergency Management
ENS	Executive Notification Service
EOC	Emergency Operations Center
EP	Emergency Preparedness
EPA	Environmental Protection Agency
EPAct	Energy Policy Act of 2005
EPRI	Electric Power Research Institute
EPZ	Emergency Planning Zone
ETV	Environmental Technology Evaluation

FACA	Federal Advisory Committee Act
FBI	Federal Bureau of Investigation
FEMA	Federal Emergency Management Agency
FOF	Force-on-Force
FOIA	Freedom of Information Act
FR	Federal Register
FRMAC	Federal Radiological Monitoring and Assessment Center
FRPCC	Federal Radiological Policy Coordinating Committee
FY	Fiscal Year
GAO	Government Accountability Office
GCC	Government Coordinating Council
GDP	Gaseous Diffusion Plant
GICNT	Global Initiative to Combat Nuclear Terrorism
GNDA	Global Nuclear Detection Architecture
GTCC	Greater Than Class C
GTRI	Global Threat Reduction Initiative
HAB	Hostile Action-Based
HEU	Highly Enriched Uranium
HHS	Department of Health and Human Services
HITRAC	Homeland Infrastructure Threat and Risk Analysis Center
HOO	Headquarters Operations Officer
HPRDS	Human Portable Radiation Detection Systems
HPS	Health Physics Society
HRCQ	Highway Route Controlled Quantity
HSAS	Homeland Security Advisory System
HSC	Homeland Security Council
HSIN	Homeland Security Information Network
HSNRA	Homeland Security National Risk Assessment
HSPD	Homeland Security Presidential Directive
I&C	Instrumentation and Control
IAEA	International Atomic Energy Agency
IASD	Infrastructure Analysis and Strategy Division
ICS-CERT	Industrial Control Systems Computer Emergency Readiness Team
ICSJWG	Industrial Control Systems Joint Working Group
IDD	In-Device Delay

IDW	Infrastructure Data Warehouse
IEEE	Institute of Electrical and Electronics Engineers
IICD	Infrastructure Information Collection Division
ILTAB	Intelligence Liaison and Threat Assessment Branch
IMAAC	Interagency Modeling and Atmospheric Assessment Center
IND	Improvised Nuclear Device
INL	Idaho National Laboratory
INMM	Institute of Nuclear Materials Management
INPO	Institute of Nuclear Power Operations
INRA	International Nuclear Regulators Association
INSAS	International Nuclear Security Advisory Service
INSServ	International Nuclear Security Advisory Service
IP	Office of Infrastructure Protection
IPPAS	International Physical Protection Advisory Service
IPRL	Intelligent Personal Radiation Locator
IPRS	Integrated Regulatory Review Service
IPT	Integrated Product Team
IRRS	Integrated Regulatory Review Service
ISCD	Infrastructure Security Compliance Division
ISFSI	Independent Spent Fuel Storage Installation
ISL	In-Situ Leach
ISN	International Security and Nonproliferation
IT	Information Technology
ITE	International Team of Experts
JAC	Joint Analysis Center
JINNI	Joint Integrated Non-Intrusive Inspection Program
LEU	Low Enriched Uranium
LLEA	Local Law Enforcement Agency
LLW	Low-Level Waste
MC&A	Material Control and Accounting
MILES	Multiple Integrated Laser Engagement System
MOA	Memorandum of Agreement
MOU	Memorandum of Understanding
MRO	Measurement and Reporting Office
MS-ISAC	Multi-State Information Sharing and Analysis Center

MTSA	Maritime Transportation Security Act
MW	Megawatts
NARAC	National Atmospheric Release Advisory Center
NASA	National Aeronautics and Space Administration
NCC	National Coordinating Center for Telecommunications
NCCIC	National Cybersecurity and Communications Integration Center
NCIPP	National Critical Infrastructure Prioritization Program
NCP	National Contingency Plan
NCS	National Communications System
NCSC	National Cybersecurity Center
NCSD	National Cyber Security Division
NEA	Nuclear Energy Agency
NEI	Nuclear Energy Institute
NESS	Nuclear Energy, Safety and Security
NEST	Nuclear Emergency Support Team
NGCC	Nuclear GCC
NGCC-R	NGCC Radioisotopes Subcouncil
NGCC-RTR	NGCC Research and Test Reactor Subcouncil
NICC	National Infrastructure Coordinating Center
NII	Non-Intrusive Inspection
NIPP	National Infrastructure Protection Plan
NIRAP	National Infrastructure Risk Analysis Program
NISAC	National Infrastructure Simulation and Analysis Center
NIST	National Institute of Standards and Technology
NJTTF	National Joint Terrorism Task Force
NMMSS	Nuclear Materials Management and Safeguards System
NNSA	National Nuclear Security Administration
NOAA	National Oceanic and Atmospheric Administration
NOC	National Operations Center
NORM	Naturally Occurring Radioactive Materials
NRC	Nuclear Regulatory Commission
NRCC	National Response Coordination Center
NRF	National Response Framework
NRP	National Response Plan
NSCC	Nuclear Sector Coordinating Council

NSCC-R	Nuclear Sector Coordinating Council – Radioisotopes Subcouncil
NSCC-RTR	NSCC Research and Test Reactor Subcouncil
NSG	Nuclear Suppliers Group
NSTS	National Source Tracking System
NUREG	U.S. Nuclear Regulatory Commission Regulation
OAS	Organization of Agreement States
ODNI	Office of the Director of National Intelligence
OECD	Organization for Economic Cooperation and Development
OMB	Office of Management and Budget
ORIA	Office of Radiation and Indoor Air
OSRP	Off-Site Source Recovery Project
OSTP	Office of Science and Technology Policy
PCII	Protected Critical Infrastructure Information
PMO	Program Management Office
PMP	Project Management Plan
PNNL	Pacific Northwest National Laboratory
POD	Partnership and Outreach Division
PRA	Probabilistic Risk Assessment
PRND	Preventive Rad/Nuclear Detection
PSA	Protective Security Advisor
PSCD	Protective Security Coordination Division
PWR	Pressurized Water Reactor
R&D	Research and Development
RAC	Regional Assistance Committees
RAIS	Regulatory Authority Information Service
RAMCAP	Risk Analysis and Management for Critical Asset Protection
RAP	Radiological Assistance Program
RAPID	Risk Analysis Process for Informed Decisionmaking
RASCAL	Radiological Assessment System for Consequence Analysis
R&D	Research and Development
RDD	Radiological Dispersal Device
RDT&E	Research, Development, Testing and Evaluation
REAC/TS	Radiation Emergency Assistance Center/Training Site
RED	Radiation Exposure Device
REP	Radiological Emergency Preparedness

RERP	Radiological Emergency Response Plan
RERT	Radiological Emergency Response Team
RES	Office of Nuclear Regulatory Research
RFI	Request for Information
RFID	Radio Frequency Identification
RIID	Radiation Isotope Identification Device
RIS	Regulatory Issue Summary
RNTRA	Radiological/Nuclear Terrorism Risk Assessment
ROP	Reactor Oversight Process
RTR	Research and Test Reactor
S&T	DHS Science and Technology Directorate
S/CT	Office of the Coordinator for Counterterrorism
SBU	Sensitive But Unclassified
SCC	Sector Coordinating Council
SGI	Safeguards Information
SHIRA	Strategic Homeland Infrastructure Risk Analysis
SIOC	Strategic Information and Operations Center
SLTT	State, Local, Tribal, and Territorial
SME	Subject Matter Expert
SNF	Spent Nuclear Fuel
SNM	Special Nuclear Material
SSA	Sector-Specific Agency
SSA EMO	Sector-Specific Agency Executive Management Office
SSACAS	State System of Accounting for and Control of Nuclear Material Advisory Service
SSI	Sensitive Security Information
SSNM	Strategic Special Nuclear Material
SSP	Sector-Specific Plan
SWAT	Special Weapons and Tactics
SWG	Security Working Group
TOPOFF	Top Officials Exercise
TRTR	National Organization of Test, Research, and Training Reactors
TSA	Transportation Security Administration
U-Mo	Uranium-Molybdenum
UF6	Uranium Hexafluoride
US-CERT	United States Computer Emergency Readiness Team

U.S.C.	United States Code
USCG	United States Coast Guard
USEC	United States Enrichment Corporation
WANO	World Association of Nuclear Operators
WINS	World Institute for Nuclear Security
WMD	Weapons of Mass Destruction
WMDT	Office of Weapons of Mass Destruction Terrorism

Appendix 2: Glossary of Terms

Buffer Zone Protection Program (BZPP). A program to bolster protective measures in the immediate vicinity of CIKR targets and, therefore, make it more difficult for terrorists to use the area for planning and launching attacks. A Buffer Zone Plan (BZP) is a document developed specifically for a given asset. After a plan has been completed and fully coordinated, it becomes the foundation for identifying training, information, equipment, and recommended buffer zone protective measures.

Byproduct Material. Generally, nuclear material (other than SNM) that is produced or made radioactive in a nuclear reactor. Also, the tailings and waste produced by extraction or concentration of uranium or thorium from an ore processed primarily for its source material content. Under the EPAct of 2005, byproduct material now also includes discrete sources of radium and other naturally occurring radioactive material, as well as accelerator-produced radioactive material.

Code of Federal Regulations (CFR). Codification of the general and permanent rules published in the Federal Register by the executive departments and agencies of the Federal Government. It is divided into 50 titles that represent broad areas subject to Federal regulation. Each volume of the CFR is published once each calendar year; interim changes are issued quarterly.

Critical Digital Assets. A digital device or system that plays a role in operation or maintenance of a critical system, or that can impact the proper functioning of that system.

Critical Infrastructure. Assets, systems, and networks, whether physical or virtual, so vital to the United States that incapacitation or destruction of them would have a debilitating impact on national security, economic security, public health or safety, or any combination of those matters.

Defense-in-Depth Philosophy. A design and operational philosophy regarding nuclear facilities that calls for multiple protective layers to prevent and mitigate accidents. It includes controls, multiple physical barriers to prevent release of radioactive material, redundant and diverse safety functions, and emergency response measures.

Design Basis Threat (DBT). A profile of the type, composition, and capabilities of an adversary. The NRC and its licensees use the DBT as a basis for designing safeguard systems to protect against radiological sabotage and theft of SSNM. The DBT is described in detail in 10 CFR 73.1(a). The term is used to clearly identify for a licensee the expected capability of its facility to withstand a threat.

Deterministic Health Effects. Effects that increase in severity as the dose increases, also called non-stochastic. This type of effect is believed to have a threshold level for which no effect is seen. Cataracts and reddening of the skin (erythema) are examples of deterministic effects. By comparison, stochastic health effects, such as cancer and genetic effects, occur by chance, without a threshold level of dose (i.e., any exposure is assumed to have some risk). The probability of stochastic effects is proportional to the dose; their severity is independent of the dose.

Emergency Planning Zones (EPZ). To facilitate a preplanned strategy for protective actions during an emergency, two EPZs around each nuclear power plant (the Plume Exposure Pathway EPZ and Ingestion Exposure Pathway EPZ). The exact size and shape of each EPZ is a result of detailed planning, which includes consideration of the specific conditions at each site, unique geographical features of the area, and demographic information.

Federal On-Scene Coordinator. The Federal official pre-designated by the EPA or USCG to coordinate responses under subpart D of the NCP, or the government official designated to coordinate and direct removal actions under subpart E of the NCP.

Force-on-Force Exercise. A two-phase, performance-based inspection designed to verify and assess the ability of NRC licensees' physical protective systems and security organizations to provide strong assurance that activities involving SNM are not inimical to the common defense and security of the facilities, and do not constitute an unreasonable risk to public health and safety.

Function. In the context of the NIPP, function is defined as the service, process, capability, or operation performed by specific infrastructure assets, systems, or networks.

Greater Than Class C (GTCC). Defined in the Low-Level Waste (LLW) Policy Amendments Act of 1985 as LLW that exceeds the Class C limits in 10 CFR Part 61.55, Licensing Requirements for Land Disposal of Radioactive Waste. This section classifies LLW as Class A, B, or C, according to the concentration of specific short- and long-lived radionuclides. This section also sets varying requirements on waste forms for disposal. Most forms of GTCC waste are generated by routine operations at nuclear power plants, fuel research facilities, makers of radiopharmaceuticals and sealed sources used in medical and industrial applications, and in moisture and density gauges and contaminated trash. GTCC waste is generally unacceptable for near-surface disposal.

Improvised Nuclear Device (IND). Quantities of high-purity (weapons-grade) uranium or plutonium that have been arranged with explosives to achieve a nuclear yield.

Integrated Protective Measures Analysis. The Comprehensive Review (CR) team's analysis and report on the site and the local community's security and response posture, with identification of gaps in desired capabilities and options for potential enhancements to close those gaps.

Integrated Response. A coordinated response from Federal, State, and local law enforcement agencies to an attack on CIKR.

Key Resource. As defined in the Homeland Security Act of 2002, key resources are publicly or privately controlled resources essential to minimal operations of the economy and government.

License. A license issued under the regulations of 10 CFR, parts 30–36, 39, 40, or 70, or by an Agreement State under its equivalent regulations. Specific licenses are issued for medical, academic, and industrial uses of nuclear material. Reactor-produced radionuclides are used extensively throughout the United States for civilian and military industrial applications, basic and applied research, manufacture of consumer products, civil defense activities, academic studies, and for medical diagnostics, treatment, and research. The regulatory programs of the NRC and Agreement States are designed to ensure that licensees safely use these materials and do not endanger public health and safety or the environment.

Material Control and Accounting (MC&A) Program. A national system of accounting for source and special nuclear material (SNM). Material control means use of control and monitoring measures to prevent or detect loss when it occurs or soon afterward. Material accounting is defined as use of statistical and accounting measures to maintain knowledge of the quantities of SNM present in each area of a facility. It also means use of physical inventories and material balances to verify the presence of material or detect loss of material after it occurs, in particular, through theft by one or more insiders.

Medical Isotope. A radioactive element (atom) used for medical purposes. Different radiopharmaceutical drugs are used for diagnostic imaging of the heart and other organs, and for therapy in treatment of cancers and other diseases.

Moderator. A material, such as ordinary water, heavy water, or graphite that is used in a reactor to slow down high-velocity neutrons, thus increasing the likelihood of fission.

Network. In the context of the NIPP, a group of assets or systems that share information or interact with each other to provide infrastructure services within or across sectors.

Non-Proliferation Agreement. A legally binding agreement between signatories to work toward prevention of the spread of WMD.

Nuclear Facilities. A term that includes all facilities that are part of the Nuclear Sector, such as commercial nuclear power plants, research and test reactors (RTRs), nuclear fuel cycle facilities, radioactive waste management facilities, deactivated nuclear facilities, facilities housing radioactive material, and radioactive source production and distribution facilities.

Nuclear Material. Uranium, plutonium, or another substance that is or may be used to extract nuclear energy (nuclear fuel), or a compound containing such a substance; thorium or another substance suited for conversion into nuclear fuel, or a compound containing such a substance; and spent nuclear fuel (SNF) that has not been placed in final storage.

NUREG Series Publications. Reports or brochures on Nuclear Regulatory Commission (NRC) regulatory decisions, containing the results of research and incident investigations, and other technical and administrative information.

Passive Radiation Portal Monitors. A detection device that provides a passive, non-intrusive means to screen trucks and other conveyances for the presence of nuclear and radioactive material. These systems are capable of detecting various types of radiation emanating from nuclear devices, dirty bombs, SNM, natural sources, and isotopes commonly used in medicine and industry.

Probabilistic Risk Assessment (PRA). A systematic process for examining how engineered systems and humans interact to ensure plant safety. The engineered systems are built and operated based on the requirements and practices for ensuring the health and safety of the public associated with the operation of nuclear power plants or other facilities that the NRC licenses.

Protected Critical Infrastructure Information (PCII) Program. The PCII Program, established by the Critical Infrastructure Information (CII) Act, creates a new framework that enables members of the private sector to voluntarily submit sensitive information regarding the Nation's critical infrastructure to DHS with the assurance that the information, if it satisfies requirements of the act, will be protected from public disclosure.

Radiation Exposure Device (RED). A device intended to expose people to radiation rather than to disperse radioactive material into the air, as a radiological dispersal device (RDD). A RED could be constructed from unshielded or partially shielded radioactive material in any form placed in any type of container.

Radioactive Material. Material that undergoes spontaneous emission of radiation (alpha particles, beta particles, and gamma rays) directly from unstable atomic nuclei.

Radiographic Image Processing. The processing of images created by exposing a photographic film or other image receptor to x-rays.

Radioisotope. A radioisotope is an unstable form of a chemical element that radioactively decays, resulting in emission of nuclear radiation.

Radiological Dispersal Device (RDD). Any device used to deliberately disperse radioactive material to create terror or harm. A dirty bomb is made by packaging explosives (such as dynamite) with radioactive material to be dispersed when the bomb goes off.

Radiological Emergency Preparedness (REP) Program. FEMA has responsibility for evaluating off-site emergency preparedness plans for commercial nuclear power plants. The REP Program was established to: (1) ensure that the public health and safety of citizens living around commercial nuclear power plants would be adequately protected in a nuclear power station accident, and (2) inform and educate the public about REP. The REP Program covers offsite activities (State and local government emergency preparedness) that take place outside the nuclear power plant boundary. On-site activities are the responsibility of the NRC.

Radionuclide. A radioisotope.

Radiopharmaceuticals. See medical isotope.

Regulatory Guide. The NRC Regulatory Guide series provides guidance to licensees and applicants on implementing specific parts of the NRC regulations, techniques used by the NRC staff in evaluating specific problems or postulated accidents, and data needed by the staff in its review of applications for permits or licenses.

Resilience. The ability to resist, absorb, recover from, or successfully adapt to adversity or a change in conditions.

Risk-Significant Sources. Radioactive materials that are considered to be Category 1 and 2 sources based on definitions of the sources in the International Atomic Energy Agency (IAEA) Code of Conduct on Safety and Security of Radioactive Sources. That document states that Category 1 sources, if not safely managed or securely protected, likely would cause permanent injury to a person who handled them or was otherwise in contact with them for more than a few minutes. It would probably be fatal to be close to this amount of unshielded radioactive material for a period of a few minutes to an hour. Category 2 sources, if not safely managed or securely protected, could cause permanent injury to a person who handled them or was otherwise in contact with them for a short time (minutes to hours). It could be fatal to be close to this amount of unshielded material for a period of hours to days.

Safeguards Information (SGI). SGI is a special category of sensitive unclassified information authorized by section 147 of the Atomic Energy Act (AEA) to be protected. SGI concerns the physical protection of operating power reactors, spent fuel shipments, SSNM, or other radioactive material. While SGI is considered to be sensitive unclassified information, its handling and protection more closely resemble the handling of classified confidential information than other sensitive unclassified information. The categories of individuals who are permitted access to SGI are listed in 10 CFR 73.2 2(b) and 10 CFR 73.59.

Source Material. Natural uranium, thorium, or depleted uranium that is unsuitable for use as reactor fuel.

Special Nuclear Material (SNM). Uranium-233, uranium-235, enriched uranium, or plutonium.

Strategic Special Nuclear Material (SSNM). Uranium-235 (contained in uranium enriched to 20 percent or more in the U-235 isotope), uranium-233, or plutonium.

System. In the context of the National Infrastructure Protection Plan (NIPP), a system is a collection of assets, resources, or elements that provides infrastructure services to the Nation.

Appendix 3: Authorities

Protection of the assets defined in this SSP requires considerable cooperation and coordination among diverse entities in the public and private sectors. Numerous legal authorities govern this work. These legal authorities and their responsibilities for sector assets are summarized below.

3.1 Department of Homeland Security

The authority of the Department of Homeland Security (DHS) is derived from the Homeland Security Act, Public Law 107-296, 116 Stat. 2135 (2002), and a number of Homeland Security Presidential Directives (HSPDs).

On December 17, 2003, the President issued HSPD-7, which "establishes a national policy for Federal departments and agencies to identify and prioritize United States critical infrastructure and key resources and to protect them from terrorist attack." The Secretary of DHS, in accordance with paragraph 29 of HSPD-7, will continue to work with the NRC and DOE to ensure protection of Nuclear Sector assets. In accordance with paragraph 25 of HSPD-7, DHS and the SSAs will collaborate with appropriate private sector entities and continue to encourage development of information-sharing and analysis mechanisms. In addition, DHS and the SSA will collaborate with the private sector and continue to support mechanisms for sector coordination such as:

- Identifying, prioritizing, and coordinating protection of CIKR; and

- Facilitating information sharing about physical and cyber threats, vulnerabilities, incidents, potential protective measures, and best practices.

A number of other statutes provide specific legal authorities for both cross-sector and sector-specific CIKR protection and resiliency programs. Examples include:

- The Public Health Security and Bioterrorism Preparedness and Response Act of 2002, which was intended to improve the ability of the United States to prevent, prepare for, and respond to acts of bioterrorism and other public health emergencies;

- The Maritime Transportation Security Act;

- The Aviation Transportation Security Act of 2001;

- The Energy Policy and Conservation Act;

- The Critical Infrastructure Information Act;

- The Federal Information Security Management Act;

- Implementing Recommendations of the 9/11 Commission Act of 2007.

Many different HSPDs are also relevant to CIKR protection, including, but not limited to:

- HSPD-3, Homeland Security Advisory System;
- HSPD-5, Management of Domestic Incidents;
- HSPD-8, National Preparedness;
- HSPD-9, Defense of the United States Agriculture and Food;
- HSPD-10, Biodefense for the 21st Century;
- HSPD-19, Combating Terrorist Use of Explosives in the United States;
- HSPD-20, National Continuity Policy; and
- HSPD-22, Domestic Chemical Defense.

Domestic Nuclear Detection Office

On April 15, 2005, the President issued HSPD-14, National Security Presidential Directive 43, and Domestic Nuclear Detection. This directive established DNDO within DHS to:

- Serve as the primary entity in the U.S. Government to further develop, acquire, and support deployment of an enhanced domestic system to detect and report attempts to import, possess, store, transport, develop, or use an unauthorized nuclear explosive device, fissile material, or radioactive material in the United States, and to improve that system over time;
- Enhance and coordinate nuclear detection efforts of Federal, State, Territorial, local, and tribal governments and the private sector to ensure a managed, coordinated response;
- Establish, with approval of the Secretary of Homeland Security and in coordination with the Attorney General and Secretaries of Defense and Energy, additional protocols and procedures for use within the United States to ensure that detection of unauthorized nuclear explosive devices, fissile material, or radioactive material is promptly reported to the Attorney General; the Secretaries of Defense, Homeland Security, and Energy; and other appropriate officials or their respective designees for appropriate action by law enforcement, military, emergency response, or other authorities;
- Develop, with approval of the Secretary of Homeland Security and in coordination with the Attorney General and the Secretaries of State, Defense, and Energy, an enhanced global nuclear detection architecture with the following implementation considerations: (1) DNDO will be responsible for implementation of the domestic portion of the global architecture; (2) the Secretary of Defense will retain responsibility for implementation of DoD requirements within and outside the United States; and (3) the Secretaries of State, Defense, and Energy will maintain their respective responsibilities for policy guidance and implementation of the portion of the global architecture outside the United States, which will be implemented consistent with relevant laws and international arrangements;
- Conduct, support, coordinate, and encourage an aggressive, expedited, evolutionary, and transformational program of R&D efforts to advance the science of nuclear and radiological detection;
- Support and enhance the effective sharing and use of appropriate information generated by the Intelligence Community, counterterrorism community, law enforcement agencies, other government agencies, and foreign governments, as well as provide appropriate information to those entities; and
- Further enhance and maintain continuous awareness by analyzing information from all DNDO mission-related detection systems.

Federal Emergency Management Agency

On December 7, 1979 the President directed FEMA to take lead responsibility for all off-site nuclear planning and response. FEMA's activities are conducted according to 44 CFR, parts 350, 351, and 352. These regulations are a key element in the Radiological Emergency Preparedness (REP) Program, established following the Three Mile Island Nuclear Power Station accident in March 1979.

FEMA rule 44 CFR, part 350 establishes the policies and procedures for the REP Program's initial and continued approval of State, local, and tribal governments' radiological emergency planning and preparedness for commercial nuclear power plants. This approval is contingent partly on State and local government participation in joint exercises with licensees. The REP Program's responsibilities in radiological emergency planning for fixed nuclear facilities include the following:

- Leading off-site emergency planning and reviewing and evaluating Radiological Emergency Response Plans (RERPs) and procedures developed by State and local governments;

- Determining whether such plans and procedures can be implemented on the basis of observation and evaluation of exercises of the plans and procedures conducted by State and local governments;

- Responding to requests by the NRC according to the memorandum of understanding (MOU) between it and FEMA dated June 17, 1993 (44 CFR, part 354, Appendix A, September 14, 1993); and

- Coordinating the activities of Federal agencies with responsibilities in the radiological emergency planning process through the Federal Radiological Preparedness Coordinating Committee (FRPCC) and Regional Assistance Committee.

3.2 Department of Transportation

The Federal hazardous materials transportation law, 49 U.S.C. 5101 et seq., and the pipeline safety law, 49 U.S.C. 60101 et seq., give the Secretary of Transportation the regulatory and enforcement authority to enhance the safe transportation of hazardous materials by all modes, and hazardous liquids and natural gas by pipeline. The Secretary also has the authority to marshal transportation in a defined area to aid in national defense and homeland security through the Defense Production Act of 1950, 50 U.S.C. App. 2071 and the Robert T. Stafford Disaster Relief and Emergency Assistance Act, 42 U.S.C. 5121 et seq. In allocating or prioritizing civil transportation resources, the Secretary, with appropriate funding from one of three agencies (DoD, DOE, or DHS) has extensive authority, in all modes, to organize transportation during an emergency. Also, the Homeland Security Act of 2002 amended the hazardous materials transportation law to include security, so the mandate now reads that the Secretary of Transportation can "prescribe regulations for the safe transportation, including security, of hazardous materials in intrastate, interstate, and foreign commerce."

3.3 Department of Energy

The AEA, as amended, 42 U.S.C. 2011 et seq., is the primary source of DOE's authority for its nuclear science, technology, and R&D activities; and nuclear weapons programs. The AEA also authorizes DOE's production, ownership, and use of special nuclear, source, and byproduct material. DOE regulations on nuclear activities are set forth in 10 CFR, parts 820, 830, and 835. The following statutory authorities govern DOE's work:

- Atomic Energy Act of 1954, as amended: Under the AEA, DOE is broadly authorized to conduct R&D in military and civilian applications of atomic energy and nuclear reactor production for the U.S. Navy; conduct the Nation's nuclear weapons programs; provide for related storage, transportation, and disposal of hazardous and radioactive waste; and regulate nuclear safety. The AEA was amended most recently by the EPAct of 2005.

- Energy Reorganization Act of 1974: Sections 104 and 201 of the act abolished the Atomic Energy Commission (AEC) created by the AEA and transferred its functions to the NRC and the Administrator of the Energy Research and Development

Administration (ERDA). Commercial licensing and related regulatory functions of the AEC were transferred to the NRC, and ERDA assumed AEC responsibility for activities that include nuclear energy R&D and operation of nuclear weapons programs.

- Department of Energy Organization Act: In 1977, ERDA was terminated and its functions transferred to the Secretary of Energy by sections 301 and 703 of the act.

Other statutes affecting DOE activities include:

- Nuclear Waste Policy Act of 1982, as amended: DOE is responsible for site characterization, construction, and operation of a geological repository for disposal of the Nation's high-level radioactive waste and SNF. DOE is also responsible for transportation of high-level radioactive waste and SNF to the repository. Section 180 of the act requires DOE to transport the waste and spent fuel in NRC-certified packages and according to NRC regulations regarding advance notification to State and local governments.

- National Nuclear Security Administration (NNSA) Act of 2000: The NNSA was established by the National Defense Authorization Act for Fiscal Year 2000. The NNSA is a semi-autonomous agency within DOE. Its mission includes activities related to national security, non-proliferation, and safety and reliability of nuclear weapons.

- Energy Policy Act of 2005 (EPAct): Among other activities, EPAct directed DOE to undertake several initiatives regarding nuclear energy R&D. Section 641 of the act provides for establishment of the Next-Generation Nuclear Plant Project, consisting of R&D and, ultimately, operation of a prototype nuclear reactor that could potentially generate electricity and produce hydrogen. Section 952 also directs DOE to conduct nuclear energy research programs, including the Generation IV Nuclear Energy Systems Initiative to develop an overall technology plan to support necessary R&D for promising technologies for new commercial reactors. Section 651(d) requires establishment of an interagency task force, with DOE membership, to report to the President and Congress on the security of radiation sources in the United States from potential threats and to develop recommendations for possible regulatory and legislative changes related to protection and security of sources.

3.4 Nuclear Regulatory Commission

The AEA, as amended, is the primary source of the NRC's authority to regulate radioactive material and civilian nuclear activities. NRC regulations are set forth in 10 CFR, parts 0–199.

The NRC and its licensees share a common responsibility to protect public health and safety; supporting Federal regulations and the NRC regulatory program are important elements in protecting the public. NRC licensees, however, have day-to-day responsibility for ensuring safe use of nuclear material. The following principal statutory authorities govern the NRC's work:

- Atomic Energy Act of 1954, as amended: Under the AEA, the NRC has broad authority to regulate (by regulation, licensing, or order) possession, transfer, and use of source, byproduct, and SNM to protect public health and safety and to provide for the common defense and security. Under AEA Section 147, 42 U.S.C. 2167, the NRC also has authority to designate information as SGI to prevent its unauthorized disclosure.

- Energy Reorganization Act of 1974: This act abolished the AEC and moved its regulatory function to the NRC, establishing the NRC as an independent regulator of certain nuclear material and facilities. The act also created what eventually became DOE. DOE addresses military uses of AEA materials, as well as nuclear energy research. Unless specifically authorized by legislation, the NRC does not regulate DOE activities, which include promotion of nuclear energy and development of nuclear material for military uses.

Other statutes that form the basis of NRC regulatory authority include:

- Nuclear Non-Proliferation Act of 1978: This act (in combination with the AEA) gives the NRC the authority to license export and import of nuclear material and equipment to ensure these items are used for peaceful purposes. For all nuclear exports, the NRC must find that export will not be "inimical to the common defense and security." No commercial export license for nuclear facilities, source material, or SNM may be issued by the NRC unless the U.S. Government and country of export have an agreement for meeting the requirements of AEA Section 123, 42 U.S.C. 10143.

- Uranium Mill Tailings Radiation Control Act of 1978: This act regulates uranium mill tailings and any remediation that might be associated with the mill sites.

- Nuclear Waste Policy Act of 1982, Nuclear Waste Policy Act Amendments of 1987, and EPAct of 1992: These acts, in combination, set forth requirements for development and licensing of Yucca Mountain, a proposed high-level radioactive waste repository being developed by DOE. In contrast to the NRC's legislatively mandated authority to regulate disposal, the NRC's ability to regulate transportation to the repository is specifically limited by the Nuclear Waste Policy Act, as amended, to the certification of transportation packages and pre-notification of shipments.

- Diplomatic Security and Anti-Terrorism Act of 1986: This act requires the Secretaries of Defense, State, and Energy and the NRC to review the adequacy of physical security standards currently applicable to SNM shipment and storage outside the United States, which is subject to U.S. prior-consent rights, with special attention to protection against terrorist acts. The act also requires these officials and the NRC to report to specified congressional committees on the results of such review. The act amends the AEA to require that each licensee or applicant to operate a utilization facility (e.g., a nuclear power reactor) fingerprint each individual who is permitted unescorted access to the facility or is permitted access to certain SGI. The act provides that all fingerprints are submitted to the Attorney General for identification and a criminal records check, with all costs paid by the licensee or applicant.

- Solar, Wind, Waste, and Geothermal Power Production Incentives Act of 1990: This act amended the AEA to require licensing of uranium enrichment facilities, other than existing gaseous diffusion plants (GDPs).

- EPAct of 2005: As part of the EPAct, the NRC is required to conduct security evaluations, including force-on-force exercises not less than once every 3 years at licensed commercial power reactor facilities. The DBT will include rulemaking and public comment. The NRC must assign a Federal security coordinator employed by the NRC in each region, and it is required to promulgate regulations establishing a mandatory tracking system for radiation sources in the United States. The EPAct establishes a Radiation Source Protection and Security Task Force to evaluate and provide recommendations to Congress and the President on the security of radiation sources in the United States from potential threats, and expands the scope of fingerprinting and criminal history checks at licensee facilities. In coordination with DOJ, the EPAct allows for use of a broader class of weapons to protect NRC-licensed or NRC-certified facilities or materials; expands criminal sanctions for sabotage of nuclear facilities, fuel, or materials; expands provisions for unlawful trespass with dangerous weapons, explosives, and other dangerous instruments; and requires the NRC to consult with DHS regarding the proposed location of new utilization facilities.

Agreement States

Section 274b of the AEA allows the NRC to relinquish its regulatory authority over certain materials and certain activities in a State if agreed-upon conditions are met. Agreement States issue licenses and regulate approximately 17,000 materials licensees, only a small fraction of which possess risk-significant radioactive material. Currently, 34 States have section 274b agreements; 3 States have announced their intention to enter into agreements. The complete list, as of May 2006, is included as table 1-4 in section 1.2.

Under the 274b agreements, the NRC interacts frequently with the States on licensing, inspection, enforcement, incident response, training, and rulemaking. The NRC provides technical assistance, primarily to Agreement States, and sponsors conferences and special workshops on topics of interest when needed. Agreement States report significant incidents involving materials to the NRC Headquarters Operations Center. More detailed event descriptions are later entered into an events database. The NRC maintains Office of Management and Budget (OMB) clearances for the needed information collections.

3.5 Federal Bureau of Investigation

In addition to the FBI's overarching terrorism response authorities as outlined in various national security and Homeland Security Presidential Directives, the following statutes apply specifically to its enforcement of statutes aimed at preventing criminal and terrorist activity involving nuclear and radioactive material:

- Atomic Energy Act, 42 U.S.C. 2011-2284;

- Prohibited Transactions Involving Nuclear Materials, 18 U.S.C. 831;

- Participation in Nuclear and WMD Threats to the United States, 18 U.S.C. 832; and

- WMD Statute, 18 U.S.C. 2332a.

As also stated in the NRP, the Attorney General, generally acting through the FBI, has lead responsibility for criminal investigations of terrorist acts or threats and for coordinating other members of the law enforcement community to detect, prevent, preempt, investigate, and disrupt attacks against the United States, including those involving nuclear and radioactive material.